Key Wc
A Journal of Cultural M

10
(2012)

edited by
Catherine Clay
Simon Dentith
Kristin Ewins
Ben Harker
Angela Kershaw
Stan Smith
Vicki Whittaker

Key Words: A Journal of Cultural Materialism

Editors: Catherine Clay (Nottingham Trent University), Simon Dentith (University of Reading), Kristin Ewins (University of Salford), Ben Harker (University of Salford), Angela Kershaw (University of Birmingham), Stan Smith (Nottingham Trent University), Vicki Whittaker.

Guest Editor for this issue: Elizabeth Allen (Regent's College, London).

Editorial Advisory Board: John Brannigan (University College Dublin), Peter Brooker (University of Sussex), Terry Eagleton (National University of Ireland Galway and Lancaster University), John Higgins (University of Cape Town), Andreas Huyssen (Columbia University, New York), Peter Marks (University of Sydney), Sean Matthews (University of Nottingham), Jim McGuigan (Loughborough University), Andrew Milner (Monash University), Meaghan Morris (Lingnan University), Morag Shiach (Queen Mary, University of London), Dai Smith (Swansea University), Nick Stevenson (University of Nottingham), John Storey (University of Sunderland), Will Straw (McGill University), Jenny Bourne Taylor (University of Sussex), John Tomlinson (Nottingham Trent University), Jeff Wallace (University of Glamorgan), Imelda Whelehan (De Montfort University).

Contributions for prospective inclusion in *Key Words* should comply with the style notes printed on pp. 201–203 of this issue, and should be sent to Catherine Clay, School of Arts and Humanities, Nottingham Trent University, Clifton Campus, Nottingham NG11 8NS, UK (catherine.clay@ntu.ac.uk).
Books and other items for review should be sent to Angela Kershaw, Department of French Studies, College of Arts and Law, University of Birmingham, B15 2TT, UK. The reviews Editor, Stan Smith, can be contacted at stan.smith@ntu.ac.uk.

Key Words is a publication of The Raymond Williams Society (website: **www.raymondwilliams.co.uk**).

Contributions copyright © The Raymond Williams Society 2012.

All rights reserved.

Cover design by Andrew Dawson.

Printed by Russell Press, Nottingham.
Distributed by Spokesman Books, Nottingham.

ISSN 1369-9725
ISBN 978-0-9531503-8-0

Contents

Editors' Preface	5
Guest Editor's Preface Elizabeth Allen	8
Rereading *The Long Revolution*: Permanent Education versus the Exclusionary Consensus John Higgins	11
Raymond Williams in the Sixties: History, Communication and Conflict Roberto del Valle	28
Raymond Williams on Culture and Society Jim McGuigan	40
The Traitor in the House Elizabeth Allen	55
The British Reception of Early Soviet Fiction 1917–1934 Ian Gasse	68
'Why, Comrade?': Raymond Williams, Orwell and Structure of Feeling in Boys' Story Papers Simon Machin	88
'The Army of the Unemployed': Walter Greenwood's Wartime Novel and the Reconstruction of Britain Chris Hopkins	103
Will Self and the Academics: Or, How to Write Satire Alan Munton	125

***

Contents

Recoveries   141

Keywords   159

Review Article   170
Jennifer Birkett

Reviews   178

Notes on Contributors   197

Raymond Williams Foundation (RWF)   200

Style Notes for Contributors   201

Editors' Preface

The current edition of *Key Words* marks the fiftieth anniversary of Raymond Williams's *The Long Revolution* with a number of essays which specifically reflect upon that text and the nature of its continuing relevance. The book itself has recently been reissued by the Welsh publisher Parthian, and is reviewed elsewhere in this issue. Williams himself could be severe on the practice of attaching significance to arbitrary dates, so our justification in marking this anniversary must rest elsewhere, on the privileged position of hindsight afforded by the transformations in culture and society since the early 1960s when Williams published *The Long Revolution*. Indeed, its later companion text, *Towards 2000*, invites just such a retrospective, insofar as it sought to analyse the competing possibilities for social change which presented themselves in the early 1980s, the period when the radical reinstatement of unmediated capitalist social relations that we now know as neo-liberalism was being initiated. John Higgins argues forcefully that one central strand of argument in *The Long Revolution* concerns the aims and purposes of education; in a wide-ranging account of some of the recent literature on higher education in particular, he detects an 'exclusionary consensus' in which other versions of education than those designed to serve the needs of a capitalist economy have been systematically ignored. For Roberto del Valle, by contrast, the distinctiveness of Williams's text lies in the political argument that it makes, which is at once a social and cultural argument also: Williams avoids the deformations of his contemporary political moment by emphasising the 'charged affective dimensions of communicable relationships'. In the third of these essays specifically directed at *The Long Revolution*, Jim McGuigan insists on the importance of Williams's book to cultural studies – widely acknowledged – but also to the sociology of culture. Williams's intellectual legacy has been carried forward in predominantly literary contexts; we need also to acknowledge and develop the continuing relevance and challenge of cultural materialism in other domains, especially in relation to naive ideas of technological determinism.

Elizabeth Allen's article on the persistent trope of treachery in Williams's novels continues the journal's critical discussion of Williams's fiction, especially in the light of the controversy over the value of the novels which aired in *Key Words* 6 and 9. The article also reminds us of the social and cultural ground out of which *The Long Revolution*, and its companion texts *Culture and Society* and *Towards 2000*, grew. Three other articles in this issue discuss various forms of twentieth-century working-class and socialist fiction, and suggest some of the actual contexts for Williams's commitment to a sophisticated realism, to which his work on the history of the novel as a form was always contributory.

Editors' Preface

Ian Gasse, in a fascinating survey of Soviet fiction published in English in the 1920s and 1930s, demonstrates the remarkable interest in, and widespread dissemination of, novels about the new society that was being created in the Soviet Union in those years. Simon Machin explores Orwell's discussion of boys' fiction, suggesting a model here for Williams's own extension of cultural analysis beyond the tight confines of high culture. Given Williams's own later ambivalence towards Orwell this is a bold suggestion; yet it does point to the actual congruence of their writing in some respects, indicated also by Williams soliciting a contribution from Orwell for the short-lived journal *Politics and Letters* in the late 1940s. Chris Hopkins, in a model analysis of Walter Greenwood's career after *Love on the Dole*, concentrates especially on the complex cultural moment of the Second World War, when contradictory pressures within the Ministry of Information could permit a progressive and social-democratic meaning to become attached to the war effort, despite Churchill's own unwillingness to broaden the war aims beyond the sheer matter of survival. The final article in this section of this issue, by Alan Munton, focuses on the contemporary fiction of Will Self, which he views as primarily satirical, and which challenges some of the tidy categories of the academy – including, perhaps, the arguments for a complex realism made by Williams himself in *The Long Revolution*.

Chris Hopkins, in his article on Walter Greenwood, discusses especially a now little-read novel, *Something in my Heart*, and this connects to a new feature in the journal, entitled 'Recoveries'. In this section we include accounts by Joseph Pridmore and Elinor Taylor of several 'working-class' oriented novels from the 1920s and 1930s. There is a large potential field of discussion here, and we hope that this section will continue to provide lively contributions to the journal.

Finally, following the new 'Recoveries' feature, in this issue we revive an early practice of *Key Words*, to which the journal's very title refers: the discussion of the social semantics of contemporary key words which Williams initiated with his own book of that title in 1976, and which has been continued in Tony Bennett's, Lawrence Grossberg's and Meaghan Morris's *New Keywords: A Revised Vocabulary of Culture and Society* from 2005. We hope that readers of *Key Words* will wish to contribute to this ongoing project. The reviews section includes a review article by Jennifer Birkett on recent books by Jonathan Bate and Thomas Docherty, which discuss the salience of Higher Education in the current political conjuncture; Birkett suggests the continuing relevance of Williams's discussion of these matters even in the changed circumstances of today.

There have been some changes to the Editorial Board of *Key Words* which should be acknowledged; following the injunction to 'welcome the coming,

Editors' Preface

speed the parting guest', we welcome Liz Allen as guest editor for this issue, and wish Dave Laing well after his departure from it. A successful year for the Raymond Williams Society should also be noted. Peter Brooker has stepped down as Chair of the Society, though he remains on the advisory board; we thank him for his long and successful service as Chair. We are very happy to welcome Derek Tatton as his replacement. The Society has been active during the year in several areas. The most prominent of these was perhaps the highly successful AGM event in Oxford in November 2011. Over 100 people attended a lecture by Anthony Barnett on 'The Long and the Quick of Revolutions: Can the Left Regain the Future from Market Fundamentalism?'. The event also marked the republication of *The Long Revolution* by Parthian Books, with a new preface by Anthony Barnett. The lecture and launch were also supported by openDemocracy and Parthian books. Also available at the event was the new edition of *The Country and the City*, introduced by Stan Smith, and published by Spokesman Books. In addition, the Society, along with the Raymond Williams Foundation, supported two further events: the Hastings conference on Raymond Williams and Robert Tressell, noted elsewhere in the Journal; and a Day School in Abergavenny on *The People of the Black Mountains*, which attracted a number of local people to a discussion of Williams's final novel. This provides an extraordinary history of the Black Mountains over the last several millennia. Finally, the Society continues to run its Postgraduate Essay competition; last year's winning entry, by Simon Machin, is published in this edition of *Key Words*.

Guest Editor's Introduction: Revolution in Hastings
Elizabeth Allen

In *Small World*, published in 1984, David Lodge offers a satirical view of the contemporary academic world in which, according to the irrepressible Morris Zapp, 'the day of the single static campus is over', many of the central characters spend their energies competing for the prestige of the UNESCO chair of Literary Criticism, a chair which is 'purely conceptual' and academics constantly jet off to conferences whose venues are indistinguishable.[1]

For the first academic conference to be held at its Hastings Centre, with the support of the Raymond Williams Society, the University of Brighton made the decision to offer a very differently conceived experience. 'Raymond Williams and Robert Tressell in Hastings: celebrating fifty years of *The Long Revolution* and the Centenary of *The Ragged Trousered Philanthropists*' was a conference firmly grounded in its locality. Hastings is Tressell's Mugsborough, where, in the first decade of the twentieth century, he worked as a signwriter and decorator and wrote the novel which has inspired the political understanding and activism of so many. Here in the 1950s, Raymond Williams taught adult education classes for the WEA while working on his non-fiction and first novel, and here in 1982 Williams gave the Tressell Memorial Lecture entitled *The Ragged Arsed Philanthropists*. While we still campaign for a blue plaque to recognise Williams's stay in St Helen's Road, Tressell's importance is more actively celebrated through the Robert Tressell Society, annual walks to explore the locations of his life and novel and collections in Hastings Museum.

The conference declared its aim as seeking 'to create a multi-disciplinary forum in which academics, researchers, trade unionists and local historians can explore the impact and legacy of the two men on contemporary research, practice and activists'. The importance of this wide-ranging recruitment, unusual for an academic conference, was confirmed by the opening keynote speaker, Stuart Laing, Deputy Vice-Chancellor of Brighton University, and was readily demonstrated by the subject matter of the papers and the list of attendees. As well as post-graduate students and specialist academics, speakers and delegates included trade unionists, a radical priest, a BBC journalist now teaching for the WEA, the chair of Hastings WEA and the Labour leader of Hastings Council. Tressell's novel refers to the Mugsborough Council, made up of thirty councillors and ten aldermen, as the Brigands and the Forty Thieves and in his Tressell lecture Williams remarks that during his own time in Hastings someone had expressed the opinion that the epithet remained appropriate:[2] perhaps the council's implicit endorsement of the subject of the

Guest Editor's Preface

conference suggests that, while the progress of *The Long Revolution* may have stalled in significant ways, some minor local progress has been achieved.

In the Introduction to *The Long Revolution* Williams writes of the need to:

> grasp the process [of the struggle for democracy, the development of industry, the extension of communications, and the deep social and personal changes] as a whole, to see it in new ways as a long revolution, if we are to understand either the theoretical crisis, or our actual history, or the reality of our immediate condition and the terms of change.[3]

While one could not, of course, claim that the day offered a representation of 'the process as a whole', it did engage not just with the work of Williams and of Tressell as 'legacy' but with the ways in which their work informs current theoretical and political debate. There was a strong emphasis on the practices of working life with reference to class attitudes and to new technologies: the relevance of Tressell's writing to trade union activism, to the contemporary 'underclass' of part-time staff in post-compulsory education and IT service support workers was raised in different papers. *The Ragged Trousered Philanthropists* was said to have given a new perspective to understanding the Poulson Affair and 'the modern Mugsborough' that it had revealed. Other papers discussed the implications of community learning in Liverpool and in Hastings, with the experience of teaching *The Ragged Trousered Philanthropists* to working-class women and creative writing to those who feel 'outside' education and culture. There was a sustained emphasis on the continuing relevance to political analysis and debate of Williams's work in *The Long Revolution* and elsewhere. Jim McGuigan, whose paper is printed here, talked of how 'the analytical acuity of such notable concepts as structure of feeling and mobile privatisation' help to 'make sense of how lived experience is related to structural transformation in the twenty-first century'. He and others commented on the extraordinary prescience of *Towards 2000* and that its date should not mark it in any way as a cut-off point. Jim McGuigan commented, since Williams's death in 1988, there has been perhaps a disproportionate emphasis on his literary legacy. Given the focus of this conference, that emphasis was slighter, but is here represented by my own paper on the significance of the trope of treachery in Williams's fiction, and its relation to his fraught class position.

There was, of course, gloom. Derek Tatton of the Raymond Williams Foundation, talking of Williams's belief that 'ordinary people should be highly educated' and the role of education in creating a participative democracy, gave an uplifting account of education in practice, with pub discussion groups on social, political and philosophical issues. Much adult education is now occurring, he said, 'underneath the radar'. But he concluded that in the race between catastrophe and education which H.G. Wells saw as the historical process, catastrophe seems to be winning. Optimism and pleasure were, nevertheless, present and legitimated in Ian Haywood's lecture on the Beano episode in *The Ragged Trousered Philanthropists* when 'a transient beam of sunshine penetrated the gloom in which the lives of the philanthropists were passed'.[4] That reading Tressell was a significant, even decisive, political experience for many was evident in a number of references made, by speakers and by delegates over coffee, to the memory of the first encounter with the text. In an introduction to the first complete edition Alan Sillitoe writes: 'I read an abridged edition … when I was nineteen and with the Air Force in Malaya. It was given to me by a wireless operator from Glasgow who said: "You ought to read this. Among other things, it is the book that won the '45 election for Labour".'[5] Indeed few people seem to have bought the book: it was a gift intended to draw the recipient into a community. As Howard Brenton's account of 'Staging Tressell' in Liverpool and Chichester with the different audience responses themselves 'producing' a different play, suggests, an ever-growing community.

Margaret Wallis, Director of the University of Brighton's Hastings campus and conference organiser, and her colleagues certainly offered delegates an experience of the significant distinction between higher education as a version of Lodge's 'small world' and the wider one with which we must engage.

Notes

1. David Lodge, *Small World* (London: Secker and Warburg, 1984), 63, 163
2. Raymond Williams, 'The Ragged Arsed Philanthropists', *Writing in Society* (London: Verso, 1984): 252
3. Raymond Williams, *The Long Revolution* (London: Penguin, 1963), 13.
4. Robert Tressell, *The Ragged Trousered Philanthropists* (London: Granada, 1965): 430.
5. Alan Sillitoe, Introduction, *The Ragged Trousered Philanthropists*, 7–10.

Rereading *The Long Revolution*: Permanent Education versus the Exclusionary Consensus

John Higgins

This article argues against the grain of a present trend to see the importance of Williams's work primarily in terms of its contribution to cultural studies. It suggests that in remembering *The Long Revolution*, we should attend to the core political challenge of the book to conceptions of the purposes of education and higher education. Viewed in this perspective, Williams's study connects to key contemporary debates on the role and purpose of higher education. By examining key documents and formulations from higher education policy over the past thirty years or so, the essay argues that Williams's insistence on the link between education and participatory democracy remains an important challenge to the current 'exclusionary consensus' amongst policy makers, one which seeks to reduce the broader social purposes of higher education to a single instrumental aim, that of servicing the economy and promoting the growth of competitive markets.

*

Introduction

Today, when *The Long Revolution* is recollected, it is usually framed in terms of the book's anticipation of the formation of the academic discipline of cultural studies.[1] It has by now become an academic commonplace to note that when Williams wrote – in the book's opening pages – that 'there is no academic subject within which the questions I am interested in can be followed through', and then went on to add that 'I hope one day there might be', that the 'academic subject' anticipated here is today's cultural studies, and commentators often then refer, for confirmation of this, to Williams's later acknowledgement (in the Preface to the second edition of *Communications*) that 'work of a long-term kind [of the sort championed by *The Long Revolution* and *Communications*] is now going on' at the Birmingham Centre.[2]

This emphasis is undoubtedly, in large part, correct. A key feature of Williams's political and intellectual project as a whole was certainly the break he initiated (or helped to initiate) in the academic study of the humanities. With the works of the 'second' trilogy – *Culture and Society*, *The Long Revolution* and *Communications* – Williams effectively subverted the binary opposition between mass civilization and minority culture that had hitherto organized academic work in the humanities.[3] In deconstructing this opposition – as he did so successfully in *The Long Revolution* and associated works – Williams helped to open up the space for the serious study and analysis of a wide range of semiotic practices – including the study of film and television – that had been cast beyond the pale of academic scrutiny since Leavis's founding pamphlet of 1930.[4]

At the same time, though, it is important to register the broader political impact that the trilogy (and perhaps particularly *The Long Revolution*) was intended to have in the larger field of public discussion and opinion, and this registration is particularly necessary if we are to assert the continuing relevance of Williams's arguments today.[5] For, with its challenging and theoretically controversial emphasis on the recognition of culture as just as important a driver of the historical changes to social life in Britain as politics (figured as the emergence of democracy) or the economy (referenced as the effects of the industrial revolution), *The Long Revolution* urged new directions not only in academic, but also in contemporary social and political understanding, both on the left and on the right. At the centre of this shift lay Williams's insistence on the relations between education and democracy, the assertion of the 'principle' (and the original title of *The Long Revolution* was *Essays and Principles in the Theory of Culture*) that education should be defined by 'what a member of an educated and participating democracy needs'.[6] Viewed from this perspective, it was *The Long Revolution*'s founding discussion and analysis of the terms of public self-understanding – its conscious bringing together of the political with the semiotic dimension of representation – that challenged the dominant ideas of the day and most aroused the ire of the book's many conservative critics, both inside and outside the context of adult education from which the book grew.

For, as Williams readily acknowledged, many key elements of *The Long Revolution* were to be found in his work in adult education in and through the 1950s. In the interviews with the *New Left Review* that make up *Politics and Letters*, he recalled how much of the book – and particularly the essays that made up Part Two – 'were topics I had taught, or was going to teach, in adult classes – the reading public, the social history of writers, the press and dramatic forms'.[7] More important, though, than the choice of the specific essays in the book, or its address to issues in the adult education movement, was its central underlying principle: the core idea of education whose importance is immediately visible in the 'unforgettable' 'degree of hostility' that the publication of *The Long Revolution* evoked, the shocked sense that – at least for conservatives – this was 'a scandalous work' (133–4).

Just why was *The Long Revolution* so scandalous?

The answer, I think, lies in the deep-rooted challenge that its view of education posed to the elitist presumptions still active in most accounts of education at the time, presumptions quite contrary to the spirit of the 'long revolution' which are re-emerging, in a differently modulated way to be sure, in today's education and higher education systems.

A precise indication of this comes through if we pay sufficient attention to even a single formulation from one of Malcolm Pittock's hostile reviews of Williams's work around the time of publication. In a Critical Forum discussion with Williams in the journal *Essays in Criticism*, Pittock cites one of the closing formulations of *Culture and Society* in order to ridicule it. The assertion, from the final paragraph of the book, reads 'The human crisis is always a crisis of understanding: what we genuinely understand we can do', but Pittock goes on to add, with deliberate provocation, 'But what happens if most of us are incapable of understanding?'.[8] For there was the rub: the 'we' of Williams's position referred to an all inclusive democratic plurality, while the 'we' of Pittock's appropriation refers to the negative image of that democratic plurality, a negative image of the kind so carefully deconstructed in Williams's devastating analysis of the term 'the masses' in *Culture and Society*.[9] Pittock's enunciation performs and works to conceal the distinction between 'the few of us' in a position to know and to teach and 'the many of them' who are at best there to be instructed.[10] This was the distinction that constituted the core of the 'cultural conservatism' that Williams saw *The Long Revolution* trilogy as challenging, embodied in figures like Eliot, 'the people who had pre-empted the culture and literature of this country'.[11]

The key figure in this conservatism was the influential poet and critical writer T.S. Eliot, whose acerbic responses to the opening up of educational opportunity represented by the Beveridge Report of 1943 and the Education Act of 1945 set the scene for the post-war debate on education which formed the background to *The Long Revolution* trilogy.[12]

In the essays gathered together as *Notes Towards the Definition of Culture* and published in 1948 Eliot had famously claimed that 'the idea of a uniform system such that no one who was capable of receiving higher education could fail to get it, leads imperceptibly to the education if too many people, and consequently to the lowering of standards'.[13] The banner of standards flourished here by Eliot had been picked up by many, amongst them Professor of Adult Education at Leeds University S.G. Raybould, who argued that adult education should be reconfigured around the idea of adult learners who sought to attain university standards in academic subjects.[14] Williams – who worked as a tutor in adult education from 1946 through to his appointment to a lectureship in drama at Cambridge 1961 – set himself against Raybould's views, and argued to retain the original emphasis of the workers' education movement on 'education for social and political emancipation'.[15] Indeed, as

Williams recalled in a 1983 memorial lecture for adult educationalist, Tony Mclean:

> The impulse to adult education was not only a matter of remedying deficit, making up for inadequate educational resources in the wider society, nor only a case of meeting new needs of the society, though these things contributed. The deepest impulse was the desire to make learning part of the process of social change itself.[16]

At the core of *The Long Revolution* trilogy was precisely this emphasis on making learning 'part of the process of social change': this was just what Williams meant by his insistence on the importance of the cultural dimension to social change and development alongside – and inextricably intertwined with – political and economic change.[17] Of necessity, education had a central role to play in the 'long revolution'.[18]

By the end of the 1950s, while Williams was sure that the old elitist structures favoured by an Eliot were on their way out, he also insisted that new struggles were imminent, against the grain of much of the 'end of ideology' social thinking of the period.[19] Thus, while he acknowledged, in 1961, that the privileges and barriers to education 'of an inherited kind' will 'in any case go down', this transformation still left open an alternative which was to become ever more stark: the crucial question of whether to replace these former privileges and barriers 'by the free play of the market, or by a public education designed to express and create the values of an educated democracy and a common culture'.[20] Writing a few years later (in the Foreword to the second edition of the third book in the trilogy, *Communications*), Williams articulated even more forcefully his sense of the new battleground around the idea of 'permanent education'.[21] In *Communications*, the idea of 'permanent education' brings together 'the concepts of learning and popular democratic culture', and emphasizes (as had *The Long Revolution* itself) 'the educational force of our whole social and cultural experience'.[22] What concerns Williams here is that, for the moment, the effective content of 'permanent education' is in reality being defined by 'the priorities and interests of a capitalist society, and of a capitalist society, moreover, which necessarily retains as its central principle (though against powerful pressures, of a democratic kind, from the rest of our social experience) the idea of a few governing, communicating with and teaching the many' – precisely the position (as we have seen above) championed by Eliot and assumed by Pittock (14–15). 'Against that kind of permanent education,' he concludes, 'already well organized and visibly extending its methods and its range, an integrated alternative is now profoundly necessary', and it was the aim of *Communications* (and, indeed, *The Long Revolution* trilogy as a whole, as well as aspects of the later *May Day Manifesto*)[23] to provide.[24]

Thus Williams in the early 1960s. And now, in 2011?

It has surely become painfully clear that universities across the world are suffering the penetration and consequent ravages of just that integration of education with capitalist priorities and interests which Williams had earlier articulated.[25] What is particularly striking in rereading the *Long Revolution* trilogy is the ease with which the central concerns around the idea of education that Williams articulated in relation to adult education in the late 1950s have returned to haunt us in relation to higher education in general, and, more specifically for the purposes of this essay, with regard to the place allotted to the humanities within higher education.[26]

We may take our bearings here from a series of reports issued by the British Academy (which was formed by Royal Charter in 1902 for the 'promotion of the humanities and social sciences') over the past decade or so.[27] All of these have, in different ways, pointed to the existence of a 'dangerously polarised debate' in higher education policy. While this policy recognizes the contribution to society and wealth creation made by the STEM disciplines (Science, Technology, Engineering, Mathematics), it fails entirely to acknowledge 'the equally important contributions made by the arts, humanities and social sciences'.[28]

How has this polarization come about?

One part of the answer at least is an ideological one: Margaret Thatcher's avowed hatred of all those academics – and notably social scientists and historians – that she saw as 'putting out poison' into the public mind, and her determination to curb the university as a site of irresponsible critical thinking. With the Education Act of 1988, Thatcher took the first decisive step in what was to become – over the next thirty years or so – a fundamental reframing of the purposes of higher education whose consequences are now painfully visible to all.[29]

Through the simple replacement of the University Grants Committee by a new University Funding Council on which, for the first time, academics were outnumbered by business people, Thatcher opened the door to an increasingly instrumental and economist view of the purposes of higher education. The dominant legitimating idea of higher education shifted from a focus on serving the public good to that of simply servicing the economy. From a commitment to promoting professional training and critical thinking across all disciplines in the sciences and humanities, the central idea of the function of higher education moved to servicing the needs of the economy in as direct and immediate a fashion as possible: precisely the stance of Williams's 'industrial trainers'.[30]

In the decades which followed, many critics have pointed to the dangers of too narrow and exclusive a focus on the economy at the expense of the other social functions of higher education, though to little avail.

When the British Academy 2010 Report suggests that the 'achievements of non-STEM disciplines are often overlooked', an interesting term is brought into play.[31] For to overlook (amongst a range of other senses) suggests both to see and yet not to see; to perceive, but not to fully process, register and allow full access to consciousness; perhaps to have read, with the eyes running across the lines of the page, but without attention to the content, and so in effect to have actively ignored.

To overlook is interesting because it suggests the complex interaction of levels of the motivated with the unintentional that makes evidence-based policy advice so challenging. The reality of overlooking exemplifies all the real world difficulties faced by evidence-based policy advice of any kind, bringing into play what I shall call here (in a deliberate recalling or retroping of Williams's great phrase, the 'selective tradition') the dynamics of exclusionary consensus.

Higher education policy over the past twenty years or so has managed to constitute the apparent paradox an exclusionary consensus. In this, an apparently general consensus is generated by the refusal of one particular perspective – with all the benefits accruing from the particular narrowness of its focus of attention, but also all the deficits necessarily resulting from its partiality – to acknowledge the existence of other perspectives, differing in interest and scope, and yet to claim for itself an unchallengeable sovereign knowledge. When such an exclusionary consensus is put in place, alternative views and arguments tend to be discounted before they are even considered. In its strongest form, exclusionary consensus works by overlooking any arguments and evidence that might question, contradict or even simply modify any of its constitutive tenets.

The formation and hardening of this global consensus – as part and parcel of the 'policy internationalism' noted by King – is easy enough to chart.[32] By 1998, the distinguished German scholar of the relations between higher education and employment, Ulrich Teichler, noted 'the increased uneasiness within higher education about undue instrumentalist pressures'.[33] In 2000, in the USA, Patricia Gumport, in an oft-cited article, could write of the shift from the 'dominant legitimating idea of public higher education ... as a social institution ... toward the idea of higher education as an industry'.[34] By 2004, the British scholar Guy Neave could suggest that 'we find ourselves in the presence of a fundamental reframing of higher education'.[35] In this reframing, higher education has moved 'from being a sub-set of the political system ... [to becoming] a subset of the economic system'.[36] In this move from uneasiness, to a tension between opposing views, to a fundamental restructuring which does not allow opposing views we may observe the formation and hardening of the current exclusionary consensus.[37]

Looking back over the period of its formation, the Scandanavian scholars Peter Maasen and Johan P. Olsen note two of the dimensions of evidence and argument that its perspective marginalizes or deletes. First, they observe the almost entire absence of a properly historical account of the university in reform policy; and second, they point to a related narrowness in the conception of the university's social roles and functions. In so doing, they – doubtless unwittingly – repeat the key lessons of *The Long Revolution*.

Reform policy displays little or no interest in the complex and varied social roles and functions that the university has played in Europe since its inception, simply tending to claim that this complex institutional legacy has been entirely superseded by present demands. Reform policy appears to have neither any significant conception of nor interest in 'the possible role of universities in developing democratic citizens, a humanistic culture, social cohesion and solidarity, and a vivid public sphere'.[38] Second, and relatedly, the value of research and teaching tends to be narrowed down to the purely instrumental, with the two components of academic activity simply identified as, and reduced to, the status of 'key instruments for economic performance and growth and mastering global competition' (7).

While reform policy and the politicians and bureaucrats who are its main proponents tend to speak with one voice, this is due to the suppression of the voices of other interested parties, and notably those of academics themselves and the university rectors who to some extent represent them. Olsen and Massen point out – in the somewhat desperate terms that show the power of the exclusionary consensus – that 'while one view has a dominant position in reform documents and speeches, there are competing views' and these include those exemplified in the Magna Charter of European Universities, who claim the university as above all 'a public institution, rooted in the Enlightenment, and serving the common good' (11, 10).[39]

In a conclusion, Olsen and Maasen offer the deliberately low-key hypothesis that 'reform strategies that reduce the complex set of roles the University has performed historically in the national context to solely an economic role in the European context is unlikely to be successful' (22). Nonetheless, this reduction continues to play a central and continuing role in European higher education policy debates, with increasingly visible and disturbing consequences. In the end, what is overlooked in reform policy is all that works to constitute the social totality, understood as that set of formations and relationships which daily weave (or unravel) the communicative fabric in which all economic activity actually subsists, and all innovation is made possible. And this is not to mention what is necessarily omitted in this survey of arguments within the exclusionary consensus itself, the simple fact that higher education in the humanities tends to address needs and goals which are simply not reducible to reigning definitions of economic livelihood and progress.[40]

The Mirage of the Professional University

Something like the cautionary hypothesis proposed by Olsen and Maasen – that the narrowing down of the university's role to solely an economic one, and the deliberate blindness to the complex social roles and functions that the university had historically played was 'unlikely to be successful' – was in fact emphasized at a much earlier stage in the formation of the exclusionary consensus (49). The fact that this was done in reports published by two very important and influential organs of reform policy, the World Bank and the OECD, but came to be subsequently ignored, is still further evidence for the structures of complex 'overlooking' at work in reform policy. Let us now briefly examine the ways in which two detailed reports – the first, presented at a World Bank seminar on higher education and development held in Kuala Lumpur in 1991 and the second issued by the OECD in 1993 – deal in particular with the question of the relation between innovation and employment (key themes of all reform rhetoric) and the humanities (a key absence in reform policy).

In 1991, Manuel Castells, one of the world's leading researchers into the influence of the development of internet technology on the global economy, presented an important report to the World Bank seminar on higher education and development. 'The University System: Engine of Development in the New World Economy' presented many of what were to become the standard tenets of reform policy, and, notably, emphases on 'the developmental potential of universities', 'the university as a productive force in the informational economy', and how the needs of the new economy 'made research increasingly important as a strategic tool to enhance productivity and competitiveness'.[41]

Yet the main thrust of Castells' arguments was to 'convey to policy makers' that it is just 'not possible to have a pure, or quasi-pure, model of the university' (211).[42] Theory has to accommodate the messy complexities of history rather than turn away from them, and Castells stressed that 'the critical element in the structure and dynamic of university systems' is, in fact, what he referred to as

> their ability to combine and make compatible seemingly contradictory functions which have all constituted the system historically and are all probably being required at any given moment by the social interests underlying higher education policies. (211)

These contradictory functions include their major social role as ideological apparatuses in which the 'conflicts and contradictions of society' (206) can be expressed and even amplified ; their powerful social function in the 'selection of dominant elites' (207); the generation of new knowledge associated with the success of 'the American science-oriented universities in the new processes of economic growth' (208), as well as the site of many core professional formations and the education of an appropriately skilled national bureaucracy (210). Given this real complexity in social reproduction as well as economic growth, Castells suggests that 'Universities will always be, at the same time, conflictual organizations, open to the debates of society, and thus to the generation and confrontation of ideologies' (211) and emphasizes that

> The technocratic version of a 'clean', 'purely scientific' or 'purely professional' university is just an historical vision sentenced to be constantly betrayed by historical reality. (212)

In fact, with regard to the centrality of innovation to any market-centred vision of the university, Castells (anticipating the conclusions of Olsen and Maasen more than fifteen years later, and articulating a variant of Williams's 'public education' stance) insists that

> One of the key elements in the development of the universities as centres of discovery and innovation is precisely the cross-fertilisation between different disciplines (including the humanities), together with their detachment vis-à-vis the immediate needs of the economy. Without the self-determination of the scientific community in the pursuit of the goals of scientific research, there will be no discovery ... there will only be scientific discovery, and connection with the world centres of scientific discovery, if universities are complete systems, bringing together technical training, scientific research and humanistic education, since the human spirit cannot be piecemealed to obtain only the precise technical skills required for enhancing the quality of regional crops. (216)

It is precisely this insistence on universities to be 'complete systems' for there to be any chance of real innovation that is lost or ignored in the rhetoric of reform policy as it hardens into an excluding orthodoxy.[43]

In similar fashion, the 1993 OECD report, *Higher Education and Employment: The Case of the Humanities and Social Sciences*, exemplifies the dynamics of this same excluding orthodoxy.[44] The report is in many ways most notable now for the fact that, while some of its findings and recommendations have been largely echoed by reform policy, other key observations and recommendations have been ignored and not taken up.

On the one hand, the report articulated what have by now become commonplaces of reform policy, particularly with regard to the low standing of the humanities and social sciences.

According to the research conducted by the OECD group, the emergence of mass higher education from the 1970s 'has had several negative consequences for higher education generally and for the humanities and social sciences especially'.[45] Massification diluted the 'traditional screening role' of higher education: 'Now that university enrolment has increased substantially, the intrinsic value of university degrees varies considerably from field to field, depending on real or perceived differences in selectivity, difficulty, student profile, and instrumental value' (50). In this situation, across all the countries surveyed in the OECD report, 'the study of H/SS [Humanities and Social Sciences] disciplines ends up low on the range of values' (50). A second and related consequence has been the 'increased emphasis on the part of employers, students, and, in many countries, of government, on the extrinsic or use value of higher education':

> More students depend on educational credentials rather than on socio-economic background for employment, more employers are looking for specifically skilled employers [*sic*], and governments are more concerned about the explicit returns on their growing investment in funding higher education. (50)

'This trend', the report emphasizes, 'further diminishes the status of H/SS disciplines because of their less obvious relevance to work' (50).

But the wording here is deliberate: 'less obvious relevance' to work does not mean no relevance, though it does indicate problems with seeking the kind of simple and direct connection between qualification and the world of work that policy makers are naturally inclined to wish were there.[46] Indeed, one of the major challenges that the report identifies for policy makers is the dramatically 'changing content and organization of work' under the impact of the increased speed of scientific and technological discovery.[47] In this situation, the report observes a significant paradox in the situation of the humanities and the social sciences, and one that disappears from later reform policy formulations.

The paradox is this: that while the ever more rapidly changing nature of work in the global network society 'dramatically enhance(s) the potential role of the humanities and social sciences', these disciplines are facing more criticism than ever before (51). It is important to quote rather than to paraphrase the OECD Report's judgement here. '[S]ome of the problems currently facing the traditional H/SS disciplines', the report observes, are 'triggered by external attitudes and value judgements which are often unjustified and discriminatory'. The

> denigration of H/SS because they are perceived as 'soft' subjects reflects excessive societal emphasis on technological advances and economic development, as well as misunderstanding of the kind of knowledge needed to deal with the contemporary complexity and ambiguity. (51)

In the end, in the view of the report, for individuals to function well in their occupations and as members of their society, higher education will need to provide

> sophisticated generic skills in the areas of communication, interpersonal relationships, and critical thinking such as can be acquired through the study of H/SS; contextual understanding of their activities requiring appropriate elements of the humanities and social sciences; and the capability of dealing with complexity and ambiguity by means of ways of knowing which differ from the traditional scientific model and are consistent with the methodologies of H/SS. (51)

In conclusion, the report recommends that these skills – located in the humanities and social sciences – 'should be integral parts of all higher education programs, technical or non-technical' (51).

That both this very direct recommendation from 1993 and Castells' careful analysis of the necessarily contradictory functions of higher education should be effectively ignored is yet further testimony to the power of the excluding consensus that came to constitute higher education policy at the close of the twentieth century, and continues to wreak havoc on the prospects for the kind democratic education envisioned in *The Long Revolution*.

Conclusion

For all the undoubted importance of *The Long Revolution* for an internal history of cultural studies in the academy, I have tried in this essay to return *The Long Revolution* to the terms of the larger public and political context the book was addressing. In particular, I have argued that such a limited reading works to obscure the link between politics and education that in fact nourished the book as a whole, and was indeed precisely the link that did most to create the immediate controversy and now largely forgotten furore that its publication created at the time. In addition, and paradoxically enough – though not paradoxically at all if you think of Williams's commitment to always taking the long view of things – I have argued that it is precisely this return to the now forgotten core of the trilogy in the commitment to public education that may best connect *The Long Revolution* to our own moment in a longer crisis and struggle.

For what is at stake, though rarely or never addressed as such in the exclusionary consensus described in brief above, are the social purposes of higher education in general. In much reform discourse, the purposes of higher education are taken to be entirely economic, and instrumental to the economy, preferring to leave aside the reality of the social bearings of education in general, and of higher education in particular. As Olsen and Maasen put it, 'reform documents give little attention to the possible role of universities in developing democratic citizens, a humanistic culture, social cohesion and solidarity, and a vivid public sphere' and they further note how there is 'no serious discussion of how a commitment to economic (as well as democratic or social) goals can be squared with academic values and the potential danger of subordinating academic curiosity for knowledge and the pursuit of truth to some external agenda. In sum, the role of Academic and Democracy is primarily defined as serving economic purposes and the growth of competitive markets'.[48]

In *The Long Revolution*, Williams had already argued that 'we often speak of the nation as if it were a large firm, with other nations as competitors' and noted how, when we 'speak of work as "the labour market"', we then go on to 'argue about education primarily in terms of the needs of "the economy"', in a marked anticipation of what were to become dominant Thatcherite and neo-liberal terms.[49] Against this, he set the need for 'a public education designed to express and create the values of an educated democracy' (186). That we have largely failed in this in the most obvious and pragmatic terms – as evidenced by the recent experience of higher education in the United Kingdom, but also in the general failure to effectively counter the exclusionary consensus of global higher education policy template – suggests that Williams's arguments for the constitutive links between education and democracy in *The Long Revolution* deserve to be reread today, if only to stress the need for renewed discussion of just what 'permanent education' might mean today.[50]

Notes

1 See, for instance, Dennis L. Dworkin 'Cultural Studies and the Crisis in British Radical Thought' in *Views Beyond the Border Country*, ed. Dennis L. Dworkin and Leslie G. Roman (London and New York: Routledge, 1993), 38; Fred Inglis, *Raymond Williams* (London and New York: Routledge, 1995), 173; Andrew Milner, *Literature, Culture and Society* (London:

UCL Press 1996), 25; John Storey, 'All Forms of Signification', in ed. Monika Seidel, Roman Horak and Lawrence Grossberger *About Raymond Williams* (London and New York: Routledge, 2010), 44.

2   See Raymond Williams, *The Long Revolution* (Cardigan: Parthian [1961] 2011), 10; Raymond Williams, *Communications* (Harmondsworth: Penguin [1962] 1973), 11.

3   Naturalism was the prime focus of the first trilogy, which included Raymond Williams, *Drama from Ibsen to Eliot* (London: Chatto, 1952), Raymond Williams, *Drama in Performance* (London: Frederick Muller, 1954) and Raymond Williams and Michael Orrom, *Preface to Film* (London: Film Drama Ltd, 1954). Williams returns interestingly to the topic of naturalism with the essay 'Theatre as a Political Forum' in Raymond Williams, *The Politics of Modernism* (London and New York: Verso, 1989), 81–94.

4   See F.R. Leavis, *Mass Civilization and Minority Culture* (Cambridge: Minority Press, 1930); and for a useful discussion of its impact on the formation of literary studies in England, Francis Mulhern, *The Moment of 'Scrutiny'* (London: New Left Books, 1979). For a detailed account of Williams's engagement with Leavis and *Scrutiny*, see John Higgins, *Raymond Williams: Literature, Marxism and Cultural Materialism* (London and New York: Routledge, 1999), 14–19; 34.

5   That the question of the trilogy's political impact is sidelined in favour of a discussion of the theoretical disagreements around the explanatory force claimed for culture in Williams's theory in the discussions with Williams conducted by the *New Left Review* and published as Raymond Williams, *Politics and Letters* (London: New Left Books, 1979) is more than unfortunate in the light of the later political developments discussed in the paper. See Williams, *Politics and Letters*, 134.

6   Williams, *The Long Revolution*, 169.

7   Williams, *Politics and Letters*, 133.

8   Raymond Williams, *Culture and Society* (London: Chatto and Windus [1959] 1967), 338; Malcolm Pittock, 'Critical Forum', *Essays in Criticism* 9 (1959): 432.

9   Where Williams acutely notes 'The masses are always the others, whom we don't know, and can't know … To other people, we also are the masses. Masses are other people'. *Culture and Society*, 299–300.

10 The same rub is apparent in the third of Marx's *Theses on Feuerbach*, with its insistence that the 'materialist doctrine concerning the changing of circumstances and upbringing forgets that circumstances are changed by men and that it is essential to change the educator himself. This doctrine must, therefore, divide society into two parts, one of which is superior to society' (Karl Marx, *Early Writings* (Harmondsworth: Penguin, 1992), 422). In this sense, is it too far-fetched to see in Williams's assertion of the 'long revolution' what Marx meant by the fact that 'changing of circumstances and of human activity or self-changing can be conceived and rationally understood only as *revolutionary practice*' (ibid.)? Similarly, is this not the basis of the links between democracy and education that form the core of the work of contemporary analyst, Jacques Rancière, whose definition of the conservative view of democracy – 'democratic life signified a large amount of popular participation in discussing public affairs, and it was a bad thing' (Jacques Rancière, *Hatred of Democracy* (London: Verso, 2006), 8) could well describe Pittock's stance – and that of the other opponents to *The Long Revolution* in the early 1960s?

11 Williams, *Politics and Letters*, 112.

12 For an account of the oppositional centrality of Eliot rather than Leavis to Williams, see Higgins, *Raymond Williams*.

13 T.S. Eliot, *Notes Towards the Definition of Culture* (London: Faber [1948] 1985), 100–1.

14 As, for instance, in his provocative study *The English Universities and Adult Education* (London: WEA, 1951).

15 In essays such as 'Figures and Highways', 'Standards' and 'A Kind of Gresham's Law' for the adult education journal *The Highway* and published in ed. John McIlroy and Sallie Westwood, *Border Country: Raymond Williams in Adult Education* (Leicester: National Institute of Adult Continuing Education, 1993), 84–8, 207–14.
16 Raymond Williams, 'Adult Education and Social Change', in Raymond Williams, *What I Came to Say* (London: Hutchinson Radius, 1989), 158.
17 John McIlroy put this well in his indispensable survey of Williams's work in adult education, writing of how '*The Long Revolution* was an inspirational book and it is difficult now to re-experience its powerful impact in the 1960s. To the idea of culture as a way of life and the struggle for a common culture Williams now added the central idea of a learning community, the cultural empowerment of the majority of the population, the excluded and disinherited who through the third phase of revolution would achieve enfranchisement in the cultural powers of meaning generation. The Learning Community reflected his experience of the democratic educational participation of the WEA but its realization would close the existing gap between education and life. These three, central intertwined ideas represented a freshened statement of the concerns of radical adult education and a programme to which existing adult education could contribute'. See John McIlroy, 'Border Country: Raymond Williams in Adult Education', in *Border Country*, 305–6.
18 Just as it did, in an intriguing and complex way, in Karl Marx's *Theses on Feuerbach*, where he writes of the need 'to educate the educator himself', Thesis III, in Karl Marx, *Early Writings* (Harmondsworth: Penguin 1992), 422) in ways that are notably picked up on and enlarged by Gramsci, always a useful comparative thinker for Williams.
19 See, for instance, J.F.C. Harrison's comment, with regard to the 'new' situation facing adult education, that is 'clear that a full employment welfare state has begun to create new social attitudes' (Harrison, cited in Higgins, *Raymond Williams*, 53), while for a notable example of the 'end of ideology' argument, see Daniel Bell, *The End of Ideology: On the Exhaustion of Political Ideas in the Fifties* (New York: Free Press, 1965). In this, Williams articulated a core resistance which exemplified or helped to explain the emergence of the 'New Left' which was, in part at least, called for precisely to face this challenge, as Dennis Dworkin reminds us (see Dworkin, *Cultural Marxism in Postwar Britain* (Durham and London: Duke University Press, 1997) 3).
20 Williams, *The Long Revolution*, 186
21 It is interesting to note that with the phrase 'permanent education' – derived, Williams suggested, from his reading of French theorists – he maps out something like the theoretical terrain covered by Gramsci's notion of hegemony, or Althusser's own reworking of that in the notion of Ideological State Apparatuses, against the usual claim (as, for instance, Storey, 'All Forms of Signification', 39) that it was only after reading Gramsci that Williams discovered the workings of power in culture.
22 Williams, *Communications*, 14.
23 For a useful reconsideration of the often neglected *May Day Manifesto*, see Stephen Woodhams, 'The 1968 *May Day Manifesto*', in ed. M. Seidel, R. Horal and L. Grossberg, *About Raymond Williams* (London and New York: Routledge, 2010), 57–67.
24 Williams, *Communications*, 15
25 For a useful survey of the penetration of these interests into secondary education, see Melissa Benn, *School Wars: the battle for Britain's Education* (London and New York: Verso 2011).
26 In this sense, the current blatant reorganization of British higher education around capitalist priorities of a narrowly-understood 'innovation' and 'employability' – not to speak of the reorganization of fee-paying structures – only presents perhaps the most extreme example of a global phenomenon in higher education policy. On these, see for

instance Stefan Collini, 'Browne's Gamble', *London Review of Books* 32 (2010): 21 and Simon Head 'The Grim Threat to British Universities', *New York Review of Books* (13 January 2011), available at nybooks.com and Christopher Prendergast 'Short Cuts', *London Review of Books* 33, no. 1 (6 January): 11.

27 See especially *'That Full Complement of Riches': The Contribution of the Arts, Humanities and Social Sciences to the Nation's Wealth* (London: British Academy, 2004) and *Past Present and Future: The Public Value of the Humanities and Social Sciences* (London: British Academy, 2010).

28 *Past Present and Future*, Foreword (n.p.).

29 For the best account of the implications of the 1988 Reform Bill for academic freedom, see Conrad Russell, *Academic Freedom* (London and New York: Routledge, 1993). Thatcher's biographer John Campbell observed that the general result of the Thatcher reforms 'was a brain-drain of talent and a demoralization of the whole academic community', and noted that 'No group in society, with the possible exception of trade-union leaders, suffered a deeper fall in status' (John Campbell *Margaret Thatcher: Volume Two The Iron Lady* (London: Vintage Books, 2008), 409). After her retirement, Thatcher herself later wrote ' that 'many distinguished academics thought that Thatcherism in education meant a philistine subordination of scholarship to the immediate requirements of vocational training', but asserted that this 'certainly no part of my kind of Thatcherism' (Thatcher cited in Simon Jenkins, *Thatcher and Sons: A Revolution in Three Acts* (London: Penguin, 2007), 124), perhaps forgetting her earlier claim that 'academics and intellectuals … are putting out what I call poison', Thatcher cited Campbell, *Margaret Thatcher*, 396, and her consequent determination to discipline the academic community into a purely utilitarian view of the universities' social function. For the view that Thatcherism is the ultimate source of the current 'undermining' of British universities (alongside some US managerial systems), see Simon Head, 'The Grim Threat to British Universities', *New York Review of Books* (13 January 2011, available at nybooks.com).

30 See the discussion developed in Williams, *The Long Revolution*, 171–4.

31 *Past Present and Future*, 5

32 As policy scholar Roger King has noted, there has been a marked increase in the international convergence of policies in higher education (and other areas of government), usually attributed (at least in part) to the extraordinarily rapid increase in the speed and ease of global communications. 'Widespread policy borrowing', he notes, 'spreading policy imaginaries by national decision-makers predicated on global comparisons and the notion of the competition-state, and the growing influence of bodies such as the OECD, underpins global convergences in government policy prescriptions.' Roger King, 'Governing Knowledge Globally: Policy Internationalism and Higher Education in the Age of Globalization', *Higher Education and Society: A Research Report* (Milton Keynes: Centre for Higher Education Research and Information, The Open University, 2010), 35.

33 Ulrich Teichler, *Higher Education and the World of Work: Conceptual Frameworks, Comparative Perspectives, Empirical Findings* (Rotterdam: Sense Press, 2009), 67.

34 Patricia Gumport, 'Academic Restructuring: Organizational Change and Institutional Imperatives', *Higher Education* 39, no. 1 (2000): 70.

35 Guy Neave, 'Higher Education Policy as Orthodoxy: Being a Tale of Doxological Drift, Political Intention and Changing Circumstances', in ed. P. Teixera, B. Jongbloed, D. Dill and A. Amaral, *Markets in Higher Education: Rhetoric or Reality?* (Dordrecht: Kluwer Academic Publishers, 2004), 142.

36 Neave, 'Higher Education Policy as Orthodoxy', 143.

37 I cite the work of social scientists here, but the observations of practicing humanities scholars were just as trenchant, and of course with more direct relevance concerning the impact of policy reform on the humanities. See, for instance, Bill Readings's deliberately

low-key observation 'the centrality of the traditional humanistic disciplines to the life of the university is no longer assured' (*The University in Ruins* (Cambridge: Harvard University Press, 1996), 3). Similarly, in one of a series of important essays regarding the impact of the new higher education policy on the humanities, Masao Miyoshi noted that 'The humanities as they are now constituted in academia are no longer desired or warranted. There is a decisive change in academic outlook and policy to de-emphasize the humanities and to shift resources to applied sciences', see Miyoshi 'Ivory Tower in Escrow', *boundary 2*, 27, no. 1 (2000): 18.

38 J.O. Olsen and P. Maasen, 'European Debates on the Knowledge Institution: The Modernization of the University at the European Level', in ed. J.P. Olsen and P. Maasen, *University Dynamics and European Integration* (Dordrecht: Springer, 2007), 9.

39 Carlo Salerno, in a powerful contribution to the Olsen and Maasen collection, also points to the same monologism and exclusionary dynamic at work in the Bologna process, noting the remarkable fact that 'the Bologna process should drag on for six years without any formal representation for the one Estate on which implementation ultimately depended – namely academia', and the absolute contrast between the 'two modes of discourse' of the European Commission and the Bologna Declaration, the Commission with its 'increasingly utilitarian, technocratic mindset, and the Bologna Declaration which (re-)instated the primacy of the cultural dimension' (Carlo Salerno, 'A Service Enterprise: The Market Vision', in Olsen and Maasen, *University Dynamics and European Integration*, 140, 141).

40 On this non-reducibility, see, for instance, Phamotse and Kissak's assertion: 'we suggest that attempts to justify the existence and pursuit of the humanities in instrumental terms are futile and misguided. We argue that their importance transcends the imperatives of utility to contribute towards the preservation and extension of what we think it means to be human, denying the constraints and logic of instrumentalism to insist upon the irreducible value of self-definition' (M. Phamotse and M. Kissack, 'The Role of the Humanities in the Modern University: Some Historical and Philosophical Considerations', *Journal of the Philosophy of Education* 42, no. 1 (2008): 49.

41 Manuel Castells, 'The University System: Engine of Development in the New World Economy' [extract], in ed. J. Muller, N. Cloete and S. Badat, *Challenges of Globalization: South African Debates with Manuel Castells* (Cape Town: Maskew Miller Longman, [1991] 2001), 211, 210.

42 Careful readers will note how Castells's use of the term 'convey' itself signals all the problems of the exclusionary consensus!

43 For a somewhat similar view on the real nature of innovation, see the more recent account by Mark Dodgson and David Gann who also emphasize the 'importance of the new interdisciplinary combinations between science, arts, engineering, social sciences and humanities, and business' (Mark Dodgson and David Gann, *Innovation: A Very Short Introduction* (Oxford: Oxford University Press, 2010), 134).

44 The report drew on research conducted in Australia, Austria, Canada, Denmark, Finland, Japan, the Netherlands, Portugal, Sweden, Switzerland, the USA and Yugoslavia, and may still represent the widest available survey. Its findings are largely confirmed by those of the Allen Report for the Canadian Social Sciences and Humanities Research Council, and notably its suggestion that 'One of the outstanding features of the knowledge-based economy will be the breadth of advanced education and skills it requires' (Robert C. Allen, *Education and Technological Revolutions: The Role of the Social Sciences and the Humanities in the Knowledge-Based Economy* (Report for the Social Sciences and Humanities Research Council of Canada, 1999), 13).

45 Organization for Economic and Cultural Development Report, *Higher Education and Employment: The Case of the Humanities and Social Sciences* (Paris: OECD Documents, 1993), 50.
46 As the noted specialist on the relations between work and higher education Ulrich Teichler observes in this regard 'researchers are likely to deliver a more complex picture than the practitioners consider desireable for making priority decisions' (Teichler, *Higher Education and the World of Work,* 18). He also points to the reality facing any planner that the reality is that '*the signals from the employment system* are more *blurred and ambivalent* than ever before' (30; his emphasis). See also the findings of the British Academy Report 2004, and Allen, *Education and Technological Revolutions*. On this, note Robert Birnbaum's observation in his useful and even entertaining study, that 'instead of recognizing that higher education's most critical goals are difficult, if not impossible to measure, institutions and systems responded by setting up goals those things that *could* be measured', *Management Fads in Higher Education: Where They Come, What They Do, Why They Fail* (San Francisco: Jossey-Bass, 2001), 84. Note also his useful warning: 'The more reasonable something sounds, the less need to subject it to critical analysis and think through its implications' (160).
47 OECD, *Higher Education and Employment*, 51.
48 Olsen and Maasen, 'European Debates on the Knowledge Institution, 9.
49 Williams, *The Long Revolution*, 132.
50 For some striking developments in this regard – and which pay due attention to Williams's work – see, for instance, Michael W. Apple, 'Rebuilding Hegemony: Education, Equality and the New Right', Wendy Hohli, 'Raymond Williams, Affective ideology, and Counter-Hegemonic Practices' and Fazal Rizvi, 'Williams on Democracy and the Governance of Education' all in ed. Dennis L. Dworkin and Leslie G. Roman, *Views beyond the Border Country: Raymond Williams and Cultural Politics* (London and New York: Routledge, 1993) and the essays collected in W. John Morgan and Peter Preston (eds), *Raymond Williams: Politics, Education, Letters* (London: Macmillan, 1993). With particular regard to the South African higher education system in this regard, see John Higgins, 'Making the Case for the Humanities in South Africa', A Research Paper for the Academy of Science of South Africa Consensus Panel Study 'The State of the Humanities in South Africa: Status, Prospects and Strategies' (2011), available through assaf.org.za. The present essay includes several paragraphs from this study.

Raymond Williams in the Sixties: History, Communication and Conflict

Roberto del Valle

The third and final section of *The Long Revolution* synthesises Raymond Williams's reconstructive project of radical practices and meanings against the background of ideological retrenchment of post-war Britain. His analysis manages to isolate the concrete material lineaments which compose and define the real antagonisms of a modern society. For Williams, these are to be found in the charged affective dimension of communicable relationships, and thus, on a fundamentally different plane from that of the ruling abstractions of 'individual' and 'society' espoused by the alternate discourses of the dominant political forces. Williams's bid for a reconstitution of (political) community through communication demands a redeployment of micro-social dynamics as constitutive of a properly alternative politics beyond the hardened ideologies of Labourism and Communism.

*

This essay presents an overview of Raymond Williams's reflections on culture and society in his 1961 book, *The Long Revolution*. In particular, it focuses on the *explicitly political* dimension of that work, that is, on the analysis of the unfolding post-war crises and on the resulting formulation of integral systemic alternatives. The bulk of the essay is thus devoted to Williams's analyses of the institutional – in the broadest sense – transformations affecting Britain in the late 1950s and early 1960s. Against a general ideological background governed by such notions and clichés as 'the mixed economy', 'affluence' or 'welfare', Williams summons a general theory of culture-and-society (after the fashion he had pioneered three years earlier in his breakthrough work) in a general political attempt to stem the cruder effects of the hegemonic consensus and its coordinated assault on democracy.

With the publication of *The Long Revolution* Williams felt that he had brought his interrogation of the 'idea of culture' (an intellectual engagement spanning his landmark book of 1958, *Culture and Society*, as well as his crucial autobiographical novel of 1960, *Border Country*) to its – first – mature conclusion. According to certain commentators, the later book attempted to counteract some of the lingering theoretical confusions harboured by *Culture and Society* – notably, the allegedly unresolved semantic instabilities in his use of the term 'culture' – 'by laying stronger theoretical and empirical foundations'.[1]

Yet as other critics have noted, the book remained characteristic of Williams's style – 'as much a collection of essays as a work with a single theme'[2] – and yet simultaneously more firmly determined to address the urgent political tasks derived from cultural analysis and less satisfactory in the overall outcome. As Fred Inglis has noted, *The Long Revolution* 'caused quite a stir, and was even more fully noticed than its older sibling'.[3] The degree of hostility which it first attracted – notably from the Right, but also from the Left[4] – coincided with Williams's full incorporation into the vanguard of the emergent New Left as a leading figure ('our best man', in Edward Thompson's words)[5] and inescapable intellectual referent.

The 'long revolution' charted by Williams in the book was, by his own admission, 'a difficult revolution to define',[6] actualising itself in different ambits, against multiple forces of reaction and conformity, and developing over an exceedingly long period of time. This complex process had three interweaving strands or lines of development, which in turn constituted 'revolutionary' processes of their own: the democratic revolution, the industrial revolution and the cultural revolution. The first accounted for the ongoing and explicit development of power struggles through which the possibility of inclusive decision-making and effective political participation was conceived. The second, for its part, was intimately connected to the productive dimension of society and the technical and scientific mobilisation of material resources. As Williams notes, '[t]he complex interaction between the democratic and industrial revolutions is at the centre of our most difficult social thinking' (11). Thirdly, and perhaps most importantly for the general emphasis of the book, the set of transformations denoted by the phrase 'cultural revolution' sought to account for the even more complex articulation of the new available means and modes of communication with the emancipatory programme for a common culture.

This latter concern offers a thematic springboard for the first section of the book, which opens with a historical analysis of creative activity and theories of creation. In it, Williams returns to the emphases of his concluding remarks in *Culture and Society*, insisting on the inseparability of individual creation from its embodiment as interpersonal meaning in a collective context. The creation of meanings, for Williams, depends on their validation by others as part of a new shared experience. The crux of artistic creation rests on its communicability and interconnectedness within a complex whole of social relations. In this sense 'communication' is synonymous with 'social process' and signals a sense of growth and transformation which cannot be abstracted from the generality of social organisation. Perhaps Williams's most striking formulation in this respect is that which renders 'communication' and 'community' interchangeable and posits them as general semantic pointers within a total articulation of social being.

The essential task is thus to reconnect the specialised areas of meaning into which an increasingly complex social totality tends to direct its diverse functions and, crucially, to reconstruct the holistic dimension which makes the links, connections and continuities among particular areas of experience operative. Following closely in the steps of the 1958 book, Williams returns to a summation of his position and general conceptualisation of cultural analysis as 'the study of relationships between elements in a whole way of life' (63). This analysis is fundamentally concerned with the organisation and patterning of the component elements in a particular historical reality. For Williams, the crucial aspect with which cultural inquiry must concern itself is not the precipitate or abstract form in which a particular artefact or mode of thinking or living is encountered, but the complex assemblage (the rules of combination, organisation and inter-relation) of the different elements in a given society. As *Culture and Society* had spelled out, the substantial core of the social whole, that matrix for which the general name of culture is often substituted, directly concerns the shared or common nature of social activity as intangible – and perhaps even unconscious – experience. The particular (whole) way of life of a given period/society is concretised in its affective texture, and this is typically found in solution, as the undifferentiated complex of attractions, distributions and compositions which define a social reality *as it is lived*. The famous concept which Williams invokes to account for this subtle quality of the social, the 'structure of feeling', thus signals the enabling condition on which culture, understood as the communicable substance of a social formation, is predicated.[7] It supplies the unconscious textures and meanings on which a sense of wholeness, of integrity and functionality, can be built.

'Our thinking about society is a long debate between abstractions and actual relationships' (120): the challenge presented by the ongoing long revolution, with its manifold components and strands of development, requires a strategic resolution of this opposition. The reduction of a society and social thinking to the levels of politics (the system of decision) and economics (the system of maintenance) is characteristic of a particular, and historically determined, description of interpersonal relations in which 'society' and the 'individual' function as the dominant abstractions. A resolution of this deadlock would necessarily require a repositioning of the terms of antagonism and resistance in a more apposite (I am tempted to say, materialist) perspective of immediate relationships and concrete assemblages (Williams would say 'identities') – indeed, of *communicable* social experience. In this respect, available formulae of oppositionality have often incurred a debilitating exposure to and complicity with, their critical target, rehearsing *en bloc* tools and elements of the hegemonic discourse. For Williams, the task of socialism must therefore reach beyond a basic substitution of priorities within an inherited conceptual and moral horizon. Rather, it must commence at the more basic level of a material configuration of affects, as the radical re-creation of a whole 'human order' (133).

In the third and final section of *The Long Revolution* Williams identifies the contemporary crisis of the 1950s and early 1960s with the breakdown or loss of 'an adequate sense of society' in this precise sense. For him, the often critical assessment of reformist or social democratic approaches to wealth redistribution and extension of opportunity rests on a fundamental distortion and lack of integral understanding of the social process: 'We think of my money, my light, in these naïve terms, because parts of our very idea of society are withered at root ... In a society whose products depend almost entirely on intricate and continuous co-operation and social organization, we expect to consume as if we were isolated individuals, making our own way' (325).

In this final section, which constitutes a departure from the general tone and orientation of the preceding chapters (and which Williams later explained as responding to 'the quite new situation of '57–9, including to some extent the discussion of *Culture and Society* itself'),[8] Williams propounds an extensive notion of communication as the proper antidote to the abundant side-effects derived from the process of abstraction which increasingly characterises modern social experience. The aggressive logic of atomisation threatens to dissolve, in a vortex of private consumption of goods and experiences, the real connections and internal coherences of a complex, industrialised, society.[9] The obscurity which befalls this steady complexification of 'our real relationships' leads to dangerous confusions regarding the actual causes of the overarching problematic. Thus, industrial production, 'large-scale organization', or even society itself and its inherent set of pressures, are variously misidentified as contributing factors to the general disorientation. The radical embeddedness of these concepts in capitalism (which insists on imposing an abstract form on them) makes their retrieval and deployment as novel formations of human relationality a most urgent task. Williams does not so much advocate a romantic recovery of a substantive/organic embodiment of the social, as a fresh re-articulation of its experience through a prioritisation of common or communicable meanings and dynamics.

For Williams, the consolidation of a 'mixed economy' and its attendant institutions in the 1950s created the conditions for an ideological recrudescence of the profit-motive and its resilient expressions in the electoral gamble. Revisionism within the Labour Party (under the executive leadership of Hugh Gaitskell and the intellectual patronage of Anthony Crosland) represented a particularly symptomatic adjustment of traditional working-class institutionality to the confused dynamics of 'affluence' and what the party's left wing characteristically described as a 'meretricious society'.[10] Its fresh projection of Britain as a 'post-capitalist' country paved the way for a smooth reinscription of socialism within a consensual system of bi-partisan alternation.[11]

Against such a backdrop of semantic and structural shifts, Williams's contention that 'the patterns of thinking and behaviour [promoted by capitalism] have never been more strong' necessarily prompts a realignment of terms and analyses which may strategically reposition the programme for a common future. The co-optation of the Labour Party, under the specific ideological conditions of revisionism, into the functional whole of capitalist society indeed marks the exhaustion of social democracy's oppositional project (328). The suggestion remains, however, in the specific endurance of symbolic loyalties, that the traditional institutions of the British left – principally the Labour Party and the unions – in their basic outline of a general social principle – cooperation – registered a viable alternative blueprint for the general functioning of society. The thrust of a reinvigorated capitalism notwithstanding, the space of possibility opened up by the continuing existence of these 'collective democratic institutions', lies in the latency or virtuality of their cultural logic, which fundamentally expresses a particular mode of (emancipated) social relationality and communicable experience (329).

The fundamental challenge for Williams remains the creation and substantiation of new meanings and directions in the articulation of social relationships: the crucial advancement of an alternative pattern of choices and identifications whereby the margin for democratic practices may be enlarged. The inherent danger of a received institutionality organised around the party system resides in the growing 'assumption that direct popular government is not what democracy is about' (337). Thus, a 'tightly organized party system and parliament seem to have converted the national franchise into the election of a court' (336).

The loss of any real sense of effective participation results from an overbearing allegiance to impersonal, abstract processes: the shifts and gradations of popular opinion are slighted in favour of results measured 'at the level of the court', rather than with direct reference to 'actual persons', in what amounts to a brand of 'conventional thinking' which, 'when it is traced to its sources, is again the tactical wisdom of a defensive autocracy' (339). This alarming estrangement from the parliamentary-democratic process is further complicated by a 'relative absence of democracy in other large areas of our lives', notably work. The extension of the principles of managerialism again witnesses a substitution of centralised decision-making for any real affirmation of democracy in the workplace. The standard socialist solution of public ownership is further complicated by the lingering bureaucratic instinct found in the public corporation model and hinted at in the customary objection that the substitution of state monopolies in those areas of activity hitherto controlled by an equally monopolistic private sector adds very little in terms of real democratisation.[12] However, the general tone of 'apathy, concession and revolt' alternately rehearsed under conditions of rampant managerialism suggests that an incomparable amelioration in terms of 'more rational and responsible solutions' would be achieved through the real extension of participative strategies.

In Williams's opinion, the inherited repertoire of distinctions allusive to birth and status further distorts the real sources of division generated by post-war British capitalism. The endurance of an older system of nobility and essentially feudal gradation within a solidly capitalist society (explained by the anomalous development of the English bourgeoisie and its consequent compromise with 'the class it had virtually defeated' in the nineteenth century (346)) survived in the systematic confusions of language and semantics: the traditional identification of an 'upper' and a 'middle' class terminologically based on hereditary distinction ('upper' and 'middle' as opposed to 'lower' in a stratification without mobility) was contrasted with the fundamentally economic determination of a 'working' class in what seemed like a radically distinct frame of reference (344–5).

The sharp increase in affluence after a period of post-war austerity contributed a further dimension to the received set of contradictions and confusions.[13] The 1950s saw an overall increase in material wealth and a corresponding growth in upward identification amongst broad layers of traditionally working-class wage earners. The general movement in patterns of consumption and the rapid expansion of consumer credit involving large sectors of the population paradoxically gave rise to an increasing convergence between the traditionally unpropertied (the working class of an earlier, proletarian, moment) and a presumptive middle class caught up in the expanding circle of credit and illusion.[14] As a result, the hegemonic doxa of 'affluence' and 'welfare' was typically premised on a blurring of real divisions often disguised by the institutionalised differential (between, for example, 'salary' and 'wage' earners): 'As we move into this characteristic contemporary world, we can see the supposed new phenomenon of classlessness as simply a failure of consciousness' (352).[15]

Williams insists on the need to produce new meanings and descriptions in order to accommodate emerging patterns: 'new kinds of work, new forms of capital, new systems of ownership' (352). However, the characteristic modulation of traditional social gradations in the new 'managed' capitalism of the 1950s operates within a general drift, not away from but towards, a general 'proletarianisation' (a generalisation of hired labour) across virtually the entire economy. Against a social background of new communities 'where work is very mixed', a split was generated between the kind of consciousness bestowed by the specific conditions of labour (which Williams terms 'trade-union consciousness') and a larger consciousness (a 'Labour consciousness') 'which has to be in terms of a mixed community and a whole society' (360). In this context, the 'affluent worker' could easily dissociate the particular realities of waged work – and the class specificities of the workplace – from a wider vision and social identity.[16] Williams recognises the potential of 1950s Conservatism (finally divested of its ominous 1930s aura) for an explicit identification, in the eyes of many people in the new socially mixed communities, with rising trends and patterns of 'learning and response': 'For at just this point, Labour seems to have very little to offer. A different version of community, a pattern of new consciousness, it has not been able to give. Its compromise policies combine the two irrelevant elements of appeal to old and fading habits and memories, and of cultural adjustment to the present social confusion' (360–1).

In this sense, both the old party left and the new revisionism appeared to perpetuate the irrelevancy of Labour descriptions to the new configurations of social interaction and consciousness, leaving 'the ruling interpretations and directions essentially unchallenged' (361). Only the re-statement of a 'real feeling of community' – an acceptance of everyone's involvement in the production of social capital, meanings, values and relations included – could break the deadlock of artificial oppositions and superimposed (and essentially false) antagonisms between different kinds of workers. The old socialist question of ownership, Williams argues, remains a central constituency of this analysis: and so, the isolation of 'that basic inequality' (the continuing ownership and control of 'social production' by only one section of the society – that represented by the class of the employers) would automatically refocus the terms of a debate overly muddled by older forms of division and residual modes of distinction.

The growth of cultural institutions in this context must capitalise on the plethora of possibilities offered by an advanced industrial society. Yet it must equally face up to the paradoxes and challenges inherent in a system of economic relations riddled, as the preceding analysis suggests, with contradictions and inequalities of a new type. Williams confronts the basic premise of the book (the notion that 'the human energy of the long revolution springs from the conviction that men can direct their own lives, by breaking through the pressures and restrictions of older forms of society, and by discovering new common institutions' (375)) with the actual state of cultural production and exchange under alleged conditions of 'post-capitalist' consensus (in the sense suggested by Crosland). In particular, the fundamental and systematic undermining of artistic freedom – torn between market dynamics and bureaucratic interference – dramatised, for Williams, 'the deepest difficulty in the whole development of our democracy'. The paradox represented by the nominal opposition and effective compromise between bureaucrat and speculator remains one of Williams's long-standing concerns in his analysis and advocacy of democratic enfranchisement for contemporary cultural institutions.[17]

The parallel crises of Labourism and Communism in the 1950s had set the specific institutional background and general ideological tone for a renovated practice of Kulturkritik[18] which sought to reactivate 'culture', understood as the reductive sphere of moral qualities and values, and concretised in selective practices, against the inertial dynamics of 'civilization' (or the general drift of mass tendencies in the society at large). Williams's work in *Culture and Society* remained within the confines of a wider attempt to vindicate this opposition for its progressive potential and harness it to the unfolding project of a nascent New Left culled from the moral and intellectual debris of the failing Communist and Labourist projects. Williams's construction of a resistant canon of critical thinking on 'culture and society' thus prefigured the radical deconstruction of the ideological alternative between paternalism – in all its guises – and assimilation to the mass trends of a new commercial culture. Francis Mulhern (72) situates the actual breakthrough in the turn of the 1960s, as the floor plan for a truly radical cultural politics is identified, not in a particular set of responses to capitalist advance, but in the empowerment of open, participative strategies of decision-making in effectively common institutional frameworks. In this sense, the transition from *Culture and Society* to *The Long Revolution* marks a resolution of the paternalist-cultural impasse in welfare Britain and a crucial enabling step in the gestation of Cultural Studies as a post-elitist, transversal mode of analysis of *all* signifying practices in society under the unitary heading of culture (78).

Williams's own definition of culture in *The Long Revolution* starts from a recognition of the 'ordinariness' which, beyond the narrow range of a selective tradition, brands all culture as a common endeavour characterised by the unspecialised complexity of social life itself.[19] It has already dispelled its lingering debt to the Leavisian category and its suggestion of a defensive elitism in the face of predatory dynamics of systemic devaluation. The tasks of reception and (de)codification imposed by the logic of canonisation (in the championing of a 'great tradition', for example) are to be replaced by a pluralist and fundamentally democratic recognition of the 'mixed' nature of the inheritance; of what is effectively an ordinarily complex genealogy of co-creation culled from 'many societies and many times as well as from many kinds of men'.[20] For the Williams of *The Long Revolution* – and its offshoot texts – the case against the modern onslaught of a mass culture imposes the promotion of the selective tradition's general availability within a common framework of reference and intervention. The danger is twofold: both the isolationist exclusivism of Kulturkritik and the debased populism of an unprincipled acceptance of the 'new' warrant obstacles to the kind of democratic enfranchisement which alone can offer a genuinely alternative social blueprint under which creativity may be acknowledged as a constitutive part of ever-expanding human faculties and affects.

Richard Hoggart's analyses in *The Uses of Literacy* – the work which is often paired with Williams's early definition of the post-war cultural problematic in *Culture and Society* – express a similar concern with the unfolding depletion of emotional and intellectual value in the advancing 'candy-floss world' of affluent capitalism. For Hoggart, the spurious reproduction of sameness – epitomised by the products of mass culture – invariably induced a chronic indifference and inability to discern or effectively respond to 'any serious suggestion of responsibility and commitment'.[21] It is worth noting that this line of cultural criticism had also been fostered, in the early years of the decade, by the Communist Party itself.[22] Characteristically, the damaging expansion of a devalued commercial culture had been linked to the hegemonic position of the United States in the post-war era and the resulting saturation of the British market with American products. Williams himself – along with critics like Hoggart – concurred with this identification of the 'synthetic anti-culture' designed for mass consumption in 1950s and 1960s Britain with the directive role of America within the capitalist world-system.[23] The special receptivity demonstrated by the British public responded, according to this native interpretation, to a deep-seated rejection of that English minority culture often decried as elitist and therefore inaccessible. The American ego-ideal encapsulated in this context a self-distancing from burdensome social distinctions of a traditional kind. Thus, as Williams noted in *Communications* (75), '[t]o go pseudo-American is a way out of the English complex of class and culture, but of course it solves nothing; it merely ritualizes the emptiness and despair'. It is the simultaneous exclusivisation of a preserved minority culture in the hands of traditional class distinctions and the condescension shown towards a 'genuinely popular tradition' which enables the cultural dominance of 'the speculators' in their colonisation of common meanings and practices.[23]

The Williams of *The Long Revolution* and the early 1960s offers what can be described as a fully consequential way out of the impasse represented by the lure of Americanisation on the one hand, and the narcissistic temptations of Leavisian minority culture on the other. And in doing so, this stage in his reflection on 'the idea of culture' can be said to surpass both his own initial sketch of a programme for common culture and the still largely continuist lines detected in *The Uses of Literacy*. Williams's resolution of the deadlock involves a shift in perspective from the internal logic of cultural self-reference (however oppositional) to the external, articulatory, emphasis on social relations and affects as the proper generative dynamics of a whole way of life.

With notions of affluence and welfare quickly fading from the general constellation of politics, reading the Williams of the early 1960s from our own critical standpoint of 2011/12 warrants some powerful effects. Rather than perceiving the radical construction of democracy in terms of a necessary extension of complex social and technological changes as an essentially outdated formula, this comes across as an invigorating admonition against the loss of opportunities for radical change, and perhaps more importantly, as a serious reminder of the unfinished nature of our shared history. Viewed from within the drama of a general exhaustion, the recommendation regains its urgency: the democratisation of culture (and society) is indissoluble from the mapping of a social whole onto a new complex of relations with their own meanings and values. It is, in other words, part and parcel of a holistic process of social re-organisation along more integrative and complex – more democratic – lines whose particular code-name, under the advanced techno-political conditions of our own conjuncture, is once again *communication*.

Notes

1. Jan Gorak, *The Alien Mind of Raymond Williams* (Columbia: University of Missouri Press, 1988), 57.
2. Fred Inglis, *Raymond Williams* (London: Routledge, 1998), 166. Inglis goes on to observe: 'It is an odd book. Part of it is hurriedly put together without proper links; parts exhibit the self-teaching of someone puzzling out questions better sorted out long ago by other people' (169–70). And Williams himself admitted in 1979 that it 'was a much more developing project even than *Culture and Society*, which of course now seems the more unified book. It was a case of bringing together certain impulses and trying to hold them in some sort of shape'. Raymond Williams, *Politics and Letters* (London: New Left Review/Books, 1979), 133.
3. Inglis, *Raymond Williams*, 170.
4. As Lin Chun has observed in his standard history of the New Left: '*The Long Revolution* received intense attack from the right, as an alert recognition of its power and quality as a serious socialist work ... A "long revolution" unaccompanied by any claim for political power and necessary means to defeat resistance is obviously gradualist with a quite utopian perspective, and this is why it was, again, fiercely criticised by the Marxist critics of the New Left'. *The British New Left* (Edinburgh: Edinburgh University Press, 1993), 51. The book also attracted important endorsements from key elements in the broad left, from Labour politician Richard Crossman, who hailed it as 'the book I have been waiting for since 1945', to fellow cultural critic Richard Wollheim, who even linked it to the 'English dream', i.e. 'the ideal of collective, unalienated folk society, where honest men work together and create together, the ideal of Ruskin, William Morris, and Leavis'. Inglis, *Raymond Williams*, 170.

5   E.P. Thompson, 'The Long Revolution (Part I)', *New Left Review* 9 (May–June 1961): 24.
6   Raymond Williams, *The Long Revolution* (Harmondsworth: Pelican Books, 1965), 10. All subsequent references to the book are given in brackets in the main text.
7   Rainer Winter has noted the affinity between Williams's concept of communication and Jürgen Habermas's theory of communicative action, which the latter author predicates on an ideal-speech situation bearing a certain resemblance to Williams's notion of a common culture of shared meanings and values. In both authors (albeit in different ways and to different effects) a primarily functional definition breeds political consequences. See Rainer Winter, 'The Perspectives of Radical Democracy: Raymond Williams's Work and its Significance for a Critical Social Theory', in ed. Monika Seidl, Roman Horak and Lawrence Grossberg *About Raymond Williams* (London and New York: Routledge, 2010). See also Andrew Milner, *Re-Imagining Cultural Studies: The Promise of Cultural Materialism* (London: SAGE, 2002).
8   'I wanted to be able to develop the position briefly outlined in the conclusion of *Culture and Society*, by a general analysis of contemporary culture and society, a wide structure of feeling in the society as it intersected with institutional developments'. Williams, *Politics and Letters*, 133.
9   Williams would later develop this analysis through the concept of 'mobile privatisation'. See Raymond Williams, *Towards 2000* (Harmondsworth: Penguin, 1985), 188; Raymond Williams, *Television: Technology and Cultural Form* (London: Routledge, 2003), 19. See also, Marita Sturken et al. (eds), *Technological Visions: The Hopes and Fears That Shape New Technologies* (Philadelphia: Temple University Press, 2004), 121; Udo Göttlich, 'Cultural Studies und das Konzept der "mobilen Privatisierung" im Spiegel der Medien und Öffentlichkeitskritik', in ed. B. Becker and J. Wehner, *Kulturindustrie Reviewed: Ansätze zur kritischen Reflexion der Mediengesellschaft* (Bielefeld: Transcript, 2006).
10 The term is Aneurin Bevan's. See Michael Foot, *Aneurin Bevan, 1945–1960* (St Albans: Paladin, 1975), 584ff. For the ideology of Labour revisionism, see its main theoretical contribution in Anthony Crosland, *The Future of Socialism* (London: Constable, 2006). See also Lawrence Black, *The Political Culture of the Left in Affluent Britain, 1951–64: Old Labour, New Britain?* (Basingstoke: Palgrave Macmillan, 2003).
11 'I conclude that the definition of capitalism in terms of ownership, whether or not it was helpful 100 years ago, has wholly lost its significance and interest now that ownership is no longer the clue to the total picture of social relationships: and that it would be more significant to define societies in terms of equality, or class relationships, or their political systems'. Crosland, *The Future of Socialism*, 46. See also Dennis Kavanagh and Peter Morris, *Consensus Politics from Attlee to Major* (Oxford: Blackwell, 1994).
12 '[S]omething is gained, however, to the extent that the state is itself democratically directed'. Williams, *The Long Revolution*, 340.
13 See Michael Sissons and Philip French (eds), *Age of Austerity 1945–51* (Harmondsworth: Penguin, 1964) and David Kynaston, *Austerity Britain, 1945–51* (London: Bloomsbury, 2008).
14 'How many supposedly middle-class people really own their houses, or their furniture, or their cars?', Williams, *The Long Revolution*, 351.
15 See also John Westergaard, 'The Withering Away of Class: A Contemporary Myth' and Robin Blackburn, 'The New Capitalism', in ed. Perry Anderson and Robin Blackburn, *Towards Socialism* (London: Fontana/New Left Review, 1965).
16 This dissociation was clearly exemplified by Alan Sillitoe in his début novel, *Saturday Night and Sunday Morning* (London: Flamingo, 1994). See Ronald Dee Vaverka, *Commitment as Art: A Marxist Critique of a Selection of Alan Sillitoe's Political Fiction* (Uppsala: Uppsala University, 1978). See also John H. Goldthorpe, *The Affluent Worker: Political Attitudes and Behavior*

(Cambridge: Cambridge University Press, 1968) and *The Affluent Worker in the Class Structure* (Cambridge: Cambridge University Press, 1969). For a different sociological perspective, see Harry Braverman, *Labor and Monopoly Capital: The Degradation of Work in the Twentieth Century* (New York: Monthly Review Press, 1974).

17 See for example his 1947 article on the 'Soviet Literary Controversy in Retrospect', in ed. John McIlroy and Sallie Westwood, *Border Country: Raymond Williams in Adult Education*, (Leicester: NIACE, 1993), 41–53.
18 Francis Mulhern, *Culture/Metaculture* (London: Routledge, 2000).
19 This recognition had been famously registered in his crucial essay of 1958, 'Culture is Ordinary', in McIlroy and Westwood, *Border Country*.
20 Raymond Williams, *Britian in the Sixties: Communications* (Harmondsworth: Penguin, 1962), 74.
21 Richard Hoggart, *The Uses of Literacy* (Harmondsworth: Penguin, 1957), 232; see also Sue Owen (ed.), *Richard Hoggart and Cultural Studies*, (Basingstoke: Palgrave Macmillan, 2008).
22 Jack Lindsay (ed.), *Arena Special Issue: The USA Threat to British Culture*, 2:8 (June/July 1951).
23 This convergence of interests between the *Arena* analysis and Williams's own was noticed by the *New Left Review* team in 1979. See Williams, *Politics and Letters*, 112.
24 Williams, *Communications*, 75.

Raymond Williams on Culture and Society[1]
Jim McGuigan

While Raymond Williams's intellectual legacy has been sustained and refreshed in mainly literary scholarship since his death in 1988, the value of cultural materialism to the social sciences has been sidelined. Williams's enormous influence on the formation of cultural studies in particular is readily acknowledged yet it tends to be taken merely for granted and his ideas are somewhat neglected. At the same time, in sociology, the currently fashionable American school of cultural sociology is distinctly uncritical, to say the least, of the neoliberal symbolic order. The article outlines the key elements of cultural materialism as an alternative sociological paradigm that has great potential for further development. Williams's path-breaking critique of technological determinism, for instance, demonstrates why digital media's impact on society should be interrogated critically. In contrast to such conventional wisdom in not only commercial hype but also sociology, the enduring insights of Williams's inspirational albeit misleadingly entitled late book of social and cultural analysis, *Towards 2000*, are emphasised.

*

> The history of our idea of culture is a record of our reactions, in thought and feeling, to the changed conditions of our common life.[2]

This article has a twofold purpose: first, and most immediately, pedagogic; the second and rather more diffusely, theoretical. I work in a university social sciences department nominally as a sociologist. However, I've always been situated in my own mind, if nobody else's, between the humanities and the social sciences. In recent years, I have found it very difficult to teach about Williams and cultural-materialist methodology to students of, for want of a better term, cultural sociology. The main reason for this is that my students do not tend to have the literary background and sufficient knowledge of history to tackle much of Williams's writings. In consequence, I have thought carefully about a selection of texts by Williams that might be readily understood by students of social science today, that is, the most social-scientific of Williams's writings.[3]

The second purpose is rather more ambitious: to save Williams from a marginal and exclusively literary/political reputation; that is, in effect, to recover his work as an inspiration for research in sociology and cultural studies. I think it is true to say that since his death in 1988 Williams's legacy has largely been in the hands of literary scholars and its enduring appreciation owes much to the sterling efforts of the Raymond Williams Society and its annual journal, *Key Words*. I am not complaining at all about Williams's continuing influence on literary scholarship but I do believe it has contributed perhaps unwittingly to deflecting attention from Williams's intellectual significance and relevance for social analysis today and, indeed, a broader-based cultural politics than the purely literary. Another and yet more significant reason for Williams's neglect in the social sciences – including media and cultural studies to some extent – has been the decline of critique in the face of neoliberal ideology, which is not unrelated to a loss of socialist conviction among the shrinking numbers of otherwise critical academics. Professional security is precarious, to say the least, in a crisis-ridden university system that is undergoing – in Britain most dramatically but also elsewhere in the world – a process of Schumpeterian 'creative destruction'. Adapting to and surviving the transformation from organised-capitalist/social-democratic principles to a thoroughgoing neoliberal 'free-market' mode of university teaching and research has become a much more urgent consideration for academics than struggling to foster human emancipation through social betterment, the orientation that animated Williams's lifetime project and his intellectual labours in the cloisters of academe.

The original publication of the recently reissued *The Long Revolution* over fifty years ago signalled Williams's sociological acumen at a relatively early stage of his career when he was only forty.[4] Its impact, in the academically fashionable word of today, was considerable though not as great on the education of socialists, of course, as Robert Tressell's *The Ragged Trousered Philanthropists*, published nearly one hundred years ago.[5] 'The long revolution' referred to the gradual formation – through struggle as E.P. Thompson was to note in his review[6] – of a culture in Britain of democratic institutions and egalitarian norms that Williams was devoted to advancing further so as to create a genuinely 'educated and participatory democracy', in one of his most resonant phrases. By the 1980s, however, Williams was, to his chagrin, identifying the lineaments of a short and abrupt counter-revolution, most notably in his last great work and bitter sequel to *The Long Revolution*, *Towards 2000*.[7]

In the mid-1970s, Williams was invited to speak about 'Developments in the Sociology of Culture' at the British Sociological Association Annual Conference,[8] a talk which led to his textbook for cultural sociology published in 1981, simply entitled *Culture*.[9] In the conference paper, as well as surveying sociological approaches to culture and critiquing the behaviourist obsession with media 'effects' that came from psychology, Williams sought to correct the positivism of much social science by advocating the use of qualitative techniques drawn from the humanities for analysing the complexity of textual meanings, including analysis of genre and narrative structures. And, in the *Culture* book, Williams aimed to produce a comprehensive framework for studying culture sociologically, covering institutions, formations and means of production, identifications, forms, reproduction and organisation. He had already been defining his cultural-materialist perspective in *Marxism and Literature*,[10] which incorporated concepts that were worked out substantively in his earlier writing, such as structure of feeling. Williams's characteristic way of thinking unfolded steadily over the years and became enriched through his encounter with the Western-Marxist tradition[11] and European-continental thought more generally from the 1960s onwards. There was no sharp break between the culturalism of the young Williams and the cultural materialism of the mature Williams. It was in the 1970s, however, that Williams theorised his *sociological* paradigm in formal terms.[12]

To appreciate Williams's distinctive and as yet insufficiently developed contribution to the social sciences, *the cultural-materialist research paradigm*, it is illuminating to compare and contrast it briefly with the presently ascendant American school of 'cultural sociology'.

The key feature of Jeffrey Alexander and Philip Smith's 'strong program [sic]' for cultural sociology is the stress on 'cultural autonomy', which they contrast with all forms of 'reductionism', including curiously enough *sociological reductionism*. No doubt their position is music to the ears of some literary theorists. For Alexander and Smith, culture is an independent variable and never a dependent variable. In consequence, 'a sharp uncoupling of culture from social structure, which is what we mean by cultural autonomy' is necessary.[13] Alexander and Smith dismiss every other school of cultural sociology as ultimately reductionist; that includes work associated with the likes of Pierre Bourdieu, Michel Foucault and Stuart Hall as well as Williams. The chief exponents of this alternative brand of cultural sociology, then, insist upon an exclusively 'textual understanding of social life' that deploys 'narrative and genre theory' (25), which are apparently its only resources. Alexander and Smith's 'cultural sociology' is thus revealed as nothing other, in effect, than a peculiarly text-bound literary theory. It is not social theory; and it makes a poor claim indeed to be considered as properly sociological. That is not all that can be said about it. American cultural sociology is idealist and also itself reductionist. It is a manifest form of *cultural reductionism* that has been used by its main exponents to furnish an ideological defence of the American way of life, no less, in what speakers of American-English would call 'liberal' circles.

In this respect, I recommend a reading of Alexander and Smith's essay, 'The Discourse of American Civil Society', for substantiation.[14] This essay examines a number of historical crises in US society – including the Watergate scandal and the Iran-Contra affair – and discovers that the American 'democratic code' always triumphs ultimately over the American 'authoritarian code'. So, although the USA is often tempted onto the dark side, the principles of an enlightened constitution inevitably defeat ever-menacing and shadowy forces in the end; which is comforting, to be sure.

Williams, on the other hand, refused to simply uncouple culture from social structure; and, in this regard, he offers something more genuinely like a cultural *sociology*. Similarly to Alexander and Smith, he recommended an attention to genre and narrative twenty years earlier than they did but that was not all he recommended. In response to structuralism and semiology, Williams refined his 'concept of culture' in the *Culture* book 'as a *realized signifying system*'.[15] For Williams, the cultural system was not the same as the social system, although the two were intimately connected together in a two-way interaction: 'This distinction is not made to separate and disjoin these areas, but to make room for analysis of the interrelations' (207). Culture, from a sociological point of view, has a measure of autonomy, but it is a relative autonomy, to turn a familiar phrase, in webs of socially structured relation that permit and facilitate agency but not the illusion of totally unconstrained autonomy, agency and freedom – call it what you will – that is extolled by American propaganda.

In 1974, Williams had already published his 'Communications as Cultural Science', which set out his conspectus for the new curriculum and research field of media and cultural studies.[16] This and the BSA paper on sociology were important for the development of social-science education during the 1970s, but most pivotal theoretically for Williams's formulation of what he later named as 'cultural materialism' was his 1973 article, 'Base and Superstructure in Marxist Cultural Theory'.[17]

At this time there was an immense revival of Western-Marxist thought taking place alongside various developments in cultural theory, including post-structuralism and postmodernism, that Williams engaged with in fashioning his own cultural-materialist position. Cultural materialism can reasonably be considered a 'paradigm' in a rather looser sense than the one meant by Thomas Kuhn,[18] though in a sense that is very familiar to the social sciences where rivalry between contending paradigms is commonplace. As the 'Base and Superstructure' article indicated, there was an evident affinity between Williams's holistic approach to culture and society and Antonio Gramsci's concept of hegemony,[19] which was also adopted fruitfully in his work by Stuart Hall,[20] one of the other major figures in the formation of British Cultural Studies.

Williams objected to the base-superstructure model of orthodox Marxism because its conceptualisation of society was insufficiently materialist, in his opinion. This may seem paradoxical since Marxists are often said to reduce everything to economic – that is, 'material' – factors, the assumption being that the super-structural institutions of politics and law, ideology and culture are all determined by and/or merely reflect economic forces and interests.

From an early twenty-first century vantage point, such economic determinism or reductionism is a very familiar refrain indeed. However, the current iteration of economic reductionism – the very opposite of cultural reductionism – does not derive from the vulgar Marxism of yore. It does not come from the Left at all but, instead, it comes from the Right of present-day politics. It is the fundamental neoliberal orientation whereby social and cultural activity is submitted relentlessly to the discipline of the market and everything is understood in monetary terms.

Moreover, it also has to be said, materialist philosophy is not exclusively about economics in any case nor should it be confused with the common-sense notion of 'materialism' as an ethical failing in which money and the acquisition of commodities matter more than relationships with people.

In philosophy, materialism is contrasted to idealism. Whereas idealism assumes that ideas alone are determining forces in the social world, materialism, on the other hand, does not have to reduce mind to matter but it does claim that sensuous human activity is where the action really is.

The point can be illustrated briefly by comparing one of Williams's key concepts, *structure of feeling*, with the German idealist notion of the *Zeitgeist* (spirit of the time), which has a certain currency today in common-sense parlance. In this regard, 'the market' is the *Zeitgeist*, but it is hardly spiritual, though it does function ideologically to mask over and obscure the political-economic forces that deploy the rhetoric of market forces – 'there is no alternative' (TINA) – as a kind of excuse or alibi for nakedly capitalist policy.

In his famous discussion of postmodernism as 'the cultural logic of late capitalism', Fredric Jameson appropriated Williams's conceptualisation of the prevailing structure of feeling to characterise it.[21] From Jameson's point of view, postmodernism is not just a set of ideas but, instead, a structure of feeling, that is, a framing of emotionality and everyday practice that is dialectically related to transnational, high-tech capitalism, whereby the human subject is disoriented and in desperate need of cartographical guidance.

Williams devoted a section of his book, *Marxism and Literature* (1977) to conceptual clarification of structure of feeling, having already used it fruitfully in practical analysis. To give a concrete example, already in the chapter on 'The Analysis of Culture' from *The Long Revolution*, Williams had traced the emergence of a structure of feeling in 1840s English literature that is most profoundly represented by Emily Bronte's *Wuthering Heights*.[22]

Also in this chapter, Williams demonstrated how a process of selection actively constructs cultural tradition or 'heritage' in specific historical circumstances; it is socially produced and likely to be revised over time; and it is by no means indisputable. The selections are made according to prevalent attitudes and interests. For instance, *Wuthering Heights* was too advanced a book to be considered important or even acceptable in its own time. It was much later that *Wuthering Heights* entered the canon of the selective tradition when the structure of feeling it articulated became more widespread.

Later, in the 'Base and Superstructure' article, Williams was to make his distinction between 'emergent' and 'residual' culture and, also, between 'alternative' and 'oppositional' orientations, distinctions that are still vital for assessing not only past developments but also trajectories in the historical present so as not to be deluded by mere novelty.

Williams complained about the treatment of culture as epiphenomenal, as though it were not of material significance, merely ideational. For him, 'signifying practice' – that is, culture in the making – is, in effect, material practice, embedded in institutionalised arrangements and relations of production through which the products of human creativity are actually made.

In a much neglected paper that was originally delivered in Zagreb during the late 1970s, 'Means of Communication as Means of Production', Williams spelt out his understanding of the materiality of cultural activity systematically.[23] His arguments here bear comparison with critical theory's culture industry/cultural industries thinking,[24] though Williams's position is more analytically detached and much less judgemental than the original musings of Theodor Adorno.[25] Williams had long been critical of elitist denunciations of the allegedly inherent and faulty properties of 'mass culture' and 'mass communications' as such.[26] He insists in a strictly sociological argument that communications are part of the productive system of society and not just secondary or superstructural phenomena. In the paper, Williams is also at pains to delineate specific forms of communication in relation to technical mediation without falling into the deadly trap of technological determinism that has been the fate of so many commentators on modern media past and present. Here as elsewhere in his writings, Williams stresses the materiality of signification and in the social realisation of significatory practice, that is, culture.

Unfortunately, as it turned out, Williams did not deliver his precise definition of cultural materialism in the Zagreb paper on the sociology of modern media but, instead and shortly afterwards, in a paper that was sparked off by controversy specifically over the purposes of literary theory, not social theory: 'Cultural materialism is the analysis of all forms of signification, including quite centrally writing, within the actual means and conditions of their production.'[27] Considering his literary background and the provenance of this definition on the occasion of fierce public dispute over 'theory' in the Cambridge English Department, it is not surprising that Williams should have remarked 'quite centrally writing'.

His remark certainly justified a strand of politicised literary history naming itself 'cultural materialism' that was proposed by Jonathan Dollimore and Alan Sinfield as a means of re-reading Shakespeare, for instance.[28] However, stressing the centrality of writing in such a manner severely understated the scope of cultural materialism as a *sociological* methodology.

It has had unfortunate consequences in closing off and, in consequence, artificially delimiting the potential applications of cultural materialism in the social sciences. This point may usefully be illustrated with reference to Williams's critique of technological determinism in the media and in society generally, which is especially germane to making sense of the dynamics of our 'digital age'.

Williams's cultural materialism has an affinity with Douglas Kellner's advocacy of multidimensional cultural analysis.[29] Such an approach seeks to articulate the interaction of conditions of production and consumption with textual meaning within specifiable socio-historical contexts. It resists one-dimensional and mono-causal explanation, which is actually the fundamental flaw of the technological determinism that, combined with neoliberal political economy, is the most prominent feature of ideological dominance around the world today.

The emergence and meaning-making properties of media are often said to be entirely reducible to direct technical innovation derived immediately from scientific discovery with inevitably beneficial results, according to the commercial hype. Moreover, we are constantly encouraged to believe, in a quasi-spiritual manner, that 'technology' (usually meaning specifically information and communication technologies these days) is the main and perhaps sole driving force of significant social change and is the solution to all conceivable problems.

Contrarily, Williams showed that the development of communication technologies and their applications result from a complex range of determinations, including cultural, economic and political factors; and that the historical outcomes of such development are never strictly inevitable.

In Williams's cultural-materialist discourse, *determination* refers to the exertion of pressure and setting of limits on human activity rather than the simple and unilinear cause and effect relation of *determinism*. Human agency matters and, in the case of technological change, *intention* is always involved, which suggests the possibility of alternative purposes and different outcomes in any given circumstance.

Williams's cultural-materialist framework for studying technological innovation, communications, cultural and social change is in constant tension with various kinds of technological determinism, from the sociological sophistication of a Manuel Castells through to the routine commercial hype for selling successive waves of new communications product, including the latest must-have gadget that promises to transform your life. Castells, of course, is wise enough to defend himself against the taint of technological determinism by pointing to the equally significant impact, in his argument, of the capitalist triumph in political economy and of the socio-cultural movements, most notably feminism, to that of the information and communication technology 'revolution' over the past forty years or so.[30] The commercial hype does not bother with such qualification and intellectual refinement, however, and the gadgets are designed to be extremely seductive in themselves anyway. At the same time, Castells continues to be read by the sociologically naive as the latest guru of technology's all-consuming power.[31]

There is no doubt that digitalisation and the various applications of computing and wireless communications have enormous consequences, for instance, with regard to television and telephony: bringing about technological convergence and proliferating communicational services and gadgets such as on-line mobile phones and multi-purpose tablets. Nevertheless, the processes by which such technologies come about and are used are much more complicated than the usual hype would suggest. Let us return to what Williams had to say, then, in order to see more clearly the problems associated with overstating the determinacy of technology.

Technological determinism assumes a linear process from scientific research and discovery to technical invention and implementation with consequential social and cultural impact, more or less unfolding smoothly over time. It is not just a simplistic model of socio-technical change but also a dominant ideological assumption, nowadays allied especially to free-market economics and politics.

Alternatively, according to Williams, technologies are developed and implemented in a complex of determinations that are not only scientific and technical but also include economic, political and cultural factors. To assume that technology is the sole cause of cultural and social change with highly predictable results – 'technology changes everything' – is a deeply flawed assumption, though it is widely believed and to a considerable extent simply taken for granted. To appreciate why technological determinism results in fallacious argumentation, it is necessary to examine how technologies have actually developed historically. Historical knowledge should encourage scepticism about exaggerated claims concerning the magical and all-transforming power of the latest technology.

The classic critique of technological determinism was formulated in Raymond Williams's book, *Television – Technology and Cultural Form*, originally published in 1974. As long ago as that, Williams was aware of most of the potential technological developments in television that have actually occurred since then and with which we are now so familiar. In this ground-breaking book, Williams discussed the multiplication of cable and satellite channels, facilities for recording programmes off the television set and rescheduling, interactivity, large-screen receivers and the rest of it.

At the time, Williams posed the question of who would gain the upper hand in controlling these developments, specifically whether they would be commanded by global capital or become a public means for fostering greater democracy and participation. He feared that the interests of big business would win out. In that, he has surely been proved right.

Williams takes the oft-stated claim that 'television has altered our world' and considers what it means. In the television book, he identifies no less than nine ways of stating the cause/effect relation between television and society, stretching from strong to weaker forms of technological determinism to, at the other extreme, what can be called social or cultural determinism.

The strongest forms of technological determinism go like this:

(i) Television was invented as a result of scientific and technical research. Its power as a medium of news and entertainment was then so great that it altered all preceding media of news and entertainment.
(ii) [...] Its power as a medium of social communication was so great that it altered many of our institutions and forms of social relationships.
(iii) [...] Its inherent properties as an electronic medium altered our basic perceptions of reality, and thence our relations with each other and with the world.[32]

The most extreme form of a contrary position – that of social or cultural determinism – on the other hand is stated as follows:

(ix) Television became available as a result of scientific and technical research, and its character and uses both served and exploited the needs of a new kind of large-scale and complex but atomised society. (12)

It is not often appreciated that, for Williams, this kind of social and cultural determinism is no better than technological determinism, though it does have the virtue of seeing television as symptomatic of historical change and not just the cause of it. The trouble with both views, however, is that they see the invention and implementation of television as a sort of accident. Williams summarised his critical attitude to both positions as follows:

In *technological determinism*, research and development have been assumed as self-generating. The new technologies are invented as it were in an independent sphere, and then create new societies or new human conditions. The view of *symptomatic technology*, similarly, assumes that research and development are self-generating, but in a more marginal way. What is discovered in the margins is then taken up and used. (13–14)

Neither of them actually tells us why television was developed at all!

Williams then goes on to outline a third way of accounting for the development of television and its relation to society:

> … [I]n the case of television it may be possible to outline a different kind of interpretation, which would allow us to see not only its history but also its uses in a more radical way. Such an interpretation would differ from technological determinism in that it would restore *intention* to the process of research and development. The technology would be seen, that is to say, as being looked for and developed with certain purposes and practices already in mind. At the same time the interpretation would differ from symptomatic technology in that purposes and practices would be seen as *direct*: as known social needs, purposes and practices in which the technology is not marginal but central. (145)

The crucial term here is *intention*, making the assumption that television was developed deliberately out of a combination of scientific knowledge produced for various reasons, the exploration of technical feasibility, the identification and creation of social needs, the testing out of possibilities etc. Inventive developments in electricity, telegraphy, photography, the moving image and radio came together around television.

It is important to note that the earliest uses of what became broadcasting, in the case of radio, during the first couple of decades of the twentieth century, were military and imperial. They were developed in order to aid the conduct of war and colonial administration. It was only subsequently that the possibilities of a *broadcast* – as opposed to a *narrowcast* – medium were explored.

Another important thing about early broadcasting – both radio and television – is that it was not inevitable for it to become a mainly domestic medium of reception. In Germany, for instance, during the 1930s, television was used limitedly as a medium of reception in public spaces, such as shopping centres, instead of the private space of the home.[33] This is a form of television that has been somewhat revived in recent years with the viewing of sport collectively in public settings such as pubs.

The development of radio and then television as a domestic medium was pioneered in the USA and Britain in relation to the general formation of mass-popular culture, widespread consumerism and the increasingly privatised experience of nuclear families during the interwar years. In the USA, wireless set manufacturers were the key players. So they were at first in Britain as well until the state intervened to set up the BBC as a separate company that soon became a publicly-owned corporation. Across the Atlantic, on the other hand, radio and television were always exclusively commercial media, set up as vehicles for advertising and sponsorship, exemplifying the thoroughgoing commodification of culture in the USA, which has now been imported into Britain and other countries that had hitherto taken 'public service' seriously.

Brian Winston has refined Williams's ideas concerning the development of communication technologies into a sophisticated model of 'how media are born'.[34] With evidence from detailed case studies, Winston demonstrates the historical contingencies of 'new media' emergence. He traces the advent of cinema, the racism of colour film chemistry, the marginalisation of 16mm film as 'amateur' until its eventual deployment in television news, the dead-end of analogue high-definition television and the limbo status of holography.

There always has to be a 'supervening social necessity' behind the emergence of a new medium of communication. In the case of cinema, the formation of a mass entertainment market and the sociality of theatre in an urban-industrial society were at least as important determinants, if not more so, than the inventiveness of 'great men', the myth of orthodox cinematic history. As well as supervening social necessities, accelerating the development of a medium at a particular moment in time, there is the brake on development that Winston calls 'the "law" of the suppression of radical potential'.[35] In the case of the denigration of 16mm film, its use thereby confined to 'amateurs' and 'subversives', classic Hollywood's expensive 35mm 'standard' was a means of controlling entry to the industry. Winston's historical researches provide considerable substantiation for the critique of technological determinism, though he rather overstates the alternative explanation of what he calls 'cultural determinism' and ignores the criticisms that Williams so acutely made of it.

Williams's major work of the 1980s was, in my opinion, mistakenly entitled *Towards 2000*. The title gives the misleading impression that it was merely a *fin-de-siècle* book which went out of date at the stroke of midnight on 31 December 1999. At the present time of writing, *Towards 2000* is actually out of print. That it was written as a sequel to *The Long Revolution* is signalled by reproducing the final chapter of the earlier book, 'Britain in the Sixties', as Chapter 2 of the later book. This may also have given the impression that Williams's last great book was as much backward- as forward-looking, more of a stocktaking of resources from the past than a refreshing means of orienting towards the future. Yet re-read now, it is manifestly evident that *Towards 2000* was a prescient anticipation of and conspectus for the circumstances and, indeed, predicament that we find ourselves in during the early decades of the twenty-first century, especially the astonishing final chapter, 'Resources for a Journey of Hope'.

In *Towards 2000*, Williams critiqued the very notion of 'post-industrial' society decisively, tackled persistent questions of nationhood and globalisation and identified the most salient issues concerning what we name today as 'neoliberalism' and the most promising sources of resistance to it, particularly urgent action for environmental protection and ecological politics in general as integral features of twenty-first century socialism.

Williams concluded *Towards 2000* with a discussion of 'Plan X', a ruthlessly 'new politics of strategic advantage'[36] that emerged from the 1970s and was represented most immediately by the stepping up of the arms' race during Ronald Reagan's first presidential term in the early-1980s. Another early feature of Plan X was not to reduce petrol consumption but to take greater command over production by the strategy of divide-and-rule amongst oil-producing states, in effect, a short-term strategy that was blithely indifferent to environmental costs and the eventual depletion of oil. The military focus was already shifting from the Cold War ahead of the collapse of European communism to the hot war zone of the Middle East.

In addition to flexing US military muscle, Plan X can readily be interpreted today as an early sighting of the hard-nosed capitalist logic at the heart of the neoliberal project, a project that is truly hegemonic on a global scale and which has had such a profound effect throughout the world over the past thirty years. Williams noted the local and indeed vanguard manifestation of neoliberalism in Thatcherism:

> Plan X has appeared recently in British politics. As distinct from policies of incorporating the working class in a welfare state, or of negotiating some new and hopefully stable relationship between state, employers and unions (two dominant policies of post-1945 governments), Plan X has read the future as the certainty of a decline of capitalist profitability unless the existing organisations and expectations of wage-earners are significantly reduced. (245)

Williams then went on to note a further feature of Plan X political economy in the British case: 'the decimation of British industrial capital itself' (245). We have seen such developments in the transition from organised to neoliberal capitalism unfold across three phases of what can still be called 'Thatcherism', after Stuart Hall:[37] Thatcherism Mark 1 (Thatcher), Thatcherism Mark 2 (Blair) and Thatcherism Mark 3 (Cameron). Williams was right, however, to call this hegemonic project 'Plan X' rather than 'Thatcherism' since it has been much more widespread than a political doctrine that is embodied in one exemplary hate figure of a nation state.

In 'Resources for a Journey of Hope', Williams said very little specifically about culture as such, though he did remark:

> There are also deep supporting cultural conditions. Plan X is sharp politics and high-risk politics. It is easily presented as a version of masculinity. Plan X is a mode of assessing odds and determining a game plan. As such, it fits, culturally, with the widespread habits of gambling and its calculations. At its highest levels, Plan X draws on certain kinds of high operative (including scientific and technical) intelligence, and on certain highly specialised game-plan skills. But then much education, and especially higher education (not only in the versions that are called business studies) already defines professionalism in terms of competitive advantage. It promotes a deliberately narrow attention to skill as such, to be enjoyed in its mere exercise rather than in any full sense of the human purposes it is serving or the social effects it may be having. The now gross mutual flattery of military professionalism, financial professionalism, media professionalism and advertising professionalism indicates very clearly how far this has gone. Thus both the social and cultural conditions for the adoption of Plan X, as the only possible strategy for the future, are very powerful indeed.[38]

The critical insights and gloomy prognostication of that passage would repay several pages of close analysis and constructive extrapolation. Instead of doing so, however, in concluding this article, it is important to note Williams's increasingly green-socialist politics. Similarly to Jurgen Habermas,[39] he supported incursions into the public sphere by campaigning social movements of 'peace, ecology and feminism'. While remaining hopeful, Williams also noted, chillingly, the sheer scale of the problems confronting oppositional forces. What he wrote in the early 1980s could equally well be said now – 'there is no real point in pretending that the capitalist social order has not done its main job of implanting a deep assent to capitalism even in a period of its most evident economic failures'.[40] Explaining how this trick has been performed and exposing it for what it really is must be a key task for critical social science. It is my sense that we still have to come to terms with the complex processes of the capitalist pleasure machine, including the sly seduction – as well as social usefulness – of technologically mediated communications; enhanced actual and virtual mobility; the social process of individualisation in work and leisure that mitigates against collective action; and the stunningly effective albeit ironic incorporation of expressions of disaffection into the cool culture of neoliberal capitalism itself.[41]

Jim McGuigan

Notes

1. An earlier version of this paper was delivered at the 'Raymond Williams and Robert Tressell in Hastings Conference', University of Brighton, 20 September 2011.
2. Raymond Williams [henceforth RW] *Culture and Society 1780–1950* (1958; Harmondsworth: Penguin, 1963), 285.
3. Because I have found it difficult to teach about Raymond Williams to Sociology and Media Studies students in a social sciences department in recent years, I decided to edit together in one volume what I consider to be Raymond Williams's most social-scientific texts (*Raymond Williams on Culture and Society*, Sage, forthcoming). A key criterion in selecting the texts for the book was that no specialist knowledge of literature or even much in the way of historical knowledge is required in order to understand them, an unfortunate though necessarily pragmatic consideration today.
4. RW, *The Long Revolution* (1961; Cardigan: Parthian, 2011).
5. Robert Tressell, *The Ragged Trousered Philanthropists* (1914; Harmondsworth: Penguin, 2004).
6. E.P. Thompson, 'The Long Revolution', *New Left Review* 9 and 10 (1961): 24–33, 34–9.
7. RW, *Towards 2000* (1983; Harmondsworth: Penguin, 1985).
8. RW, 'Developments in the Sociology of Culture', *Sociology* 10 (1976): 497–504.
9. RW, *Culture* (London: Fontana, 1981).
10. RW, *Marxism and Literature* (Oxford: Oxford University Press, 1977).
11. Perry Anderson, *Considerations on Western Marxism* (London: New Left Books, 1976).
12. Jim McGuigan and Marie Moran, 'Raymond Williams and Sociology' (forthcoming).
13. Jeffrey Alexander and Philip Smith, 'The Strong Program in Cultural Sociology – Elements of a Structural Hermeneutics', in J. Alexander, *The Meaning of Social Life – A Cultural Sociology* (New York: Oxford University Press, 2003), 13.
14. Alexander and Smith, 'The Discourse of American Civil Society', in Alexander, *The Meaning of Social Life*, 121–54.
15. RW, *Culture*, 207.
16. RW, 'Communications as Cultural Science' (1974); in Christopher Bigsby (ed.), *Approaches to Popular Culture* (London: Arnold, 1976), 27–38.
17. RW, 'Base and Superstructure in Marxist Cultural Theory', *New Left Review* 82 (1973): 3–16.
18. Thomas Kuhn, *The Structure of Scientific Revolutions* (Chicago: University of Chicago Press, 1970).
19. Quintin Hoare and Geoffrey Nowell Smith (eds), *Selections from the Prison Notebooks of Antonio Gramsci* (London: Lawrence & Wishart, 1971).
20. Stuart Hall, *The Hard Road to Renewal – Thatcherism and the Crisis of the Left* (London: Verso, 1988).
23. Fredric Jameson, *Postmodernism, or, the Cultural Logic of Late Capitalism* (London: Verso, 1991).
22. RW, *The Long Revolution*, ch. 2 'The Analysis of Culture', 61–95.
23. RW, 'Means of Communication as Means of Production' in his *Problems in Materialism and Culture* (1978; London: Verso 1980), 50–63.
24. See Heinz Steinert, *Culture Industry*, tr. Sally-Ann Spencer (1998; Cambridge: Polity, 2003).
25. J.M. Bernstein, ed., *The Culture Industry – Selected Essays on Mass Culture, Theodor Adorno* (London: Routledge, 1991).
26. See Jim McGuigan, 'Reaching for Control – Raymond Williams on Mass Communication and Popular Culture', in ed. W. John Morgan and Peter Preston, *Raymond Williams – Politics Education Letters* (London: Macmillan, 1993), 163–88.
27. RW, 'Marxism, Structuralism and Literary Analysis', *New Left Review* 129 (1981): 64–5.

28 Jonathan Dollimore and Alan Sinfield (eds), *Political Shakespeare – New Essays in Cultural Materialism* (Manchester: Manchester University Press, 1985).
29 Douglas Kellner, 'Critical Theory and Cultural Studies – The Missed Articulation', in ed. Jim McGuigan, *Cultural Methodologies* (London: Sage, 1977), 12–41.
30 See, for instance, Manuel Castells, 'An Introduction to the Information Age', *City* 7 (1997): 6–16.
31 Although John Naughton is not sociologically naive, even he reads Castells to some extent as a McLuhanite technological determinist in *From Guttenburg to Zuckerberg – What You Really Need to Know About the Internet* (London: Quercus, 2012).
32 RW, *Television – Technology and Cultural Form* (London: Fontana), 11.
33 Anthony Smith, 'Television as a Public Service Medium', in his edited *Television – An International History* (Oxford: Oxford University Press, 1995), 78.
34 Brian Winston, 'How are Media Born and Developed?', in ed. J. Downing, A. Mohammadi and A. Sreberny-Mohammadi, *Questioning the Media – A Critical Introduction* (1990; London: Sage, 1995), 54–74.
35 Brian Winston, *Technologies of Seeing – Photography, Cinematography and Television* (London: British Film Institute, 1996).
36 RW, *Towards 2000*, 243.
37 Stuart Hall, 'The Great Moving Right Show', in ed. S. Hall and M. Jacques, *The Politics of Thatcherism* (London: Lawrence & Wishart, 1983), 19–39.
38 RW, *Towards 2000*, 246–7.
39 Jurgen Habermas, *Between Facts and Norms – Contributions to Discourse Theory of Law and Democracy*, tr. William Rehg (1992; Cambridge: Polity, 1996).
40 RW, *Towards 2000*, 54.
41 See my efforts to address these issues in my book *Cool Capitalism* (London: Pluto, 2009). I will be developing the themes touched upon here in a future article that draws upon Williams's enduring academic and political inspiration, provisionally entitled 'Mobile Privatisation and the Neoliberal Self'.

The Traitor in the House
Elizabeth Allen

The article examines the significance of the trope of treachery in the fiction of Raymond Williams. It argues that two main narrative strands can be distinguished in its construction, one essentially autobiographical and the other a recurring and complex response to a historical episode. The central argument is that the compulsive focus on the figure of the 'traitor' is driven by Williams's sense that, in his move from his Welsh working-class community to Cambridge high tables, he has committed an act of treachery. While Williams's non-fiction is clear and emphatic in its rejection of 'Cambridge values', his fiction articulates a more complex and haunted sense of the implications of that move. Explanation is routinely offered but the article argues that the repetition and the textual energy expended on the justification supports the case for a profound unease on the author's part. The article also examines the role played in the novels by the story of the Massacre of Abergavenny and the ways in which it is used, unsuccessfully, to position the traitor as the Other and to lay his ghosts.

*

Nid Oes Bradwr yn y ty hwn. There is no traitor in this house. Such was the assertion on the cards issued to the slate quarrymen of North Wales during the bitter strikes of 1900–1903 in the Penrhyn quarries and displayed in the windows of their homes in Bethesda.[1] The dispute created a deep division in the community between the strikers and the strike breakers. Most of the cards remained in the windows for over two years: when a card was removed from a window it was a sign that another quarryman had been forced back to work.

A recent reproduction of the card has an odd double significance for the study of the fiction of Raymond Williams. It appears in a pamphlet campaigning for the establishment of a Museum of People's History in Wales, an institution eerily reminiscent of the Institute and Library of Industrial Wales which Williams invented in *The Fight for Manod* with the purpose of offering its Directorship to Matthew Price, so enabling his permanent return to Wales.[2] More significantly in terms of this article, the accusatory *bradwr*, traitor, not only has a central place in his novel *Loyalties* but is a significant element in the trope of treachery which dominates his fiction. From *Border Country* to *People of the Black Mountains,* and most emphatically in *Loyalties*, traces or full-blown narratives of treachery appear. Two main narrative strands, however, may be distinguished: while the move away from Pandy and Wales into a different place and class is understood as treachery, this 'autobiographical' strand runs alongside a historical instance of treachery, the massacre committed by the Norman knight William de Braose at Abergavenny, the town nearest to Pandy. These apparently very different narratives interweave in a complex and compulsive manner. Although treachery in the novels includes narratives of the traitor as an alien who breaks trust with his guests, his lover or his country, they are haunted by a bitter belief that there is in fact 'a traitor in the house', and by the fear that their author is that traitor.

Williams's fiction continuously seeks for an appropriate cultural form and for a narrative that will mediate the realities of contemporary political and social relations; the desire to identify and lay the ghost of the traitor can be read as an important impetus towards the adoption of the variety of different genres that characterise his fiction. While the non-fiction is explicit on Williams's adherence to class and place, the fiction, that part of his work which he valued most highly, articulates contradictions and complexities only latent elsewhere. In his essays, from the early 'Culture is Ordinary'[3] to the late essay written for the collection *My Cambridge* which asserts; 'It was never *my* Cambridge',[4] (added emphasis) the sense is of a writer clear as to where the battle lines are drawn and to where he is situated in those lines. Yet the narrative of the fiction suggests an altogether less easy relationship between origin and current position. His writing always exists in a tension between the personal and the collective, enacting what can be characterised as a private drama: Tony Pinkney has described it as 'shot through with private resonances and impulses ... infiltrated by subterranean currents of anger, anxiety and crisis'.[5] It is the move from the home village of Pandy to Cambridge which generates a powerful source of anxiety, one which the novels seek compulsively to exculpate. In the first edition of *Keywords*, Terry Eagleton refers to the tensions in Williams's writing engendered by the moves between class and place as the 'formative and typical historical experience'.[6] Yet the narrative structures of his fiction are pervaded by a deep unease that the representative crisis is not altogether an adequate motive for the move. The very repetition of the story of exile has the paradoxical effect that, while it stands as the exemplary story of a generation, simultaneously suggests that this is a narrative which is personal and compulsive.

The protagonist in each of the first five novels is required to negotiate the route from his original place and class without falling into collusion or despair. This move, considered in the opening pages of the first novel, *Border Country*, and the subject of a pivotal element in *People of the Black Mountains*, his last, is at once necessary, disabling and disloyal. The betrayal is figured always in spatial terms. Over and over, the boy from the borders of Wales and England moves east, away from the mountains to the flat plains, from a culture of intimacy to one which privileges the objective, the abstract. Even in those novels, where the move east is not represented directly but a generation in the past – *Second Generation* and *The Volunteers* – although the protagonists, Peter Owen and Lewis Redfern, live in Oxford and London, Wales as their place of family origin is significant in their psychological and political positioning.[7] *The Volunteers* also offers Mark Evans, who in his move from Wales has both compromised his earlier radical politics and his integrity by abandoning his wife for a much younger woman.[8] In *Border Country*, Matthew Price's parting from his family in the village of Glynmawr for Cambridge is the central theme, while in *Loyalties* a similar move by Gwyn Lewis, taken from the mining community of the South Wales valleys to Cambridge, is also explicitly offered as a question of conflicting principles and loyalties. Interestingly, a significant part of the case made by the Welsh critic James Davies, who attacks Williams as having, through his long exile in England, progressively lost a true sense of Welsh social practice, is that he moved to 'the far side of England' – the implication being that he would have retained more Welsh identity and integrity had he moved no further along the A40 than, say, to Chippenham.[9] Over and over the move is performed, and over and over great textual energy is expended to explain and expiate a perceived guilt of exile, a perceived betrayal of the place of origin.

It is tempting to see the narrative in its clearest and bleakest form in its last representation, the episode in Williams's posthumously published novel *People of the Black Mountains*, 'The Coming of the Measurer', set in 2000 BC. Measurement is consistently a key concept in Williams's fiction. *Border Country* opens with historian Matthew Price's concerns over the validity of the methodology which the discipline insists on his using: 'ways of measuring'[10] which he perceives as deforming human relations. At the end of *Second Generation*, Harold Owen understands the methods of Peter, his academic son, as inimical to the needs of his class: 'He just wants to measure.'[11]

In 'The Coming of the Measurer', Dal Mered, old and making his way home to die in the Hills of the Bluestones, southwest Wales, comes to the 'simple, well-ordered, well-provided' settlement of Lanoluc in the Black Mountains.[12] It is a moment when mythic ways of understanding natural phenomena are challenged by scientific observation, when human being perceive themselves as detached from nature and so able to observe and measure. Dal Mered has been, for thirty-four years, one of the new people, the Company of the Measurers of Menvandir, on the great plain where can be found the already ancient stone circles now called Stonehenge. This way of living where 'we do not herd or grow but … measure the whole world', Mered understands as the 'growing point of the whole world' (176). The knowledge can be, as Mered demonstrates, of practical application to a farmer/hunter community, but primarily this is knowledge not as instrumental but for its own sake. To pursue knowledge in a spirit of disinterested inquiry rather than directly to improve the human lot need not, of course, be morally suspect. The way in which the change is so situated in this story is one which is arguably the paradigmatic move in Williams's fiction and the source of the trope of betrayal. The symbiotic division of labour whereby the company study the world while others provide their sustenance and benefit from the applications of that study, turns into crude exploitation. However much the material conditions of those who supply them with food and labour may deteriorate, the Measurers refuse to accept any compromise in their own way of life. Faced with refusal by their 'workers', they use their knowledge of an imminent solar eclipse to inspire terror and abort a rebellion. They go on to enforce laws that oblige 'packs of men' to undergo training as if they were dogs and, in a rather ill-considered phrase, to 'make their movements together' (180). So, although Mered has not lost his love of his 'science', disillusion with its corruption has sent him westwards to his old home. The Measurers are shown as bent on disclaiming the material conditions on which they are ultimately dependent. This is the 'disastrously wrong pattern' that in *Second Generation* (two millennia later or twenty years earlier in Williams's writing career) Peter Owen identifies as academic life, alienation of learning from human need and which causes him to see academics as operating as a 'priestly caste'.[13] The novels offer a series of dramatisations of the dangerous seductions of the Measurer's Move and the distances, moral as well as spatial, to which such a move commits those who succumb. Driven by intellectual curiosity and the pressures of history, they move east from the Black Mountains to the plains. Like Mered they are angry, ill at ease, out of place. The parallels with Williams's own trajectory are irresistible and the novel is continuously alert to the accusation that such a move may be opportunist escapism or even betrayal: the Company joined is morally suspect.

The nature of betrayal in the fiction is ever-present but not in a single form and the defences which are offered shift from explicit dialogues on guilt and betrayal to the construction of narratives which seek to counter indirectly any charges which might be made. 'I feel that I'm being blamed. Blamed for something that is quite inevitable', protests Matthew Price in *Border Country*.[14] And indeed the text supports his protestations of innocence, encouraging us to see Matthew as of those living in a social 'border country' and, like Thomas Hardy, a man 'caught by his personal history in the general structure and crisis of relations between education and class'.[15] The account that Matthew offers is of a loss of agency. He explains to Morgan Rosser thus:

A part of a whole generation has had this. A personal father and that is one clear issue. But a father is more than a person, he's in fact a society, the thing you grew up into ... We've been moved and put into a different society.[16]

Matthew does, though, have the opportunity to make a choice. Morgan Rosser, who after the political disillusionment of the outcome of the General Strike has become a successful entrepreneur, offers him a job in his expanding business: 'Not as anyone's employee, but getting ready when the time comes, to take things over. That's what I'm offering you, Will' (312). Will is thus given a clear, and clearly significant, choice between going away to make his own way in a presently uncertain future or becoming the son-in-law and heir apparent. But, as the Devil with Christ in the wilderness, the offer is not that which might truly tempt. For the significant absence in Williams's fiction is the man who might serve as role model for refusing the Measurer's Move: the working-class activist defined not solely in terms of commitment and integrity but by an understanding of local, national and international processes. Nor do we find any representatives of an alternative Welsh tradition: the scholarship boy who takes an Oxbridge degree but, crucially, resists its seductions and heads home. In Gwyn Jones's novella 'I was Born in Ystrad' the narrator attends an English university where he is, he notes, 'one of their very nicest little doctored toms, a collier's son with the outlook of a French aesthete'. Having laboured as a teacher in Cardiff, with a shift into the stunningly surreal, he becomes a leader in a failed socialist Welsh revolution. Williams, though, does not offer us even a less aspiring working-class hero than this. Such a figure might have been modelled on Williams's own activist and articulate father who is, in *Border Country*, 'separate[d] out' into the in many ways admirable but inarticulate Harry Price and the 'restless, critical and self-critical' and morally less admirable Morgan Rosser.[17] Matthew's move into exile is protected by the nature of the choice that he is offered.

The Measurer Sons are not like the Angry Young Men, Matthew's contemporaries, who make unlovely accommodations and no new commitments. Joe Lampton's move to his room at the top is enabled by his ability to reject and despise the 'dead Dufton, dirty Dufton, dreary Dufton' from which he has escaped.[18] Matthew may move east but he remains in dialogue with the values of the place of origin, values significantly strongly associated with his father: 'His whole mind seemed a long dialogue with his father – a dialogue of anxiety and allegiance, of deep separation and deep love.'[19] And crucially, he, like the other Measurers, returns: psychologically at the end of *Border Country* and physically and permanently, through that post with the Institute and Library of Industrial Wales, at the end of *The Fight for Manod*. This pattern of return, which marks Williams's own reading and writing practice,[20] is compulsive in the novels. In *People of the Black Mountains*, the return is performed in the contemporary framing story by Glyn and re-enacted in different periods by the Measurers Dal Mered and Karan and the escaped slave of the Roman invaders, Berin.[21] Even those characters, like Peter Owen in *Second Generation* and *The Fight for Manod*, and Lewis Redfern in *The Volunteers*, who have been brought up elsewhere return, even if temporarily, to 'the warm Welsh embrace'.[22]

The betrayal, then, can be read as superficial and temporary. The Measurers are, nevertheless, in their exile, shape-shifters. For Matthew the obvious change is the adoption of his official name of Matthew and the rejection of the name, Will, by which he was known in boyhood. Dal Mered too is an adopted name: 'For the boy Ranan was now in another life. He did not belong in the life of a measurer.'[23] There are other significant changes in the move. In *Second Generation* Peter Owen berates his supervisor Robert Lane, whose father was a compositor for his 'surrender' to middle-class mores: 'Did you have to become like them? Did you have to change your whole voice, your body, every bit of yourself?'[24] Lane, a philanderer, is not a Williams figure, but the attack is an uncomfortable echo of Morgan Rosser's more measured and saddened response to the Matthew who returns to the village to visit his dying father. Matthew seeks to distance himself from the category that Morgan identifies as 'your senior colleagues and their colleagues and masters … that lot' by commenting: 'They're not bad. They're just like foreigners, when you come where it matters.' But Morgan will not accept the distinction:

> They're exactly like you, and that's the fact, Will. It's you think you're different, but you're getting more like them. With the occasional kick, you know. A rude noise round the corner when you think they're looking.[25]

Williams knows too, of course, the social instrumentality of personal guilt. Peter Owen in *Second Generation*, son of working-class activists and now studying for his doctorate in a city clearly based on Oxford, understands the advantages of the individual accepting personal responsibility for weakness for a political system that oppresses his class: 'He could take the confusions, the betrayals into his own person, he would no longer criticize the life that engendered them and the system that sustained them. Having broken in himself he would have made the system safe.'[26]

So the debate is highlighted but it is not dealt with. Socio-economic pressures, lack of agency, minor acts of rebellion, pain and confusion, even the final return: these are not enough. Those who leave have been, even if it involves the collusion of the families they have left, educated into a class bound to injure their own people: 'It was really as if, oppressed by an enemy, a people had conceived its own liberation by training its sons for the enemy service' (138).

But the Measurer son is not the only traitor who haunts these texts. We have too the historical narrative of the de Braose knight who held Abergavenny Castle and perpetrated his own Night of the Long Knives with a massacre of the Welsh princes. This story, hinted at in *Border Country*, represented in a contemporary form in *Loyalties* and finally given in full in *People of the Black Mountains*, sits appropriately within a discourse of Welsh history suffused with the language of treachery. It is, nevertheless, deployed in the later novels in a manner which is highly suggestive for reading the significance of the Measurer Son and the question of the traitor within the house.

Welsh history, both ancient and modern, abounds in instances of treachery. In the twentieth century the most powerful examples are those of the 1926 General Strike with its long echoes into the miners' strikes of the 1970s and 1980s. Anne Perkins has commented on the 'language of betrayal' in 1926 that pervaded South Wales following the decision of the non-mining unions to return to work.[27] Neither was this sense a merely historical detail: Patrick Hannon says that during the 1984–85 strike, a new generation of miners were bitter at the way 'the other unions had let them down in 1926'.[28] In 1984 the language of treachery also underpinned Margaret Thatcher's identification of the miners as 'the enemy within'.[29]

The discourse of earlier Welsh history too is marked by this emphasis on betrayal. 'From the beginning there was treachery' claims a mediaeval Welsh historian. Citing this, J. Beverley Smith comments:

> Many are the references to the 'oppression and treachery' of the Normans in the territory of the Welsh people, but there was an acknowledgement too that foreign intervention exacerbated internal strife and frequently provoked desertion and betrayal.[30]

This emphasis is a 'trenchant theme' from Mordred's betrayal of Arthur, told in Geoffrey of Monmouth's history, onwards, a work which, says Smith, 'had an overwhelming and oppressive influence upon Welsh historical consciousness for several centuries to come' (ibid.). Myths are, of course, responsive to political need and Glanmor Williams, in his account of mediaeval and Tudor Wales, emphasises 'how a people may brood in centuries of defeat on their traitors, creating a mass of mythical lore and prophetic legends to compensate for their losses and sustain their hopes'.[31] An account by Harri Webb, a late twentieth-century literary and political journalist, in his account of the death of Llywelyn ap Gruffyd in the struggles against Edward I, continues to insist on the centrality of treachery: 'Llywelyn fell, isolated, deserted and betrayed, hardly more in death than in life.' The tribal leaders were 'unreliable, faithless, treasonable,' the villages 'eager to denounce neighbouring villages for their treachery'.[32]

While Williams's recorded reaction to this version of earlier Welsh history, as offered to his interviewers in *Politics and Letters*, is one of unambiguous rejection,[33] the response of the boy Will in *Border Country* is altogether more nuanced. In an account rich in the kind of metaphor and details which Williams was to say outraged him with their false positioning of his country and people, the schoolmaster tells the story of the death of the 'head and shield of the Cymri [who] fell by the treachery of his own men'.[34] Yet the boy Will 'years later ... was to remember it word for word'. The grandiose claim on which the story ends: 'The body of the brave Gruffyd ap Llewellyn died, but his memory will live on for ever in the hearts of the sons and daughters of Wales', is, ironically, borne out in the body of the boy Will.

These ghosts of treachery are raised early in *Border Country*. Matthew Price, just arrived from London at his home village of Glynmawr, has fallen asleep reading the county history. It talks of 'the church ... distinguished by its relics, including a gown and brooch of Jane Latimer, reputed mistress of Robin de Braose ... that there is a Norman roodscreen and an ancient camp and the bloodiest of the border castles and the stone of Treachery and the gown of the reputed mistress of Robin de Braose' (81–82). The act of treachery signalled here by the stone, the bloody castle and the Braose name is the first mention in Williams's fiction of the Abergavenny massacre of 1175, an act which a terse twelfth-century annal describes thus: 'Seisyll ap Dwynfal and Geofrey his son (and many others of Gwent) were treacherously slain by William de Braose at Abergavenny.'[35] The massacre, under the title 'The Abergavenny Murders,' is the subject of an episode in *The Eggs of the Eagle*, the second volume of *People of the Black Mountains*, where the specific cynicism and brutality of the events are emphasised but subdued to the overall sense of the narrative sequence, the repeated and determined oppression of the weaker by the powerful, the calculated erasure of a community's economic bases and cultural practices.[36] But while this episode has at last given full voice to the story that has haunted earlier texts, it is the echoes and traces in those earlier texts which are more suggestive in terms of Williams's understanding of treachery and its relation to class and to national and to international formations. It is in *Loyalties* that his need to deny 'the traitor in the house' is demonstrated most acutely and in its least resolved form.

A central figure here is a twentieth century Norman and a twentieth century Braose, scion of 'an old diplomatic family'.[37] This Norman Braose is not guilty of the treacherous slaughter of Welsh men or the ordering of the dashing to death of babies before the eyes of their mothers. But, as a computer scientist who passes information to the Soviet Union, he is a traitor to his country, and he is also guilty of betraying the trust of Nesta, a young woman from a South Wales mining family, whom he seduces, impregnates and abandons. In his actions he manages to combine the various actions defined under 'betrayal' and 'treachery' – the violation of trust, the leading astray and seduction, the desertion in time of need, the attempts to overthrow the state to which the offender owes allegiance – fairly comprehensively. An upper-class Englishman, the name that links him so firmly to the perpetrator of the Abergavenny Massacre makes him a pawn of destiny, the oppressive outsider predestined to betray.

Nesta marries the miner Bert Lewis who becomes the adoptive father of Gwyn, the child born of her brief liaison with Norman Braose, and the issue of treachery is complicated by the strongly Oedipal plot. Gwyn's responses to the acts and values of his two fathers collapse the personal/political binary. That collapse poses a serious problem for a novel which in its opening framing sequence insists on such a distinction being preserved as its loss reduces the integrity of the social dimension. The grandson of Braose, Jon Merritt, recruited to work on a television programme on British dissidents argues that:

> There is a difference between dissidents and quirky individuals. The upper-class radicals … none of them seem to me quirky at all. Individuals, yes, but mainly with different principles, different ideas of society … If the dissent is only a quirkiness, everything important is devalued. (6)

It is arguable that the construction of Braose, who manages to be both seducer and, in an echo of Clifford Chatterley, sexually dysfunctional, itself performs just this reductive manoeuvre.

The novel never suggests that Braose's political activities are simply to be condemned. In his first interview with his natural son he raises questions of 'divided loyalties' and modes of fighting that are 'beyond legitimacy': although these concepts remain unexplored, the sense is of a man exhausted by interior debate (266–269). The defence offered by his sister, Emma, and her son is one of rigorous attention to dates and names which 'prove' that he never undertook any action that might be considered treacherous. They present him as the innocent who has covered for the double dealings of his former colleague and friend Monk Pitter, to whom the deceits were an intellectual game, uninformed by moral or political beliefs. Gwyn response here is unequivocal: '*Braose bradwr*' he announces and explicates: '*Bradwr* is Welsh for traitor' (305). The situation is shown to be yet more morally and politically complicated when Pitter, in a discussion with Gwyn, simultaneously admits to treachery and mounts a strong defence of the position adopted by himself and by Braose during the war and the post-war period. He situates actions and decisions in their historical moment, suggests that the concepts of loyalty and treason are historically constructed and seeks to convince Gwyn of the complexity of the endgame:

> Traitor, without doubt, is a definable quality. There are genuine acts of betrayal of groups to which one belongs. But you have only to look at shifts of alliance and hostility, both the international shifts and within them the complex alliances and hostilities of classes, to know how dynamic this definable quality becomes. (317)

Gwyn's response to the conflicting accounts is a 'dazed uncertainty'. He rehearses, to himself and to his wife Jill, 'an interrupted uncertain, always scrupulously qualified, narrative' which interleaves the alternative readings he has been offered, concluding only that the narrative is 'obsessive in its continuing uncertainty' (331). Yet when Gwyn confronts Braose on his Gloucestershire estate the arguments are set in very different terms.

Now there is no indication of Gwyn's harbouring any doubt: he is full of rage and rejection. The specific terms in which he represents Braose's treachery are those of class: his, says Gwyn, has 'always been a class of betrayers' and of alignment with alien powers which have deformed the perception of the native growth of socialism (359). Gwyn here allies himself firmly with the values of his adoptive father. Bert Lewis fought for socialism in Spain and in Wales, an allegiance to place and to values which, Braose taunts Gwyn, is, because of his education and profession, no longer available to him. But Gwyn, unlike Matthew Price and Peter Owen, demonstrates little sense that he suffers from the Measurer's guilt. While he finds it painful to negotiate the tensions of the circumstances of his birth, there is no evidence that he shares Peter Owen's analysis that working-class sons who move into the professional classes have thereby enrolled with the enemy. For, in making the Measurer's Move, to the east and into the Company, Gwyn is effectively kidnapped. Having grown up in Wales with his mother Nesta and adoptive father Bert Lewis he has been, Bert tells his aunt Emma Braose, 'advised for Cardiff'. Cardiff, Emma, the Communist Part activist, makes clear is an inadequate academic institution for her nephew. 'I want him to go to Cambridge. I really want him to fly.' Bert comments: 'It's for him to say in the end' (152). Yet there is no textual representation of Gwyn's response to this plan, and the next episode opens with Emma's discussion with Mark Ryder, a Cambridge don who has conducted one of the interviews: Gwyn is effectively absent from his own interview. The sense of inevitability, almost of the predetermined outcome of a fairy story, is enhanced by Bert's later deathbed analysis of the control exercised over Gwyn: 'Letting Emma watch over you ... to turn up when you was ready and get you back to Cambridge where you belonged' (256). Gwyn believes himself to have maintained the agency which allows him to practise the values of his family, class and place. Now, the 'dazed uncertainty' which tormented Gwyn after his meeting with Pitter has vanished, the confrontation with the class enemy is stark and he is able to produce a smooth and coherent narrative of treachery and loyalty. Invited to lunch, he responds: 'Do you think I would enter your house?' Braose's final action is the slamming of his door, thereby leaving Gwyn guilt-free outside and the traitor immured within the house (356–366).

Thus at this point the treachery that has haunted the novels and its protagonists has been successfully 'nailed' as a class, and perhaps, too, a national failing. The coming together of the two narratives of treachery has allowed the Measurer son to demonstrate his loyalty to his people while the twentieth-century Braose shows that he remains the villain, the traitor to his country and his principles. Yet the very coherence of this story, the satisfactory slam of the door, rides roughshod over the complexities and ambiguities which the text has produced. In the frame sequence which ends *Loyalties* the young researcher Jon Merritt resists the seductions of being employed on a glamorous series on 'The English Radicals and Romantics during the French Revolution' in order to focus on the 'shape and pressure' of the lives of men like his grandfather Norman Braose and Monk Pitter, 'people in real and uncertain situations' (374). It suggests that Williams, despite the heavy weight of authorial will he has expended to identify the traitor in the house, is not finally convinced and continues to agree with Jon Merritt that there are 'questions to ask'.

People of the Black Mountains can be seen as offering another approach to a possible resolution. The novel opens with an acknowledgement of the tension that needs to be negotiated between the 'personal' and the 'common' experience, the anxious need to negotiate the relation between the 'old deep traces' and the individual ideal of some new and specific purpose:

> The mountains were too open, too emphatic to be reduced to personal recollection ... What moved, if at all, was a common memory over a common forgetting ... there might be the sense of *tabula rasa*: an empty ground on which new shapes could move. Yet that ideal of a dissident and dislocated mind, that illusion of clearing a space for wholly novel purposes, concealed, as did these mountains, old and deep traces along which lives still moved.[38]

Yet the paradigmatic Measurer, Dal Mered, suggests a possible reconciliation to those later members of his company:

When I left Menvandir, I was an old man but I was not tired of measuring. When I get back to where I was born I shall go on measuring. But I shall measure as I have always measured, for the measuring itself and because it delights me. I will not give signs, for I am not a priest but a Measurer. (178)

Can this reconciliation and homecoming, the renunciation of the dangerous powers of the priestly caste while retaining the skills that this 'enemy training' has given, offer the answer to the exile's guilt? Superficially attractive, it has about it a sense of exhaustion, of leaving the life of action to tend one's garden. It fails, even as the identification of Norman Braose as the traitor in the house, seemed to offer another tactic for allaying guilt, yet finally the novel's structure denies its simple certainties. The figure of treachery refuses to remain safely in the house of the Norman Establishment figure, the returning Measurer is a wounded and isolated figure. The move eastwards once made, the footsteps cannot be effaced.

Notes

1. *The Welsh Slate Museum Handbook*, National Museum of Wales 2002, 43.
2. Huw Lewis, *The Campaign for a Museum of People's History for Wales* (Cardiff: Welsh Assembly, 2005).
3. Raymond Williams, 'Culture is Ordinary', in ed. Robin Gale *Resources of Hope* (London: Verso, 1989), 3–18.
4. Raymond Williams, 'My Cambridge', in ed. Francis Mulhern *What I Came to Say* (London: Hutchinson, 1989), 3–14.
5. Tony Pinkney, 'Raymond Williams and the Two Faces of Modernism', in ed. Terry Eagleton *Critical Perspectives* (Cambridge: Polity, 1989), 20.
6. Terry Eagleton, 'Raymond Williams, Communities and Universities', *Keywords* 1 (1998): 34.
7. The Owen brothers, Harold, the father of Peter, and Gwyn, come from the iron-working villages just west of Gwenton, the market town where Matthew Price attends the grammar school. Raymond Williams, *Second Generation* (London: Chatto and Windus, 1964), 29. Journalist Lewis Redfern is near the end of the novel discovered to be of Welsh parentage. 'Both your parents' parents went from South Wales to Birmingham. In the thirties, to get work.' Raymond Williams, *The Volunteers* (Cardigan: Parthian, 2011), 227.
8. Williams, *The Volunteers*, 170.
9. James A. Davies, 'Not Going Back But Exile Ending: Raymond Williams's Fictional Wales', in ed. W.J. Morgan and Peter Preston *Raymond Williams' Politics, Education and Letters* (London: St Martins Press, 1993), 119.
10. Raymond Williams, *Border Country* (Cardigan: Parthian, 2006), 4.
11. Williams, *Second Generation*, 345.
12. Raymond Williams, *People of the Black Mountains: The Beginning* (London: Chatto and Windus, 1989), 157.
13. Williams, *Second Generation*, 137, 151.
14. Williams, *Border Country*, 348.
15. Raymond Williams, *The English Novel from Dickens to Lawrence* (London: Hogarth, 1985), 81.

16. Williams, *Border Country*, 351.
17. Williams, *Politics and Letters: Interviews with the New Left Review* (London: New Left Books, 1979), 282.
18. John Braine, *Room at the Top* (London: Penguin, 1959), 97.
19. Williams, *Border Country*, 20.
20. Frederic Raphael, '*Raymond Williams' Bookmarks* (London: Cape, 1975), 162–5.
21. Williams, *People of the Black Mountains: the Beginning*, 3; episodes 'The Coming of the Measurer' and 'Earthstorm', *Eggs of the Eagle*, 'Berin Returns to Banavint.'
22. Williams, *The Volunteers*, 222.
23. Williams, *People of the Black Mountains: the Beginning*, 176.
24. Williams, *Second Generation*, 83.
25. Williams, *Border Country*, 352.
26. Williams, *Second Generation*, 306.
27. Anne Perkins, *A Very British Strike* (London, Macmillan, 2006).
28. Patrick Hannon, *When Arthur Met Maggie* (Bridgend: Seren, 2006). Hannon identifies other perceived traitors such as Ramsay Macdonald and Roy Jenkins, for re-inventing himself in an English image, 95–8.
29. Seamus Milne, *The Enemy Within: Thatcher's Secret War Against the Miners* (London: Verso, 2004).
30. J. Beverley Smith, *The Sense of History in Medieval Wales* (Aberystwyth: Aberystwyth University College, 2001), 12.
31. Glanmor Williams, 'Prophecy, Poetry and Politics', in ed. H. Herder and H.R. Lyons, *British Government and Administration* (Cardiff: University of Wales Press,1974), 86.
32. Harri Webb, 'At the Ford of Irfon', in ed. Meic Stephens *A Militant Muse* (Bridgend: Seren, 1998), 45.
33. Raymond Williams, *Politics and Letters: Interviews with New Left Review*, 28.
34. Williams, *Border Country*, 210–11.
35. J. Williams ap Ithel (ed.), *Annalles Cambriae* (1860), Courtesy J. Beverley Smith.
36. Raymond Williams, *People of the Black Mountains: Eggs of the Eagle* (London: Chatto and Windus, 1990), 213.
37. Raymond Williams, *Loyalties* (London: Chatto and Windus, 1985), 17.
38. Williams, *People of the Black Mountains: the Beginning*, 11.

The British Reception of Early Soviet Fiction 1917–1934
Ian Gasse

Early Soviet fiction, unlike early Soviet cinema and visual and graphic art, is little known in Britain, despite a large number of contemporary translations appearing during the 1920s and early 1930s for a British reading public, some of which was eager to know about the lived experience of the new Soviet society. The article provides an overview of the varied fiction published in Britain from the time of the Revolution to the first Soviet Writers' Congress in 1934, when 'socialist realism' was decreed the sole acceptable model for future Soviet fiction. The article provides a brief historical context and initial exploration of some of the material factors determining the publication of this fiction, and suggests that much more of it should be known than the few novels that appeared in the influential Penguin Modern Classics series from the 1960s onwards.

*

> It would be an extraordinary thing if out of an upheaval in the lives of a hundred and thirty million human beings, an upheaval in which two quite different ways of looking at life were engaged in mortal combat, no new literature were to be born.
> Arthur Ransome, Introduction to Yuri Libedinsky, *A Week* (1923)

The early Soviet period, from the end of the civil war to the termination of the New Economic Policy (NEP), is generally seen as extraordinarily productive culturally with, in particular, major achievements in cinema and the visual arts putting the Soviet Union on the world stage, and making awareness of these achievements part of the general knowledge, within Britain, of twentieth-century Soviet culture. Yet the early Soviet fiction of the same period, down to the official announcement of 'socialist realism' at the inaugural Congress of Soviet Writers in 1934, has not survived at all well in Britain.

While language is clearly a major factor, the Soviet fiction of the period known to British readers appears effectively to be that provided by the Penguin Modern Classics imprint of the late 1960s and 1970s, which largely comprised four major figures, Isaac Babel, Boris Pasternak, Mikhail Sholokhov and Yevgeny Zamyatin, and a handful of novels and stories: *Red Cavalry*, *The Last Summer*, *Quiet Flows the Don*, *Virgin Soil Upturned* and *We*. Of these, the last, written in the Soviet Union and published in Europe and America in the early 1920s, was not published in the USSR until the 'glasnost' years of the late 1980s. To this short list must be added three more writers of the time whose work has been rediscovered and made available in Britain. Mikhail Bulgakov and Andrei Platonov both worked in difficult conditions throughout the period. Bulgakov in particular wrote works such as *The Master and Margarita* 'for the drawer', not expecting circumstances favourable to its publication in Russia to emerge for many years. Alexandra Kollontai, a commissar in the first Soviet government who later fell from official favour, became relatively well known in Britain during the feminist moment of the 1970s, when she was hailed as a pioneer and her short stories widely re-translated and re-published. A fourth fairly well-known Soviet author is Ilya Ehrenburg, but, while some of his early novels were published here during the 1920s and early 1930s (one of which, *The Love of Jeanne Ney*, was made into a successful feature film by the German director, G.W. Pabst), Ehrenburg's fiction did not become generally known in Britain until the pro-Soviet enthusiasms of the Second World War and the short-lived 'thaw' in the Cold War during Krushchev's early ascendancy.

The overall result of this limited postwar publishing history is that the period of almost unprecedented and rapid social, political, economic and cultural change in Soviet Russia, following revolution, civil war and the establishment of the world's first 'socialist state', as it was lived, felt, recorded and expressed in the period's fiction, remains largely unknown in Britain. It is the purpose of this brief and preliminary study to identify the Soviet fiction which did appear in Britain during the 1920s and early 1930s, to locate it within the development of early Soviet literature from 1917 to 1934, and to outline some of the factors influencing contemporary British publishers in their decisions about what Soviet fiction they might publish.

The present article is a provisional attempt to offer, for a twenty-first century readership that may be unfamiliar with the early cultural history of the Soviet Union, a survey of this fiction in the light of Raymond Williams's model of 'dominant, emergent and residual' modes of literary production. It also seeks to illustrate the ways in which the material practices of the British publishing industry in the 1920s and 1930s influenced the selection of the Soviet fiction made available to the British reading public.

The Soviet Context: 'War Communism' through NEP to Five-year Plans

From the end of the period of 'war communism' in early 1921 to the announcement of the first five-year plan in 1928/9, Soviet Russia experienced seven years under the mixed system of the New Economic Policy (NEP), introduced by Lenin in 1921 to 'save the revolution' and hold the fabric of Soviet society together, following peasant uprisings in Tambov and elsewhere and the Kronstadt naval mutiny in Petrograd. The partial restoration of small-scale capitalism under NEP was a compromise response to the dangerous situation facing the Bolsheviks, characterised by the almost complete breakdown of the economy and widespread civil unrest, which threatened the Bolshevik hold on power.

At first, NEP, though greatly resented by rank-and-file Bolsheviks as a partial restoration of capitalism, proved economically successful and by 1926 much of the Soviet economy was functioning at or near the levels of the pre-war period in 1913. Agriculture had recovered to a level whereby cities and towns once again had more or less adequate food supplies and the prospect of being able to sell their surplus produce on the market gave peasants the opportunity to 'enrich themselves', in Bukharin's phrase, and feel they had a stake in the new society, after the excesses of 'war communism'. However, by 1927/8, although harvests continued to be more or less adequate, grain was once again not reaching the cities in sufficient quantities and the nature of the old-fashioned methods and capitalist context of agricultural production became the subject of much debate, with increased criticism of the policy of 'facing the countryside', which had been one of the key elements of NEP, designed to help build a socialist economy gradually, using increasing agricultural surpluses both to acquire foreign technology and provide investment for industry.

By 1927 also, a threat of war and a growing awareness of the creation of both a new NEP bourgeoisie and increasingly affluent peasants, the kulaks, contributed to an increasing opposition to NEP and focused greater attention on the imperative of developing a modern and efficient industrial economy, to meet Soviet security and production needs and provide adequate employment for the growing urban working-class population, being fuelled by the migration of poorer peasants to the cities.

These economic and political developments led to a growing emphasis on centralised planning for the economy, in order to develop heavy industry and provide infrastructure and armaments, and take control of the agricultural sector so as to guarantee reliable food supplies for the urban population. From 1928, and as a result of Stalin's more fully established power base, these factors led to the adoption of the policies associated with 'socialism in one country', based on intensive industrialisation and the enforced collectivisation of agriculture, enshrined in the five-year plans.

Ian Gasse

The Impact on Soviet Fiction

These changing economic and political conditions also impacted on cultural production. The dislocation of economic activity during the revolution and civil war created material shortages and severe production difficulties for cultural industries and the death toll from both international and civil wars seriously reduced the skilled labour force needed for the speedy restoration of cultural as well as other industries.

Alongside the economic and political changes and debates was a series of ideological debates about the role of culture in Soviet society. Whilst Lenin and other leading Bolsheviks acknowledged and encouraged the important role of culture in helping to create the ideological conditions for the new society, their views on what that culture should be were relatively traditional, based on a broad acceptance of realism in literature, film and visual art. However, the dissemination of Marxist ideas had encouraged a widespread application of Marxist doctrine to the role of culture, resulting in theorists such as Plekhanov, Bogdanov and others exploring ideas about the development of a specifically proletarian culture.

Although Proletkult, the organisation Bogdanov initiated to encourage proletarian culture and disseminate literary and other artistic skills amongst the working class, had its independence and activities much curtailed in late 1920 at Lenin's behest, because of its potential challenge to the new state's cultural authority, the underlying idea of a distinctive class-conscious and politically driven proletarian culture became widespread amongst a younger generation of Bolshevik cultural practitioners and activists, who established a range of groups expressing militant views about the development of proletarian writing and other proletarian art.

During NEP, much of the focus of the struggle for socialism shifted to this 'cultural front'. Many of the older Bolshevik leaders – Lenin, Trotsky, Bukharin and Lunacharsky – backed by the country's most respected author, Maxim Gorky, argued for the need to master and learn from established nineteenth- and early twentieth-century Russian literature, and in the case of Trotsky and Bukharin to defend the new writing of the non-communist 'fellow-traveller' novelists, who acknowledged the reality of the revolution and the new Soviet society. The more radical groups, on the other hand – October, On Guard, the Russian Association of Proletarian Writers (first VAPP, later RAPP) and the Futurist-inspired Left Front of the Arts (LEF) – adopted uncompromising positions based on a complete rejection of inherited bourgeois culture. They were also highly critical of those writers who continued to be published – for example, Boris Pilnyak, Ilya Ehrenburg and the various members of the Serapion Brotherhood, a group of writers insisting on their political independence – who were either not proletarian in origin or not active within the radical groups.

The development of Soviet fiction during the 1920s and early 1930s took place against a background of these continuing and often acrimonious debates. From 1921, when the publishing and printing industries recovered sufficiently to allow for the publication of novels again, until 1928, when the cultural political agenda associated with the onset of the first five-year plan and collectivisation of agriculture required writers (along with artists and other cultural workers), as well as proletarians and peasants, to participate in the building of 'socialism in one country', there was a period of comparative freedom of expression, with novels appearing which explored the not always flattering realities of post-revolutionary society and NEP Russia as they were being experienced and lived.

Dominant, Emergent and Residual

The emergence of fiction writing after the revolution took place in a society that, unusually, no longer had an inherited dominant culture imposed and reinforced by traditional state cultural institutions, as these had been largely swept away by the revolution and civil war. Most of the established writers and intellectuals of the last years of Tsarism either left the country to live in exile (some were deported in 1922) or initially refused to have anything to do with the Bolsheviks, assuming they would not long remain in power.

In addition, as with much of the rest of the economy, the Russian publishing and printing industries were at this time vastly reduced in scope. In 1921 printing capacity was a quarter of what it had been before the war and paper supplies one twenty-fifth of the pre-war figure.[1] The predominant form of literature immediately after the revolution was poetry, which required less in the way of paper and time for its production than fiction and could be disseminated orally through the social conventions of a 'café society'. New prose fiction did not begin to re-appear in any quantity until the establishment of NEP, which provided both the necessary economic conditions for the revival of the publishing industry, with a more or less viable market, more private publishers, and a political atmosphere in which a range of different views could be at least partially tolerated, thus allowing for a range of fictional writing once again to become possible.

The struggle for dominance in this field of cultural activity was, from the outset, characterised by much open hostility, recrimination and personal vindictiveness, particularly on the left. Notwithstanding Lenin's often quoted 1905 remarks about freedom of expression – 'everyone is free to write and say whatever he likes, without any restrictions'[2] – the view of the radical proletarian groups was that literature had to be focused on the imperative of curtailing and ultimately eliminating residual bourgeois literature and 'individualist' values to replace them with the collectivist values of the emerging proletarian culture.

The proletarian groups – October, On Guard, RAPP – were consequently highly critical of much of the fiction that appeared in *Red Virgin Soil*, the 'thick' literary-artistic journal established in 1921, with the express approval of Lenin, Krupskaya and Gorky, under the editorship of Alexander Voronsky, as the main vehicle to promote, encourage and showcase new Soviet writing. The criticism of the journal stemmed from the fact that, in order to guarantee an adequate level of quality, Voronsky gave more space to established and 'fellow-traveller' writers, such as Boris Pilnyak and Alexei Tolstoy, than to emerging proletarian authors like Fyodor Gladkov.[3]

This struggle for dominance amongst the competing literary groups was only finally resolved in 1932 when the Party abolished them all, irrespective of political orientation, and established the Union of Soviet Writers as the sole writers' organisation. However, this Stalinist conclusion had not seemed inevitable during the earlier 1920s and in 1925 the Party passed a resolution adopting an apparently 'liberal' position of tolerance, allowing for and acknowledging the 'fellow-travellers' as well as encouraging proletarian writers:

> The hegemony of proletarian writers is, as yet, non-existent, and the Party ought to help those writers to earn for themselves the historical right to such a hegemony [...] [T]act and care are essential in dealing with the fellow-travellers. The Party must evince tolerance towards transitional ideological forms. They must vigorously oppose any frivolous and contemptuous treatment of the old cultural heritage, as well as of literary specialists. Communist criticism ought to dispense with any tone of literary command – the Party cannot bind itself to support any particular tendency in the sphere of literary form [...]. The new style will be created by other methods, and the solution of this problem is not yet pressing – the Party should therefore encourage the free competition of various groups and tendencies in any given field. The Party cannot allow, by decree or proclamation, any legal monopoly of literary production on the part of one group or literary organization, and cannot grant this monopoly to any group – not even to the proletarian group itself.[4]

In the event, this provided only a temporary respite and attacks on Voronsky soon began again, leading to his removal from the editorship of *Red Virgin Soil* in 1927 and the shifting of power, with Party backing, to a single literary organization, RAPP, for the four years from 1928 to 1932,[5] as the first phase of a 'cultural revolution' from above.

The changing distribution of influence and power between the 'fellow-travellers' and the proletarian groups was reflected in the fiction that several of the 'fellow-travellers' produced during the later 1920s and early 1930s. Pilnyak, whose 1922 novel, *The Naked Year*, included explicit modernist experimentation, was, by 1930, producing *The Volga Flows to the Caspian Sea*, a novel making at least some concessions to the need to support the drive to industrialisation of the five-year plan.[6] Leonov – whose early novels *The Badgers* and *The Thief*, reflected his own ambiguous attitude to the revolution and NEP society and, in the latter novel, involved formal experimentation similar to that of André Gide in *The Counterfeiters* – set his two subsequent novels, *Sot* and *Skutarevsky* within five-year plan contexts. Likewise, Ehrenburg's *Out of Chaos* and Veresaev's *The Sisters* showed a marked shift to themes reflecting the new economic and political circumstances, whereas their earlier work had been more ambiguous about or, in Ehrenburg's case, even critical of, Soviet reality.

By 1934 most of the 'fellow-travellers' had accepted the new reality, fallen silent,[7] or begun writing 'for the drawer'. By then, also, more proletarian fiction was being published, by such authors as Avdeyenko, Chumandrin, Ilyenkov, Ostrovsky and Panferov, some of whom, Fadeyev and Sholokhov for example, were beginning to produce more accomplished work. What could be described as a new 'dominant' fiction, designed to 'remould the mentality of people in the spirit of socialism',[8] was thus achieved as the direct result of Party intervention and as part of the cultural revolution imposed across all Soviet creative activity. Those writers who failed to recognise the new reality were encouraged to acknowledge their errors or find themselves, at the least, expelled from the Writers' Union, to become isolated and unpublished.[9] The brief period of 'emergent' Soviet fiction was over for a generation.

Early Soviet Fiction in Britain to 1934

The quantity of early Soviet fiction appearing in Britain during the 1920s and early 1930s was considerable, with almost fifty titles published. Of these, at least ten (that is, more than 20 per cent of all titles) quickly sold out their first editions and were re-published in cheaper second edition reprints within a year or two of their original publication.[10] The appetite for this fiction in the 1920s followed a period during the Edwardian years when Russian literature in general had been of growing interest for parts of the British intelligentsia and reading public, with a series of new or, indeed, first editions of some nineteenth-century Russian novels appearing, which helped to consolidate the status of Russian fiction in Britain. Amongst others, the Woolfs' Hogarth Press, founded in 1917, became a substantial publisher of some of this literature.

The creation of the first 'workers' state' in 1917 increased the interest in Russian society and culture in Britain, particularly amongst the labour and trade union movements and the progressive intelligentsia. Visits and delegations to the Soviet Union by representatives of these groups took place throughout the 1920s, and the British Society for Cultural Relations with the USSR was established, by H.G. Wells and others, in 1924, as a mark of the increased level of interest in the Soviet Union. Moreover, Soviet Russia was seen to be expanding economically during the NEP years at a time when the British economy was in at least partial decline.

This was thus a time of considerable optimism for some on the left in Britain, with what appeared to be an historic destiny, involving the end of capitalism and of the exploitation of the working class, taking shape. It was also a time when a comparatively new party of the left, Labour, became the established opposition, and briefly a minority government, formally recognising the Soviet Union in February 1924, and also of the early years of the newly formed Communist Party of Great Britain. In this context, there was clearly a substantial potential readership for literature of or about the Soviet Union.

The Fiction Itself

In considering the appearance of this fiction in Britain, I want to highlight some of the ways in which the practices of the British publishing industry during the period materially affected what was published, in order to provide an example of how such practices can be seen to contribute to the selection process of what may be available to a reading public at any one time, and therefore of what may be more generally known about a foreign literature. Briefly, the commercial – and political – values of British publishers were central in determining what amongst this new Soviet fiction became available to the reading public, though some of the details of the exact mechanisms by which this occurred warrant further research: for example, how publishers became aware of the new titles, how they acquired the rights to publish them and how willing the Soviet authors were in assisting them.[11]

A personal note is appropriate here. I became interested in this fiction when embarking on a PhD at Manchester University, which was to be about some aspect of the culture of Soviet Russia under NEP, a period when it seemed that the Stalinist political and cultural outcomes of the 1930s were not yet a foregone conclusion. As I found and read the fiction of the 1920s, I was surprised to discover several novels about subjects I had assumed would not be permitted to be available in the 'capitalist west' or even acknowledged by the authorities in Soviet Russia itself.

For example, in one of the earliest of the Soviet era novels, *Tashkent* (1921), Alexander Neverov wrote openly about the famine of 1920/21; in *Chocolate* (1922), the communist writer Alexander Tarasov-Rodionov recounted the story of a loyal communist arrested, interrogated and executed, anticipating the themes explored in Arthur Koestler's 1940s novel, *Darkness at Noon*; in *The Embezzlers* (1927), Valentin Kataev described an NEP underworld of seedy bureaucracy and aristocracy that seems to belong to Tsarist Russia; and Ilf and Petrov constructed their comic picaresque tales about aristocrats and opportunists chasing across an impoverished country pursuing imagined wealth in *Diamonds to Sit On* (1928) and *The Little Golden Calf* (1931). N. Ognyov explored the chaos of aspects of early Soviet education in *Diary of a Communist Schoolboy* (1926) and *Diary of a Communist Undergraduate* (1928); Ehrenburg and Leonov described the squalor and poverty of NEP Russia in, respectively, *A Street in Moscow* (1927) and *The Thief* (1927); and Panteleimon Romanov uncovered some of the problems of adjustment to Soviet society for pre-revolutionary intellectuals in *Three Pairs of Silk Stockings* (1930), and of the changing relations between the sexes in *Without Cherry Blossom* (1925) and *The New Commandment* (1927).

Of the fiction more directly connected with revolution and civil war which was, at least initially, officially approved, Boris Pilnyak and Konstantin Fedin created two of the most formally ambitious novels in, respectively, *The Naked Year* (1922) and *Cities and Years* (1924),[12] each of which experimented in different ways with modernist innovation. Of the communist writers exploring these themes, Alexander Fadeyev was among the first of the 'proletarian' authors to be credited with success, by applying 'Tolstoyan' techniques of characterisation, in *The Nineteen* (1927), a novel about Red partisans attempting to evade both Whites and Japanese troops in eastern Siberia. Serafimovich, in *The Iron Flood* (1924), and Furmanov, in *Chapaev* (1923), which later became a successful socialist realist film, also provided popular and officially approved accounts of the civil war. Veresaev, a 'fellow traveller', wrote a more nuanced account in *The Deadlock* (1924), which highlighted both Red and White excesses as the front ebbed and flowed across a Crimean town, and Libedinsky produced *A Week* (1922), which presents credible characterisation of both Reds and Whites, despite his strong identification with the Bolshevik cause.[13]

Finally, there are the industrial novels and novels of collectivisation, which were often heralded as examples of the new Soviet fiction. The first successful industrial novel, Gladkov's *Cement*, appeared in *Red Virgin Soil* in 1925, and was duly acclaimed as the first authentic proletarian novel about the building of the Soviet economy, as well as containing an account of the problems of sexual equality in the new society. Pilnyak's *The Volga Flows to the Caspian Sea* (1930) is interesting in terms of the author's increasing accommodation to the required kind of fiction, while Leonov's *Sot* (1930) provides an example of another author's move towards greater, though by no means complete, orthodoxy in subject matter. However, Valentin Kataev's *Forward, Oh Time!* (1932) is probably the most satisfying of these industrial novels. In it he demonstrates an extraordinary ability to write in a markedly different style from that of his earlier comic novel, *The Embezzlers*, and creates a novel of considerable excitement and tension, based on the unlikely subject of an attempt by a group of shock workers in Magnitogorsk to break the world record for laying concrete. Sholokhov's *Quiet Don* (1928) chronicles the impact of revolution on a Cossack village, while Panferov's *Brusski* (1928) describes aspects of the problems of agricultural collectivisation from a communist perspective.[14]

Soviet Fiction Published in Britain, 1917–1934[15]

Year	Author/Title/Soviet Publication Date[16]	Publisher
1923	Yuri Libedinsky/*A Week* [1922]	George Allen & Unwin
1924	Boris Pilnyak/*Tales of the Wilderness* (stories) [1920/2]	Routledge
1925	ed. Alexander Chramoff/*Flying Osip: Stories of New Russia*	Fisher Unwin
1927	Vikenti Veresaev/*The Deadlock* [1924]	Faber & Gwyer
1928	N Ognyov/*Diary of a Communist Schoolboy* [1926]	Gollancz
	Boris Pilnyak/*The Naked Year* [1922]	Putnam
1929	Isaac Babel/Red Cavalry (stories) [1926]	Knopf
	ed. Jonathan Cournos/*Short Stories out of Soviet Russia*	Dent
	Ilya Ehrenburg/*The Love of Jeanne Ney* [1924]	Peter Davies
	Alexander Fadeyev/*The Nineteen* [1927]	Martin Lawrence
	Fyodor Gladkov/*Cement* [1925]	Martin Lawrence
	Valentin Kataev/*The Embezzlers* [1927]	Ernest Benn
	ed. Joshua Kunitz/*Azure Cities* (stories)	Modern Books
	N Ognyov/*Diary of a Communist Undergraduate* [1928]	Gollancz
1930	Ilya Ilf & Evgeny Petrov/*Diamonds to Sit On* [1928]	Methuen
	Mikhail Ilin/*Quiet Street* [Not known]	Secker

Year	Author/Title/Soviet Publication Date	Publisher
	Josef Kallinikov/*Women and Monks* [Not known]	Secker
	Alexander Neverov/*Tashkent, City of Bread* [1921]	Gollancz
	Fyodor Panferov/*Brusski* [1928]	Martin Lawrence
	Panteleimon Romanov/*Without Cherry Blossom* [1925]	Ernest Benn
1931	Josef Kallinikov/*Land of Bondage* (stories) [Not known]	Grayson & Grayson
	Leonid Leonov/*Sot* [1930]	Putnam
	Leonid Leonov/*The Thief* [1927]	Secker
	Vladimir Lidin/*The Apostate* [1928]	Jonathan Cape
	Panteleimon Romanov/*Three Pairs of Silk Stockings* [1930]	Ernest Benn
	Vyacheslav Shishkov/*Children of Darkness*	Gollancz
1932	Ilya Ilf & Evgeny Petrov/*The Little Golden Calf* [1931]	Grayson & Grayson
	Mikhail Ilin/*My Sister's Story* [Not known]	Secker
	ed. S Konovalov/*Bonfire: Stories out of Soviet Russia*	Ernest Benn
	Boris Pilnyak/*The Volga Flows to the Caspian Sea* [1930]	Peter Davies
	Nina Smirnova/*Marfa: A Siberian Novel* [Not known]	Boriswood
	Alexei Tolstoy/*Imperial Majesty* [1932]	Elkin Mathews & Marrot
1933	M Chumandrin/*White Stone* [Not known]	Martin Lawrence
	Ilya Ehrenburg/*A Street in Moscow* [1927]	Grayson & Grayson
	Vasili Ilyenkov/*Driving Axle* [1931]	Martin Lawrence
	V Matveyev/*Commissar of the Gold Express* [Not known]	Martin Lawrence
	ed. G Reavey & M Slonim/*Soviet Literature: An Anthology*	Wishart
	Panteleimon Romanov/*The New Commandment* [1927]	Ernest Benn
	Alexander Tarasov-Rodionov/*Chocolate* [1922]	Heinemann
1934	Alexander Avdeyenko/*I Love* [1933]	Martin Lawrence
	Valentin Kataev/*Forward, Oh Time!* [1932]	Gollancz

Ian Gasse

Year	Author/Title/Soviet Publication Date	Publisher
	Alexandra Kollontai/*Free Love* (stories) [1923]	Dent
	T Oduluk/*Snow People: A novel* [1934]	Methuen
	Panteleimon Romanov/*On the Volga* (stories)	Ernest Benn
	Mikhail Sholokhov/*And Quiet Flows the Don* [1928 on]	Putnam
	Sergei Tretyakov/*Chinese Testament* [1933]	Gollancz
	Vikenti Veresaev/*The Sisters* [1933]	Hutchinson
	Alexandra Voinova/*Semi-Precious Stones* [Not known]	Heinemann

British Publishing and Early Soviet Fiction

Publishing in Britain during the inter-war years was subject to the same general conditions as the rest of the British economy. A short postwar 'boom' was followed by a sustained period of economic depression while, at the same time, the industry experienced greater 'competition' from cinema and radio as increasingly popular general cultural activities. On the other hand, literacy was effectively universal and the growing widespread use of electricity in the home provided a much-improved general environment for reading. The National Book Council (later League) was set up in 1925 to promote leisure reading, and the commercial opportunities of bookselling were reflected in the growth of book clubs, such as Gollancz's Left Book Club, from 1929 onwards.[17]

Within this context several new publishers, some of whom were to publish at least some Soviet fiction, established themselves during the 1920s and 1930s, including Jonathan Cape (1921), Ernest Benn (1923), Peter Davies (1925), Victor Gollancz (1927), Martin Lawrence (1927), Wishart (1927), Boriswood (1931) and Lovat Dickson (1932),[18] reflecting an increasing demand for books – from 1919 county councils were empowered to provide public libraries – and the growing demands of aspiring authors.

The market for fiction included private buyers, a much smaller number than is now the case,[19] public libraries, the commercial circulating libraries, which were still very important,[20] and educational institutions. Despite the general economic conditions, new publishers were clearly persuaded that there were genuine opportunities to establish successful new publishing houses, and the experiences of Ernest Benn, Victor Gollancz and Allen Lane bear this out.[21]

The three leading publishers of Soviet fiction in Britain from 1917 to 1934 were Martin Lawrence, Ernest Benn and Victor Gollancz, publishing

The British Reception of Early Soviet Fiction 1917–1934

respectively seven, six and six titles. Martin Secker published four, Putnam and Grayson & Grayson three each, Peter Davies, Dent, Heinemann and Methuen two each, with single titles published by George Allen & Unwin, Boriswood, Jonathan Cape, Elkin Mathews & Marrot, Faber & Gwyer, Fisher Unwin (who were acquired by Benn in 1926), Hutchinson, Knopf, Modern Books, Routledge and Wishart. Some of them, like George Allen & Unwin, Jonathan Cape, Heinemann and Routledge also published other Soviet-related material, whether literature or non-fiction.[22]

The questions that arise are, first, what motivated these firms in publishing Soviet fiction and, second, how they decided what to publish. According to the contemporary publisher, Stanley Unwin, of George Allen & Unwin,[23] publishers in the interwar years made their money from authors who were already well known, so that their publishers could be reasonably sure of a ready market for the next title by a given author, assuming the standard and focus of the new work was comparable to those of previous titles. Victor Gollancz's concern to take established authors with him from Ernest Benn, when he set up his own firm, confirms this view.[24] However, this factor could not initially have been the case with any of the Soviet fiction. There would, therefore, appear to be three possible reasons for their investing in Soviet fiction.

The first, notwithstanding Unwin's remarks, was straightforwardly commercial; publishers believed it worth testing at least one example of the new Soviet fiction on the British reading public to see how it sold. Several publishers clearly felt there was sufficient general curiosity about 'ordinary life' in the Soviet Union amongst a large enough portion of the British reading public to justify the expense of publishing at least one Soviet title to see what happened. Two examples illustrate the success and failure of this kind of approach.

Despite Unwin's own view that publishers never made money from translations because of the extra royalties incurred, to translator as well as author,[25] his own company, George Allen & Unwin, published the first Soviet novel to appear in English, *A Week*, by Yuri Libedinsky, in 1923. It was translated by Arthur Ransome, *The Guardian*'s Russia correspondent, who was himself an Allen & Unwin author, and its publication in Britain seems to have been largely speculative, based on Ransome's own judgement and enthusiasm. 'Back in Riga,' he writes in his *Autobiography*, 'I made a translation of one of the books I had brought out of Russia, *A Week* by Iury Libedinsky. This was the best of the short novels in which some of the younger writers were trying to show the revolution in terms of human beings. I do not think I could have found a better specimen of the new writing.' It was duly published in both Britain and America but, according to Ransome, 'attracted little attention'.[26]

Allen & Unwin published no more Soviet novels, though they continued to publish other material on the Soviet Union.

For Ernest Benn, on the other hand, the experiment was comparatively successful. Of the six titles Benn published between 1929 and 1934, five of them went to a second impression or a cheaper, reprinted edition within eighteen months or two years of initial publication. This did not, however, lead to a general commitment by Benn to Soviet fiction and seems to have been the result of finding an author who proved saleable. Four of Benn's six titles were novels or short story collections by Panteleimon Romanov, typically about themes connected with the new sexual mores of post-revolutionary Soviet society; another was Valentin Kataev's comic picaresque novel, *The Embezzlers*, about two state trust employees who abscond with thousands of roubles on an extended spree.

Benn also used a kind of sensationalism in advertising the Romanov titles. The prosaically entitled *Comrade Kislyakov* became, when published by Benn, *Three Pairs of Silk Stockings* and *The New Commandment* was originally trailed as *The Wives of the Commissar*.[27] But rather surprisingly, given this start, Benn published no more Soviet fiction after 1934, perhaps owing to the departure of the firm's Russian 'expert', Stephen Graham, who had 'edited' and provided introductions to Benn's first three examples of Soviet fiction. There was no preface or introduction by Graham – or anyone else – to Benn's edition of Romanov's *The New Commandment* (1933) or the collection of his short stories, *On the Volga* (1934).

The second reason for publishing Soviet fiction was the more disinterested one that the literary significance of the work was such that a publisher felt it should be available to British readers, irrespective of whether it made money.[28] Contemporaneously – up to 1934 – only Babel's *Red Cavalry* seems to have been judged to be in this category.[29]

The final reason was that the work was judged to be important politically. The novels published by Martin Lawrence, the British Communist Party publisher, were largely in this category and, indeed, with the exception of Libedinsky's *A Week*, and Sholokhov's novels, none of the early Soviet 'political fiction' was published by any of Britain's more mainstream publishers. The policy of Martin Lawrence appears to have been to ensure that Soviet Russia's new proletarian fiction, by authors like Chumandrin, Fadeyev, Furmanov, Gladkov, Ilyenkov and Panferov, all of whom were or had been members of RAPP, should be available, and promoted, to the British reading public, as part of the Party's wider political ambitions.[30]

Of these three reasons for publishing Soviet fiction, the first was clearly the most common, as publishers attempted to mine a vein of general curiosity about and interest in 'everyday life' in Soviet Russia. The titles of the four collections of short stories published during the period all stressed the 'newness' or Soviet nature of Russia in their titles. John Cournos, in his foreword to the Dent anthology, claimed that the stories 'have a value for the faithful picture of Russian life as it is lived today; far more faithful [...] than the picture presented by the political or sociological observer'.[31] Alexander Chramoff, in his introduction to the Fisher Unwin anthology, stated that 'The chief object of this book [...] is to acquaint the Western reader with the life of New Russia through the works of the best native writers now resident in Russia',[32] and S. Konovalov, in his preface to the Ernest Benn selection, indicated that the aim of the anthology was 'To show the Russia of today through fiction, and to give at the same time representative examples of its literature [...]'.[33]

Stephen Graham, who was instrumental in helping select the early Soviet titles published by Ernest Benn, emphatically agreed with this approach. Introducing Valentin Kataev's novel, *The Embezzlers*, he argued that the novel 'gives a picture of Russia done by a Russian who is living in Russia now, and this is more real in detail and colour than any picture given us by a mere visitor to the country'.[34] In his preface to the Panteleimon Romanov novel, *Three Pairs of Silk Stockings*, also published by Benn, he went further: 'Since I have been debarred from entering Russia it has been my hobby to read most of the literature coming out of Soviet Russia in the original, partly for my own pleasure and instruction and partly with a view to having the most interesting books translated and published. As regards the latter, there is one test which I apply to Russian books at the present time: it is, do they answer the question – *How do the people live?* In my opinion almost any book which gives a credible answer to that question ought to be translated.'[35]

The other most prolific British publisher of early Soviet fiction, after Martin Lawrence and Ernest Benn, Victor Gollancz, seems not to have had anything like the same commercial success as Ernest Benn with titles going quickly to reprints: none did.[36] Nevertheless, Gollancz continued to publish Soviet fiction throughout the 1930s, with a further four titles appearing, three of them by Alexei Tolstoy, from 1935 to 1937. Gollancz stood perhaps midway between Ernest Benn and Martin Lawrence in terms of motivation for publishing the fiction, as he was clearly politically committed to and interested in the socialist society that Soviet Russia then appeared to be creating, as well as being a successful commercial publisher.

One assumes that Gollancz, like Benn, and presumably the other commercial publishers, had someone like Graham monitoring the fiction being published in Russia, in order to be alive to what might prove a success if published in Britain. Of Gollancz's early Soviet titles, Alexander Neverov's novel, *Tashkent*, which describes experiences connected with the 1921 famine and a young boy's attempts to save his family from starvation, was highly popular in the Soviet Union, and may have seemed likely to repeat its success in Britain.[37] Other popular contemporary novelists in the Soviet Union during the 1920s were, amongst the 'fellow travellers', Ehrenburg, Seifullina, Veresaev, Shishkov, Alexei Tolstoy, Lavrenev, Romanov, Ivanov and, amongst the 'proletarian writers', Gladkov, Serafimovich and Libedinsky.[38] Of these, only Lavrenev failed to have anything published in Britain during the period up to and including 1934.

Success for a foreign novel in Britain in the 1920s and 1930s appears to have meant selling out a first edition of 1,500 copies, which retailed at anything from five shillings (25p) to seven shillings and sixpence (37.5p), within about eighteen months or so of initial publication. Reprints tended to be priced at three shillings and sixpence (32.5p), though this was still comparatively expensive; really cheap novels cost sixpence or even less.[39] Advertising on a first edition novel could, according to Unwin, involve as much as 20 per cent of gross receipts, so the opportunity for profits on a first edition was slight.[40] Ways of reducing risk were therefore at a premium and several British publishers collaborated with US publishers to share translation and print costs. Gollancz had an arrangement with Payson & Clarke,[41] Heinemann with Doubleday and Methuen with Harpers. Both the US and British editions of Ilf & Petrov's *Diamonds to Sit On* (1930), published respectively by Harpers and Methuen, were printed by Jarrolds of Sheringham.

For Martin Lawrence, collaboration – with a Soviet publisher – was politically as well as economically motivated. Evidence of the collaboration appears in several novels, with Avdeyenko's *I Love*, Chumandrin's *White Stone*, Ilyenkov's *Driving Axle* and Serafimovich's *The Iron Flood*, all printed in Moscow and published by the Co-operative Publishing Society of Foreign Workers in the USSR, the forerunner of the Moscow Foreign Languages Publishing House, but given a Martin Lawrence dust jacket and/or binding.

Despite the range of novels published, the high literary quality of some of them and the comparative commercial success of Ernest Benn, only Babel and Sholokhov (who may have been deemed more saleable by Penguin in the 1960s and 1970s as a result of winning the 1965 Nobel Prize for Literature) among the Soviet writers published in Britain during this period survived to be accorded the 'modern classic' status by Penguin noted above. The reasons for this require a more detailed study than is possible here, involving an analysis of the evolving general political climate in Britain, the commercial instincts and marketing activities of publishers, the nature of the British reading public of the time, the interest shown by British authors in the fiction, the attitudes of the significant reviewing journals and magazines, and the continuing marginal existence of the political and alternative publications that may have been more sympathetic to or interested in the fiction. Sheila Hodges, in considering the success of Gollancz's Left Book Club in her study of the Gollancz firm, reminds us of part of the prevailing 'structure of feeling' of the interwar period: 'Conservative opinion – which included most of the press and the booksellers – tended to ignore "progressive" books, an attitude which was compounded by the general indifference of the public to anything touching on politics. Moreover, there was a kind of unspoken law that literature and politics didn't mix.'[42]

Later, after the end of the Second World War, the termination of the wartime alliance with the Soviet Union and the onset of the Cold War, combined with knowledge of Stalin's domestic atrocities, the demonstrable military effectiveness of the Red Army and the waning of the earlier enthusiasm for Soviet Russia as a utopian experiment of worldwide significance, made it possible for the Soviet Union to be more convincingly depicted and seen as a powerful threat to the international order and western society. Within this context, Soviet fiction of the early interwar years could be seen to have less appeal for both the British reading public and British publishers. For most westerners after the Second World War, the future was American and the deliberate cultural promotion of the American way of life, via cinema, television and other media, made that future seem immediate, exciting and accessible. What Soviet fiction did make headlines and seep into the popular consciousness in Britain was principally the novels of Pasternak and Solzhenitsyn, which were often crudely exploited as Cold War propaganda. A different historical trajectory and a different general attitude to the Soviet Union in postwar Britain would probably have been necessary for more early Soviet fiction to have been included in the Penguin Modern Classics list. Nevertheless, the historical and literary interest and value of a substantial number of the novels suggests they would not have been out of place in the Penguin imprint. They would certainly have provided a greater and more nuanced understanding of early Soviet society.

Acknowledgements

I am grateful to Lynne Attwood, Dave Cope and Linda Edmondson for comments on earlier drafts of this article.

Notes

1   For this and other aspects of early Soviet publishing history, see Gregory P.M. Walker, 'Soviet Publishing since the October Revolution', in ed. Miranda Beaven Remneck, *Books in*

Russia and the Soviet Union: Past and Present (Cambridge: Cambridge University Press, 1991), 59–91.
2. V.I. Lenin, 'Party Organisation and Party Literature', in V.I. Lenin, *On Literature and Art* (Moscow: Progress Publishers, 1970), 25.
3. For a detailed history of *Red Virgin Soil*, see Robert A. Maguire, *Red Virgin Soil: Soviet Literature in the 1920s* (Ithaca: Cornell University Press, 1987).
4. Quoted in Marc Slonim, *Soviet Russian Literature: Writers and Problems 1917–1967* (1967: New York, Oxford University Press), 49.
5. For a full account of RAPP and its activities, see Edward J. Brown, *The Proletarian Episode in Russian Literature 1928–1932* (New York: Columbia University Press, 1953).
6. Pilnyak had particular reason for trying to regain favour with the authorities after he published a short story, *The Tale of the Unextinguished Moon*, in 1926, which appeared to be based on the incident in which the Red Army commander Frunze had been compelled to have surgery, against his will, by Stalin and had died 'under the knife'.
7. At the 1934 Congress of Soviet Writers, five years before his arrest, Isaac Babel stated that he was writing in a new genre, 'silence' – see Edward J. Brown, *Russian Literature since the Revolution* (Cambridge, MA: Harvard University Press, 1982), 94.
8. See A.A. Zhdanov, 'Soviet Literature–The Richest in Ideas, The Most Advanced Literature', in ed. H.G. Scott, *Soviet Writers' Congress 1934: The Debate on Socialist Realism and Modernism* (London: Lawrence & Wishart, 1977), 24.
9. See the experience of Panteleimon Romanov described in Max Eastman, *Artists in Uniform: A Study of Literature and Bureaucratism* (London: George Allen & Unwin, 1934), ch. IX.
10. Almost another forty volumes of Soviet fiction appeared in the years between 1935 and 1939, before the Second World War disrupted the normal workings of the British publishing industry.
11. Because the Soviet Union was not a signatory to the Berne Convention on copyright, Soviet authors were often keen to have their work published in western countries as this gave them copyright protection.
12. Fedin's novel did not appear in English until 1962.
13. Libedinsky went on to produce a series of novels through the 1920s – *Tomorrow*, *The Commissars*, *The Making of a Hero* – which explored the adjustment of communists to the evolving Soviet society. Unfortunately, none of these has ever been published in English so what would potentially have been an interesting example of a writer's development in the early Soviet Union is unavailable to English readers. However, by the last of these novels, Libedinsky was being accused of becoming preoccupied with the individual psychology and personal life of his communist hero, not the development of the society. His status was consequently undermined.
14. Many of these books can still be found in original editions via the abebooks website (www.abebooks.com).
15. These lists have been compiled using two 1940s bibliographies: A. Ettlinger and J.M. Gladstone, *Russian Literature, Theatre and Art, A Bibliography of Works in English, Published 1900–1945* (London: Hutchinson, 1946) and Philip Grierson, *Books on Soviet Russia, A Bibliography and Guide to Reading 1917–1942* (London: Methuen, 1943). There are some discrepancies between the two sources regarding Soviet fiction published in Britain in the interwar period, hence my caution about a definitive figure for the number of titles published. Where possible, I have used copies of the novels themselves to settle any contradictions, but not all are readily available, notwithstanding the usefulness of the abebooks website (www.abebooks.com).

16 I have excluded Maxim Gorky's post-1920 fiction from the list on the twin grounds that from 1921 to 1928 he was living in exile and that the subjects of his post-revolutionary novels were always located in the period prior to the revolution.
17 I am indebted to John Feather's *A History of British Publishing* (London: Routledge, 1988) for much of this detail: see particularly chapters 16 and 17.
18 See *The British Book Trade Directory 1933* (London: Whitaker & Sons, 1933), published on behalf of The Publishers' Association of Great Britain and Ireland and the Associated Booksellers of Great Britain and Ireland.
19 According to Sheila Hodges in her study of the Gollancz publishing house, 'Fiction, then as now, was purchased almost entirely by the libraries'; see Sheila Hodges, *Gollancz: The Story of a Publishing House 1928–1978* (London: Gollancz, 1978), 50.
20 My own copies of Panteleimon Romanov's short stories, *On the Volga* (London: Ernest Benn, 1934) and the anthology, *Soviet Literature*, edited by George Reavey and Marc Slonim (London: Wishart, 1933), have labels indicating they once belonged, respectively, to the British Sailors' Society Ocean Libraries for Merchant Seamen and W.H. Smith & Sons Library, the latter available at 1d per day, with a minimum loan charge of 3d.
21 Feather, *A History of British Publishing*, ch. 17.
22 For example, George Allen & Unwin published Trotsky's *Literature and Revolution* (1925) and Max Eastman's critique of Soviet literature, *Artists in Uniform* (1934), as well as an annual *Soviet Union Year Book*, and Routledge published the first British study of Soviet literature, by Gleb Struve, in 1935.
23 Unwin published his own *The Truth about Publishing* in October 1926, with a second edition a month later and third and fourth editions in 1929 and 1946. In discussing publishers' newspaper advertising, he says, 'I do not believe that many people buy books merely because they see them advertised. […] it is the following books by the same author that derive the maximum benefit from any extensive advertising. What better justification could there be for the claim that a publisher needs a definite option upon subsequent work before embarking upon any big campaign?', 252.
24 The established authors allowed Gollancz to innovate and experiment with new writers – and some Soviet fiction: see Hodges, *Gollancz*, chs I to III.
25 Unwin, *The Truth about Publishing*, 313–4.
26 Rupert Hart-Davis (ed.), *The Autobiography of Arthur Ransome* (London: Jonathan Cape, 1976), 305.
27 'Benn's New Spring List, *The Publisher & Bookseller*, 3 February 1933, 142–3.
28 According to André Schiffren in *The Business of Books* (London: Verso, 2000), this 'enlightened' attitude amongst some publishers was a characteristic of publishing prior to the corporate takeover of the industry in the later twentieth century.
29 Yuri Olesha's *Envy*, published by the Woolfs' Hogarth Press in 1936, could claim to be another. The Hogarth Press specialised in *belles lettres* and had published Gorky's *Reminiscences of Tolstoy and Chekhov* in the 1920s and 1930s.
30 There appears to be no Martin Lawrence archive from which to establish that this was the case.
31 John Cournos, *Short Stories out of Soviet Russia* (London: Dent, 1929), viii.
32 Alexander Chramoff, *Flying Osip: Stories of New Russia* (London: T. Fisher Unwin, 1925), 16. A Publisher's Note at the front of the book explains: 'The work of the young Russian writers whose art has been influenced by the Russian Revolution, and has found its fullest expression during that great upheaval, is as yet totally unknown in this country. This volume is an attempt to present the more characteristic productions of a representative group of these writers.' *Flying Osip* was the first such anthology.
33 S. Konovalov, *Bonfire: Stories out of Soviet Russia* (London: Ernest Benn, 1932), v.

34 Valentin Kataev, *The Embezzlers* (London: Ernest Benn, 1929), 7.
35 Panteleimon Romanov, *Three Pairs of Silk Stockings* (London: Ernest Benn, 1931), vii.
36 The information about reprints comes from A. Ettlinger and J.M. Gladstone, *Russian Literature, Theatre and Art*, passim. Gollancz, of course, may have had larger print-runs.
37 For an analysis of contemporary surveys of Soviet reading preferences, see Evgeny Dobrenko, *The Making of the State Reader: Social and Aesthetic Contexts of the Reception of Soviet Literature* (Stanford: Stanford University Press, 1997), ch. 2.
38 Dobrenko, *The Making of the State Reader*, 48.
39 See Q D Leavis, *Fiction and the Reading Public* (London: Chatto & Windus, 1932), 26–7.
40 Unwin, *The Truth about Publishing*, 259.
41 Hodges, *Gollancz*, 20–21.
42 Hodges, *Gollancz*, 123.

'Why, Comrade?': Raymond Williams, Orwell and Structure of Feeling in Boys' Story Papers

Simon Machin

The essay examines Orwell's 'Boys' Weeklies', his ground-breaking 1940 study in the development of cultural studies, which looked at boys' story papers published by the right-wing press and their considerable following amongst working class readers. It traces the development of the boys' periodical from its murky origins in the penny dreadful through growing respectability in the *Boy's Own Paper* and mass appeal in the *Gem* and *Magnet*. Using Williams's concept of structure of feeling, as refined and developed in *The Long Revolution*, the essay looks at the spirited riposte by Charles Hamilton, the creator of the populist Greyfriars schools stories, to Orwell's attack. Hamilton staunchly defends a working class sensibility that valued patriotism, decency and self-respect. The article concludes by looking at Williams's own ambivalent attitude to Orwell's 'absence of roots' and also Orwell's impatience with the conservative mindset of the proletariat.

*

In March 1940, while Raymond Williams was preparing for the preliminary stage of the Cambridge Tripos, a groundbreaking piece by George Orwell, 'the first important essay of its kind written in England',[1] filled almost a third of the London literary magazine, *Horizon*. By looking seriously at a lowbrow subject, the content, tone and style of ten story papers, five owned by the Amalgamated Press and five by D.C. Thomson & Co, 'Boys' Weeklies' was a signpost to the (then) less travelled academic pathway, where culture is ordinary. In it, Orwell anticipated a break with the contemporary Leavisite orthodoxy of high-mindedness – in this instance about the value of studying the popular press – the aspiring undergraduate was to make in a different direction from the procedures of practical criticism over a decade later.

But Orwell did more than inspire the voyage out from close reading. He posed a question, appropriated within this essay's title, about a gap in left-liberal writing ('popular imaginative literature is a field that left-wing thought has never begun to enter'[2]) which I explore in both its immediate and wider contexts, since it was problematised by Williams and addressed in evolving ways, in fiction as well as cultural criticism, during his writing career. The immediate question is why a Left-wing boys' paper does not exist in Britain to rival the pre-war *Gem* and *Magnet*.

At first glance such an idea merely makes one slightly sick. It is so horribly easy to imagine what a Left-wing boys' paper would be like, if it existed. I remember in 1920 or 1921 some optimistic person handing round Communist tracts among a crowd of public-school boys. The tract I received was of the question-and-answer kind:

Q. 'Can a Boy Communist be a Boy Scout, Comrade?'
A. 'No, Comrade.'
Q. 'Why, Comrade?'
A. 'Because, Comrade a Boy Scout must salute the Union Jack, which is the symbol of tyranny and oppression', etc, etc.

Now, suppose that at this moment somebody started a Left-wing paper deliberately aimed at boys of twelve or fourteen. I do not suggest that the whole of its contents would be exactly like the tract I have quoted above, but does anyone doubt that they would be *something* like it?[3]

Behind the silky denunciation of propaganda lies the thornier matter of why reactionary and nationalistic stories have such a hold over a large swathe of lower-class juveniles, and how the radical critic should approach this sensibility or, to use Williams's term, 'structure of feeling'. The first part of this essay will examine the development of boys' story papers in the late nineteenth century, when their hegemonic influence was established at a time when social access to populist publishing and state-sponsored education was broadening. The second will explore the ways in which Williams developed the concept of structure of feeling in the period leading up to *The Long Revolution* to explain the relationship of aesthetics to class allegiance in the era of mass communication; and also Williams's uneasiness with Orwell's implied attack on the reading practices of the industrial working class.

Orwell's instinctive recoil from what radical school fiction might look like is the counterpart to the discomfiture with which critics have approached the real content of boys' story papers even when confidently inferring connections in what was in practice an obscure and ephemeral publishing milieu. This results in much commentary being an equivalent of the Rorschach Test in which the observed patterns in the historical record reveal as much about the analyst as the assumed content. For example, 'Boys' Weeklies' makes the dogmatic assertion that the boarding-school world that dominated the *Gem* and the *Magnet* was inspired by Kipling's *Stalky & Co.*, and in this belief its author is almost certainly wrong, for reasons linked to personal preoccupations.[4] We know this because of the spirited rejoinder to Orwell's attack from a single source, published in the subsequent issue of *Horizon* somewhat to the surprise of Orwell who suspected that the *Gem* and *Magnet* stories were the work of a syndicate. Charles Hamilton who as Frank Richards was the prolific and sole architect of Greyfriars and as Martin Clifford of St Jim's convincingly refutes the evidence for Kiplingesque derivation. This is derived, firstly, from a limited overlap in slang terms, such as 'jape', which Hamilton notes is extant in Chaucer and 'frabjous' which appears in Carroll, and secondly by the shared name of a master, Prout, although in Hamilton's view '[n]o two characters could be more unlike'.[5] Hamilton's disclaimer carries weight because Orwell does not disclose exactly why he believes *Stalky & Co.* to be the precursor, nor why stories preparing adolescent boys for personal participation in the Empire should attract lower-class readers not destined for this commission. For the United Services College at Westward Ho!, 'the Coll', functions as a proving ground for the rising imperial generation of administrative cadets and army subalterns, who made up a substantial group within the intended readership. With the benevolent connivance of a hero-worshipped headmaster, the triumvirate of Stalky, M'Turk and Beetle rehearse the qualities of resourcefulness and independence[6] that will be required on the North-West Frontier, where the narrative concludes. It is not that Orwell is wrong to emphasise high jinks. It is simply that the world of Greyfriars belongs to a purely domestic tradition of scholastic mayhem, dateable to the 1860s – with no strategic, colonial purpose.

Derivation is, in fact, an issue over which Hamilton is curiously evasive, claiming that his style is his own, and not capable of imitation. Although this argument forcefully rejects the insinuation of hack writing, it ignores the structural indebtedness of the Greyfriars and St Jim's repertory which Orwell correctly observes as 'carefully graded, as to give every type of reader a character he can identify himself with'.[7] In this regard it can be confidently stated that the first author for boys' story papers to establish 'the standard repertoire of schoolboy types who were to constitute the stock company of fiction: the sneak, the sulky boy, the easy-going boy, the untidy, boy, the duffer, the dandy, the growler, the bully, the scapegrace'[8] was Talbot Baines Reed, an early writer-volunteer[9] for the *Boy's Own Paper* (*BOP*) in the 1880s, very much convinced of its mission to provide appropriate role models in the characters of the school story. To examine the motivations behind Reed's major popular success, *The Fifth Form at St Dominic's*, is to come upon the central issue of ideology that caused Orwell to pen his exploration into the conservative and strangely disconnected world of Greyfriars.

Orwell acknowledges that the atmosphere of Hamilton's institutions resembles nineteenth-century rather than modern public schools; and the presentation of this atmosphere was originally a deliberate contrast to what was available as popular reading material for Victorian boys. Despite the fear of pecuniary loss amongst its founding committee at the Religious Tract

Society, the *BOP* was established as an antidote to a class of publication known as the 'penny dreadful'. The dreadful in early Victorian times had followed the sensational tradition, which as well as dealing with tales of the unexpected, chronicled stock underworld types, such as highwaymen and pirates. But as the century progressed, as Patrick Dunae observes, 'the connotations of the term had changed; instead of referring to long-running serial publications which had been read by both sexes and all ages, the term came to be applied almost exclusively to boys' periodicals of the lowest stratum'.[10] Weekly parts now featured characters with unnatural abilities, like Spring-Heeled Jack, or unconventional appetites, like Sweeney Todd, alongside rebellious juveniles.

The violence and anti-authoritarian behaviour of the boy-heroes in these story papers led to public concern whether proletarian and lower middle-class youths were being influenced to delinquency. The historian John Springhall has successfully recovered evidence of the literary field of offending publishing houses, centred upon Fleet Street, and of the grubbing relays of writers who developed the characters, recycled the plots and redrew the boundaries of taste for this sub-genre of romance. Establishing a fixed form was far from the original intention of the Victorian story paper, whose survival was dependent upon volume and the rehashing of material at speed. Springhall is, nonetheless, able to cite 'Boys of Bircham School', whose first instalment appeared on 8 June 1867 in *The Young Englishman's Journal*, as the prototype of the school story in a boys' weekly periodical.[11]

In addition to the Dickensian overtones of Dotheboys Hall, George Emmett's serial contained several of the ingredients that were still evident over seventy years later: the battle of wills between head, masters and pupils, floggings, a comic foreigner, wordplay, pranks, slapstick, physical cruelty, and snobbery. However, the circulation wars between the publishing firms of the Emmett Brothers and Edwin Brett in the 1870s, to name but two, created competition for ever-increasing thrills. This led to the main boy protagonists of each house, Tom Wildrake and Jack Harkaway, forsaking school for exotic adventures overseas with their former companions. Springhall estimates that the circulation of *Boys of England*, featuring Harkaway's dare-devil escapades, rose by 1871 to 250,000 copies which, given wide sharing, would mean a weekly readership of one million.[12]

The sheer volume of story papers led to concern that more respectable juveniles were also being tempted to sample this fare, a view expressed by the Seventh Earl of Shaftesbury to the Religious Tract Society in 1878: 'It is creeping not only into the houses of the poor, neglected, and untaught, but into the largest mansions, penetrating into religious families and astounding careful parents by frightful issues.'[13] Shaftesbury's jeremiad is at one end of the spectrum of public opinion; in surveying penny weekly part novels in 1874,

The Bookseller concluded that no word would do a reader any serious harm and that many antics amounted to no more than healthy schoolboy 'defiance'. Differences of perspective were less significant in practice than the tactics to be adopted when the Religious Tract Society's alternative reached bookstalls in 1879. As Richard Noakes observes 'the architects of the *BOP*, and its even more popular sister periodical, the *Girl's Own Paper*, recognised that in order to displace the 'penny dreadful' the new periodical would have to ape some aspects of these lower publications'.[14]

The success of the *BOP* was therefore going to be dependent on a curious synthesis of religious idealism and worldly-wise publishing élan. Evangelical high-mindedness guaranteed that losses would be underwritten (and unnecessarily because a surprising annual surplus was generated initially), that free copies would be distributed through the national Sunday School network, and that the periodical would be designed to appeal to a wide cross-section of boy readers. Professional expertise ensured high production values, a bias towards incident and excitement and away from explicit moralising, and a two-tier pricing policy with weekly parts aimed at lower class apprentices and a monthly directed to middle-class families. If tensions continued to exist between the overseeing RTS committee and acting editor over what should or could appeal to boy readers, the school stories of the *BOP* managed to instil a value conducive to the *zeitgeist*: uplift. From its first edition, which featured an article entitled 'My First Football Match', penned anonymously by Reed, the *BOP* conveyed the atmosphere of the elite public school to those not privileged to experience it at first hand. Perhaps surprisingly, the same was true of its author, who, like Hamilton after him, had never attended one and was dependent upon the reminiscences of friends.

When contrasted with the penny dreadful, at the level of narrative an exchange was being offered to the reader: realism for sensation, consistency of tone for extravagant description, and subtle characterisation for humorous caricature. *Fifth Form at St Dominic's*, serialised in 1881 and published in book form in 1887, introduced many of the plot elements that were to become standbys in the following decades for Reed's imitators: the upstanding pupil wrongly accused of a social crime; his humiliation, proud isolation and final vindication; the decline and final exposure of the school wastrel; inter-year or group rivalries; broken and restored friendships; low-life villains, often publicans and gamblers, who ensnare out-of-bounds schoolboys; boating accidents; storms and heroic rescues. Its popularity is the result of skilful characterisation conveyed through believable dialogue, and an awareness of the attractiveness to young minds of the chivalric romanticism of *Tom Brown's Schooldays*, and to a lesser extent the lachrymose *Eric*.

As Williams reminds us in *The Long Revolution*, the Public Schools Act of 1868 led to the reorganisation of secondary education on a narrow class basis.[15] These new educational institutions inevitably attracted the interest of all sections of society, whether the frisson of curiosity for those debarred from entry or the clamour of engagement for those potentially within their charmed and widening circle. Boarding schools by their very nature broke with the established practice of domestic tutelage, and somewhat paradoxically, they threw the privileged boarder back on his own resources. The two previously-mentioned and formative schoolboy fictions, by Hughes and Farrar, were published within a year of each other, in 1857 and 1858 respectively, a year before Samuel Smiles published *Self-Help*. A new boy comparing their approach in order to break the code of appropriate behaviour at any public school would have found them invaluable. They are reliable guides to acceptable contemporary conduct across a range of issues. For example, they make it clear that homesickness should never to be admitted to and, for a similar reason, sisters and mothers never mentioned. They sanction verbal expressions of male friendship but limit the confession of religious scruples only to close friends. They condone fighting when limited to boxing, present fagging as a legitimate and bullying as an unfortunate test of endurance, and in a moral descent depict cribbing as dubious, ragging teachers as reprehensible, breaking bounds as deviant, smoking as unacceptable, public houses as ruinous, and 'taking up' or consorting with younger boys as damnable. For the Christian Socialist Hughes, the Anglican Headmaster Farrar and the Congregationalist Reed, religious feeling is truly manly and by extension boyish, and crucially the prism through which all other school activities, mandated, condoned and illicit, are refracted. As the religious impulse of the Evangelical Revival waned in the 1880s and 1890s, the new dogmas of playing the game and empire filled the void for the elite minority. But throughout these changes the vicarious enjoyment of privilege, what Orwell calls snob value (perhaps particularly to those, as it were, looking in through locked iron gates) remained ingrained.

The first decade of financial success for the *BOP* was not lost on potential new entrants to the market, even though low-life rivals like Brett's *Boys of England* continued to appear, and a fellow religiously-inspired periodical *Young England*, published by the London Sunday School Union, was emboldened to enter the lists on 3 January 1880. As MacDonald acknowledges, an ethically-based magazine is vulnerable to inroads in its market share, when changes in social attitudes – to militarism, for example – allow competitors to make it seem old-fashioned. When *Chums*, aimed at a solidly middle-class audience, first appeared in 1892, it maintained an evangelical tone, and included articles about the everyday lives of ordinary working men. But to improve circulation, *Chums* soon employed a lighter tone, promoted imperialism, simplified its appearance and became more sensational. It also included anecdotes, jokes and cartoons,[16] a format not dissimilar to *Tit-Bits*, a digest for adults of excerpts from other published sources, pioneered by George Newnes in 1881. Catering for the upper end of the social spectrum, *The Captain*, launched in 1899, carried a more sophisticated tone. It also popularised P.G. Wodehouse's public school stories, where cricket stood in for any more lofty moral ambition, and the effete good manners of Psmith banished the possibility of religious soul-searching.

The final development into the ultimately conservative world described by Orwell occurred when, in Boyd's words, '[t]he publication of boys' story papers mirrored [...] trends in the magazine industry as it shifted from individual entrepreneurs in the Victorian period to highly capitalised proprietorship within the context of the limited company in the twentieth century'.[17] The major figure in the reconfiguration was Alfred Harmsworth, later Baron Northcliffe, the founder of *The Daily Mail*. Having learned the journalistic trade on the staff of *Tit-Bits* under Newnes, Harmsworth established a London publishing house at 26 Paternoster Square and in the 1890s with his brother Harold, later Baron Rothermere, entered the popular market for story papers with *Boys' Home Journal*, *Boys' Friend*, and most significantly *Marvel*, which cut the sale price to a halfpenny. It included a complete novella as well as adventure and detective fiction, and marketed itself explicitly as a 'healthy contrast' to the penny dreadful.

Because of his detailed understanding of printing technology and the importance of establishing distribution channels through the railways and the small newsagents described by Orwell, Harmsworth was able not just to anticipate the sort of reading material craved by the newly literate market assisted by the Board Schools of the 1870 Education Act, but to deliver it almost literally to the doorstep. The family publishing venture developed into The Amalgamated Press and in the new century nurtured the prolific talent of Hamilton in the *Gem* from 1907 and *Magnet* from 1908. The effectiveness of its marketing ended any pretensions of the *BOP* to be a periodical for mass weekly readership and it retreated into monthly publication in 1914. Having forced the now venerable *BOP* to redefine its market, the Harmsworth titles were themselves challenged by the entry of D.C. Thomson, the Scottish publishers, into the field with a series of more vivid, violent and experimental papers (*Adventure*: 1921, *Rover* and *Wizard*: 1922, *Skipper*: 1930, *Hotspur*: 1933). This forced the Amalgamated Press to update and respond in kind (*Modern Boy*: 1928, *Triumph*: 1924, *Champion*: 1922) completing the list specifically considered in 'Boys' Weeklies'. Yet British story paper violence was a far cry, as Orwell was keen to point out, from the coarse and sadistic American equivalent, and continued to absorb juvenile readers within a timeless, conventional, politically unaligned, patriotic and fantastical world.

When Cyril Connolly agreed to print 'Boys' Weeklies' in a highbrow magazine with a limited circulation at the end of the phoney war, the projected book from which it was selected, *Inside The Whale and Other Essays*, had only just been accepted for publication by Victor Gollancz.[18] Since Orwell did not anticipate a response from one specific purveyor of Greyfriars it is difficult to make out at whom his rather provocative salvoes about the apolitical and subjugated consciousness of the bulk of the British lower middle and working classes were aimed. Tellingly, as if in ironic endorsement of his findings, the paper shortage following the German invasion of Norway ended the careers of the *Gem* and *Magnet*, whereas, through the intervention of Harold Nicholson, a friend at the Ministry of Information, *Horizon* was to access stocks that enabled it to continue to publish. Charles Hamilton's riposte to Orwell in 1940 raised a number of questions over the accuracy of his analysis. But an academic response, looking again at the growth of the nineteenth-century reading public, had to wait until the publication of *The Long Revolution* in 1961, the year Williams returned as a lecturer to the Cambridge which the Etonian Eric Blair had failed to reach – to the chagrin of his teachers.

In his preface to *The Long Revolution*, Williams appealed for it to be seen as part of a ten-year project that also encompassed both his groundbreaking *Culture and Society* of 1958, and debut novel, *Border Country* of 1960. The project can itself be seen as a retort to Orwell, an attempt to merge popular imaginative fiction with a leftist redefinition of culture which follows the same signature blurring of the literary tools of fiction and commentary. And if, as Fred Inglis suggests, the overarching intention is to repudiate 'the Eliot-Leavis line [...] that industrial civilization has created an indiscriminate mass of people closed or obdurate to any but the easy, escapist pleasures provided for commercial profit',[19] then the third and final book is the most thoroughgoing in its sociological examination of nineteenth- and twentieth-century cultural developments. However, structurally, *The Long Revolution* is still in thrall to the methods of practical criticism from which its author drew his living between 1946 and 1961 in the Oxford University Delegacy for Extra-Mural Studies.

That *The Long Revolution* should hark back to a critical paradigm as well as being exploratory is no surprise since Williams also admits in his preface that he did not anticipate the public debate stimulated by *Culture and Society*, and had redrafted the present book to take account of this discussion. He goes further, admitting to having 'risked an extension and variety of themes well beyond the limits of any kind of academic prudence, for what seems to me the good reason that there is no academic subject within which these questions I am interested in can be followed through'.[20] *The Long Revolution*'s tripartite form reflects the experimental quality of Williams's thinking, his intention to valorise the struggle of the working class to achieve universal suffrage, develop a political consciousness and gain educational opportunities whilst considering the influence of mass communications and culture upon them. Part 1 is an enquiry into the nature of artistic creativity and its social reception, with a specific concentration on the 1840s, the decade in which Chartism articulated a radical proletarian consciousness and the industrial working class began to be discussed and represented in serious literature. Part 2, the most sociological and least reflective, is an account of the development of education, reading, the popular press, standard English and literary forms. Part 3, a personal analysis of Britain in the 1960s, reflects his argument that the relation of art to society is so complex as to be irreducible.

Williams's sectionalised approach is both an inevitable result of fresh theory-making and perhaps a desire not to come too directly at a complex question raised by Orwell: why growing political self-definition and better education has not led working class readers to abandon Greyfriars and its like for more contemporarily realistic and artistically satisfying fare. In its breadth, *The Long Revolution* could not expect to cover specifically the development of school fiction, although Williams does acknowledge the social importance of *Tom Brown's Schooldays* in changing public attitudes positively towards non-domestic education (65). He is also conscious that a strand of nineteenth-century literature had ideological designs on its readers, and notes in passing how '[r]espectable schemes of moral and domestic improvement become deeply entangled with the teaching and implication of particular social values, in the interests of the existing class society' (57). Opposition to imposed cultural norms is also noted, since Williams's interest in the social history of dramatic forms allows him to identify an authentic form of working class entertainment largely free from hegemonic interference, the music hall tradition. But his writing about this form is not celebratory: the experience of a night at the music hall is not brought to life. There is no specificity here to rival the novelistic opening of 'Boys' Weeklies' where the ranks of 'vilely printed' magazines in the provincial newsagents are so vividly realised.

Even more problematically, culture is defined hierarchically in Part 2, its ideal form still carrying figuratively an Arnoldian capital C. Although two further definitions are added, the corpus of intellectual and imaginative work over time and a particular way of life, Williams still appears to anticipate a form of gradualism through which training in aesthetics will alter the reading practices of the uneducated: '[t]he whole argument about "cheap literature" has been compromised by its use as a form of class-distinction, whereas the real problem is always the relation between inexperience and the way this is met' (169). This aside is made in the context of Matthew Arnold's condemnation of railway bookstalls and their deleterious influence on the middle classes – in his view people with a low standard of life. Williams includes this viewpoint to buttress the historical evidence that the middle classes 'made all the same mistakes and were as evidently exploited' (169) as the working class. The political rallying-call is clearly intended to be optimistic but within a few pages a more realistic admission is made: '[T]he kind of attention required by serious literature is both personally and socially only variously possible.' And most unusually, Williams is drawn into evaluative question-begging about light reading: '[w]e can all see the difference between relatively harmless and harmful drugging' (172). It is not totally apparent that Orwell would agree on the dividing line. Nonetheless, it would be unreasonable to exaggerate the critical dependency upon a Leavisite model at the expense of emerging developments in thought from a commentator for whom communication always represented an 'actual living change' (35) and *The Long Revolution* affords the opportunity for the elaboration of his evolving understanding of cultural materialism.

In writing about the challenge of how to classify cultural preoccupations of another time and place, Williams revives an idea first experimented with in the 1954, *A Preface to Film*.[21] 'The term I would suggest [...] is *structure of feeling*: it is as firm and definite as 'structure' suggests, yet it operates in the most delicate and tangible parts of our activity: it is the particular living result of all the elements in the general organization.'[22] The applicability of the concept to school fiction to a world which has consolidated its own unconscious values will be apparent when juxtaposed against Orwell's description of a dominant trope: '[a] constantly recurring story is one in which a boy is accused of some misdeed committed by another but is too much of a sportsman to reveal the truth.'[23] The reflex that makes tale-telling a solecism might be beyond the explanatory powers of a contemporary schoolboy, just as evaluating the socio-cultural causes of the convention might tax a later political theorist, and Williams is right to foreground the complexity. Structure of feeling is also used tactically as a sideswipe at a too simplistic Marxist base/superstructure model, on the basis, in Eagleton's words, 'that it is far too static and mechanistic to account for social formation'.[24] There is a sense in which *The Long Revolution* is exploratory, a form of thinking aloud, and the decision to separately compartmentalise its structural, historical and political accounts may arise from an awareness of how large a field, the sociology of culture, is being mapped. If the articulation is still stiff, it nevertheless points towards developments in a theoretical framework for the discussion of aesthetics, mass production and class difference that would take place across the Channel.

Bridget Fowler is surely correct to highlight the commonalities between 'structure of feeling' and Pierre Bourdieu's 'habitus',[25] the individual complex of dispositions, associations and cultural assumptions, derived from daily connection to a socio-economic group, that is elaborated with particular regard to aesthetics in *Distinction*.[26] Although Bourdieu was born into a not dissimilar working-class background in France, his theoretical approach has an objectivity missing from Williams (or indeed Orwell) who place themselves within the world (perhaps even the structure of feeling) that is adumbrated and sometimes draw unsubstantiated conclusions from personal experience. Additionally, because Bourdieu is deliberately trying to find a *via media* between a deterministic and charismatic understanding of art in society, he is able to break down the oppositional tension between structure and feeling, and observe, sometimes playfully, the cultural experiments, rhetorical devices and money-making gambits perpetrated by writers, publishers and critics in the cultural field of production.[27]

Bourdieu's analysis of the literary field is particularly helpful for genre fiction, and since the 1990s very illuminating work has been done on the writers' market created by magazines like the *Boy's Own Paper*[28] (which included Baden Powell and Conan Doyle), and especially the breakthrough that Sherlock Holmes represented to serial fiction in middlebrow magazines from the 1880s.[29] The concept also makes sense of the cultural posturing that is part of the relatively good-natured banter between Hamilton and Orwell. The former cannot resist expressing his surprise at being allowed to appear in a 'highbrowed' periodical, unmistakable from 'the fact that *Horizon* contains a picture that does not resemble a picture, a poem that does not resemble poetry, and a story that does not resemble a story'.[30] In the pained and pedantic tone of his reply, Hamilton resembles nothing so much as a genteel Victorian novelist.

But the most specifically helpful contribution made by Bourdieu to an evaluation of boys' story papers is his exploration of depth hermeneutics and the interpretative struggle faced by the reader, in which he unwittingly employs the term, code, so germane to public school fiction:

> A work of art has meaning and interest only for someone who possesses the cultural competence, that is, the code, into which it is encoded […] The conscious or unconscious implementation of explicit or implicit schemes of perception and appreciation […] is the hidden condition for recognizing the styles characteristic of a period, of a school or an author, and, more generally, for the familiarity with the internal logic of works that aesthetic enjoyment presupposes.[31]

Orwell is in no doubt that he has the measure of the reading competence demanded by Greyfriars; on the basis of little more than anecdote he develops a class-based taxonomy outlining at what age, if at all, readers move on.[32] The spectrum runs from public schoolboys who outgrow the *Gem* and *Magnet* by the age of twelve to working class habitués who maintain a life-long addiction. That Rhodes and Baden Powell had a no less nostalgic pleasure in returning to the pages of the *BOP* in Africa may have been unknown to Orwell, as may the quantitative processes of analysis that would have contradicted or supported his assertion. But cooler reflection would surely have led him to accept how much of his own prejudicial reading is fed into the famous dismantling of the comfortable public school fantasy:

> The year is 1910 – or 1940, but it is all the same. You are at Greyfriars, a rosy-cheeked boy of fourteen in posh, tailor-made clothes, sitting down to tea in your study on the Remove passage after an exciting game of football which was won by an odd goal in the last half-minute. There is a cosy fire in the study, and outside the wind is whistling. The ivy clusters round the old grey stones. The King is on his throne and the pound is worth a pound [...] After tea we shall sit round the study fire having a good laugh at Billy Bunter and discussing next week's match against Rookwood. Everything is safe, solid and unquestionable. (90)

The intention is satirical, and the technique familiar from Lytton Strachey,[33] consisting of the stockpiling of well-turned phrases that purport to reflect an interiority of thought, whilst being a selective pastiche aimed at casting the subject in a poor light. It is a *tour de force* likely to impress an editor, but a stumbling block to a Left-wing academic expecting consistency of political outlook. Williams responded in kind by proposing alienation as the problem in his 1971 Orwell monograph: '[w]hen he is in a situation, he is so dissolved into it that he is exceptionally convincing, and his kind of writing makes it easy for the reader to believe that this is also happening to himself. The absence of roots is also the absence of barriers.'[34]

Williams here exhibits a tendency that also characterises the debate between Orwell and Hamilton: the construction of an understanding of the reader or mass audience through personal assumptions about how any literary text will be interpreted – what Jonathan Rose, the cultural historian, has termed the 'receptive fallacy'.[35] Fortunately, as a result of the development of archival resources and research tools within the emerging discipline of book history in the 1990s, it has been possible to ground a theoretical discussion of reader response within the historical reality, by looking at nineteenth- and early twentieth-century working-class memoirs. This resource has enabled Rose to examine the available responses to boys' weeklies (by those motivated enough to record their reactions) in his section, 'Greyfriars' Children', affording him (and the reader) the opportunity to adjudicate between Orwell and Hamilton.

It is probably undeniable that by their very literacy, the memoirists quoted by Rose are atypical of their wider reading cohort. Nevertheless, immediately apparent is their strength of engagement with the Greyfriars 'code', and the sophisticated capacity to translate its values to very different and quite inauspicious surroundings, thereby conferring on the elite lassitude of Harry Wharton and Co. an extraneous, gritty dignity. The translation takes place with a full awareness of its capacity to be what Rose terms 'bourgeois cultural hegemony',[36] and a full-throated gratitude for those values which echoes Hamilton, and in some cases, a heroically understated tenacity that convicts Orwell of a lack of imaginative sympathy. What is even more surprisingly evident, however, is the intellectual gap in Orwell's argument: as Rose points out ' [o]ne could enjoy Frank Richards and still become a socialist or even a Communist' (331). Several examples are cited of politically aware readers who contradict the assumption of supine indoctrination in 'Boys' Weeklies', none more august than a future director of the *New Statesman*, C.H. Rolph, but the most striking witness is surely Guy Aldred, an anarchist who, in place of Greyfriars, veered into reading American dime detective novels, the sort of fiction that was beyond the pale even for Orwell. When questioned over the disparity between pursuing revolutionary politics and following champions of law and order, he replied with a comment that should give pause to any student of reader response theory: ' [w]e often get out of our reading what we put into it' (322).

If this developing discipline, the history of audiences, is providing salutary answers to questions first posed under a different rubric, the sociology of culture, by pioneers like Williams, it is also a surprising source of satisfaction that 'the past was more intricate and nuanced than he sometimes allowed'.[37] Nor should we be surprised that literature for children is a very early subject for the contesting of ideology in cultural materialism. In her influential book on the impossibility of children's fiction, Jacqueline Rose proposes that 'the history of children's fiction should be written, not in terms of its themes or the content of its stories, but in terms of the relationship to language which different children's writers establish for the child. How therefore do these [...] works present their world to the child reader; what are the conditions for participation and entry that they lay down?'[38] The boy reader *will* be fought for ideologically; his ability to successfully negotiate contested territory on his own terms is a recent discovery. It has become customary to describe Raymond Williams as a theorist inhabiting border territory, never quite able to dispense with extra-literary considerations when evaluating prose. Another way of viewing his position would be to regard him as a cultural optimist, structure of feeling being a carefully sculpted phrase used to respect the indurate quality of humanity, recognising that we are always and everywhere more than readers. And on balance there is considerable evidence to vindicate the rose-coloured proposition that a dingy suburban tobacconist can indeed be hallowed ground.

Simon Machin

Notes

1. Michael Shelden, *Friends of Promise: Cyril Connolly and The World of Horizon* (London: Octopus Publishing Group, 1990), 45–6.
2. George Orwell, 'Boys' Weeklies', *George Orwell: Essays* (London: Penguin, 1984), 100.
3. Orwell, 'Boys' Weeklies', 99.
4. That Orwell should cite such an extreme precursor as Kipling is influenced by his own unhappy memories of private education. Shelden notes that Connolly also commissioned Orwell to write 'Such, such were the joys' a reminiscence of the preparatory school they both attended, which was regarded as too libellous to print (47). Orwell's repudiation of his birth name Eric Arthur Blair is connected to his dislike of the Christian name, Eric, the eponymous hero of Farrar's most famous novel, which Orwell cannot bring himself to mention in the text of 'Boys' Weeklies', substituting the less familiar *St Winifred's* (82).
5. Charles Hamilton, 'Frank Richards Replies to George Orwell', in ed. Sonia Orwell and Ian Angus, *The Collected Essays of George Orwell* (Harmondsworth: Penguin, 1970), 531–40.
6. Stalky is a term in schoolboy slang, meaning 'clever, well-considered and wily, as applied to plans of action; and "stalkiness" was the one virtue Corkran toiled after'. Rudyard Kipling, *The Complete Stalky & Co.* (Oxford: Oxford University Press, 1987), 13.
7. Orwell, 'Boys Weeklies', 86.
8. Jeffrey Richards, *Happiest Days: The Public Schools in Fiction* (Manchester: Manchester University Press, 1988), 106.
9. Richards confirms that Reed transferred the copyright of the stories to the RTS for a nominal fee because of his belief in their work (106).
10. Patrick A. Dunae, 'Penny Dreadfuls: Late Nineteenth-Century Boys' Literature and Crime', *Victorian Studies* (1979): 134.
11. John Springhall, '"The Boys of Bircham School": The Penny Dreadful Origins of the Popular English School Story, 1867–1900', *History of Education* 20, no. 2 (1991): 93.
12. Springhall, 'The Boys of Bircham School', 87.
13. Dunae, 'Penny Dreadfuls', 139.
14. Richard Noakes, 'The Boy's Own Paper and Late-Victorian Juvenile Magazines', in *Science in the Nineteenth-Century Periodical: Reading the Magazine of Nature* (Cambridge: Cambridge University Press, 2004), 155.
15. Raymond Williams, *The Long Revolution* (London: Chatto & Windus, 1961), 138.
16. Robert H. MacDonald, 'Reproducing the Middle-class Boy: from Purity to Patriotism in the Boys' Magazines, 1892–1914, *Journal of Contemporary History* 24, no. 3 (1989): 523.
17. Kelly Boyd, *Manliness and the Boys' Story Paper in Britain: A Cultural History, 1855–1940* (Basingstoke: Palgrave Macmillan, 2003), 25.
18. George Orwell, *The Complete Works of George Orwell*, XI, ed. P.H. Davison (London, Secker & Warburg, 1998), 422–3.
19. Fred Inglis, *Raymond Williams* (London: Routledge, 1995), 148.
20. Williams, *The Long Revolution*, ix–x.
21. Raymond Williams and Michael Orrom, *Preface to Film* (London Film Drama, 1954).
22. Williams, *The Long Revolution*, 48.
23. Orwell, 'Boys' Weeklies', 82.
24. Terry Eagleton, 'Base and Superstructure in Raymond Williams', in *Raymond Williams: Critical Perspectives*, ed. Terry Eagleton (Cambridge: Polity Press, 1989), 165.
25. Bridget Fowler, 'The Cultural Theory of Bourdieu and Williams', *Key Words: A Journal of Cultural Materialism* 3 (2000): 116–7.
26. Pierre Bourdieu, *Distinction: A Social Critique of the Judgement of Taste* (London: Routledge & Kegan Paul), 1986.

27 See, for example, 'The Field of Cultural Production', in ed. Randal Johnson, *The Field of Cultural Production: Essays on Art and Literature* (Cambridge: Polity Press, 1993).
28 In addition to Noakes, 'The Boy's Own Paper and Late-Victorian Juvenile Magazines', see Aileen Fyfe, *Science and Salvation: Evangelical Popular Science Publishing in Victorian Britain* (Chicago and London: Chicago University Press, 2004).
29 Peter D. McDonald, *British Literary Culture and Publishing Practice 1880–1914* (Cambridge: Cambridge University Press, 1997), 118–72.
30 Hamilton, 'Frank Richards Replies to George Orwell', 531–40.
31 Bourdieu, *Distinction*, 6.
32 Orwell, 'Boys' Weeklies', 84–5.
33 Lytton Strachey, *Eminent Victorians* (Oxford: Oxford University Press, 2003).
34 Raymond Williams, *Orwell* (Glasgow: William Collins, 1971), 88.
35 Jonathan Rose, *The Intellectual Life of the British Working Classes* (New Haven, CT: Yale University Press, 2001), 4. Rose acknowledges his own debt to the reconstruction of a detailed history of reader response from memoirists by David Vincent in *Bread, Knowledge and Freedom: A Study of Nineteenth-Century Working Class Autobiography* (London: Methuen, 1982) and by John Burnett, David Vincent, and David Mayall (eds), *The Autobiography of the Working Class: An Annotated, Critical Bibliography*, 3 vols (New York: New York University Press, 1984–89).
36 Rose, *The Intellectual Life of the British Working Classes*, 323.
37 Editors' Preface', *Key Words: A Journal of Cultural Materialism* 8 (2010): 5.
38 Jacqueline Rose, *The Case of Peter Pan or The Impossibility of Children's Fiction* (London: Macmillan, 1994), 78.

'The Army of the Unemployed': Walter Greenwood's Wartime Novel and the Reconstruction of Britain
Chris Hopkins

This article explores Walter Greenwood's completely forgotten wartime novel *Something in My Heart* (1944), which is of note both as a sequel to his influential novel *Love on the Dole* (1933) and as a novel which explicitly focuses on the war as an opportunity to put right the social injustice and political mismanagement of the 1930s. The novel focuses on two unemployed Salford men in the late 1930s and on their contribution to the war effort once they have joined the RAF at the beginning of the war. The article argues that the political motivations of Greenwood's novel in arguing for a very different post-war Britain are influenced both by his experience of pre-war censorship and his sense of the political possibilities opened up by the Ministry of Information's stress on the idea of 'the People's War'.

*

Walter Greenwood is, of course, famous as the Salford author of the best-remembered 1930s depression novel, *Love on the Dole*, a novel which had considerable impact and which suddenly changed, or fulfilled, the direction of his own life. Thus, January 1933 brought him a letter from Jonathan Cape, which Greenwood quotes as starting simply, 'Dear Sir, We will publish your novel'. Greenwood's 1967 memoir, *There Was A Time*, also comments, 'I was on the threshold of a wonderful year, though this I did not know'.[1] In fact this is the memoir's last comment on the 1930s, for the remaining brief chapter looks back at Hanky Park from the time and place of the 1960s demolition-site which is preparing the ground for the Salford Shopping Precinct. This ending, with its comparison of the period 1900–1933 with the period of the post-war welfare state and 1960s prosperity in particular, is clearly making a point about the ending of that (particular) impoverished world, and about social progress. It is also making a point about Greenwood's own life: with the publication of *Love on the Dole* he left that life behind in a personal sense, at least, and took up the desired life of a writer – and that is a story he does not wish to pursue in his memoirs beyond this founding point.

In fact, very few others have wished to pursue Greenwood's life as a professional writer much beyond the publication of *Love on the Dole* either, and, as this article will suggest, that has led to the neglect of some interesting texts and their contexts. Thus his own memoir gives no account of how this eventful acceptance letter immediately or in the longer term impacted on his life after 1933 – leaving us to fill in very broadly for ourselves what happened to him by leaping over the space between 1933 and 1966 (only one critic has devoted any attention at all to his novels after *Love on the Dole,* but even he does not discuss Greenwood's one wartime novel).[2] For if *Love on the Dole* remains his most significant work, ignoring his other work of the 1930s as well as his later work has sometimes left him as a rather contextless author beyond the context for *Love on the Dole* itself – accepting in effect his own memoir's rhetorical closure of his life in 1933, and also perhaps a stereotyped view of working-class writers as able to write only a single successful work directly from experience (a view which perhaps played a considerable part in some reviewers' responses to his novels after *Love on the Dole*).[3]

In fact, he lived for the rest of his life as a professional author, writing new works and adaptations right up until the late 1960s, and publishing four more novels in the 1930s and one wartime novel, on which this article will focus, with the slightly un-warlike seeming title *Something in My Heart* ('an absurd title', one review says[4]), in 1944. From 1934 onwards, he made a living not just through fiction publication but also through the journalistic commissions which increasingly came his way. By 1938, he had been a professional writer for five years, and had been living in Cornwall and London for two years. Indeed, by 1938 he had become not just an author but himself an agent for a variety of kinds of creative artist, for in that year he co-founded with his accountant, a Mr Park, his own stage and film agency and production company, called Greenpark, after its two originators.[5] It may also be worth noting before going on to discuss Greenwood's wartime novel that the company went on to make government 'information films' during the war.[6] It seems possible that this activity, and his other indirect contacts with the wartime Ministry of Information (MOI) through the curious change of heart about a film version of *Love on the Dole* in 1940, may have brought Greenwood an awareness of the MOI's potential reach and developing political complexities, and that this may have influenced the genesis, shape and message of *Something in My Heart*, which so interestingly and insistently revisits *Love on the Dole* from the perspective of the war.

Before discussing *Something in My Heart* in its own right, it is important to set out the context of Greenwood's experience of constraints on political expression and the power of state apparatuses suddenly to alter their own rules. The surprising decision to make a film version of *Love on the Dole* in 1940, when 1935 and 1936 screenplays had been subject to extensive and insuperable objections from the British Board of Film Censors, has often been noted. Thus, the British Board of Film Censors' reports on the proposed 1935 film said that the film was 'a very sordid story in very sordid surroundings' and was anxious about both political and sexual issues:

> The scenes of mobs fighting the police are not shown in the stage-play, but only described. They might easily be prohibitive. Even if the book is well reviewed and the stage play had a successful run, I think this subject as it stands would be very undesirable as a film.
>
> I do not consider this play suitable for production as a film. There is too much of the tragic and sordid side of poverty and a certain amount of dialogue would have to be deleted and the final incident of Sally selling herself is prohibitive.[7]

The best and fullest account of how, in factual and political terms, this impossible film became possible is given by Caroline Levine in her excellent article, 'Propaganda for Democracy: the Curious Case of *Love on the Dole*'.[8] According to a letter written to *The Guardian* (3 April 1984) by Ronald Gow, co-writer with Greenwood of the play version of *Love in the Dole* (1935):

> … in 1940 he and Greenwood were summoned to meet with J. Brooke-Wilson, the Secretary of the British Board of Film Censors. 'Brookie' told the two writers that they must turn their dramatic script into a screenplay without delay. 'This film's got to be made', he reportedly told them. 'We've got a tip from someone "higher up". I can say no more'. (867)

Further, Gow recalls that the context was a British sensitivity to criticism in the US, with 'headlines in the American press saying, "Britain Bans Workers' Film"; and in 1940 this was thought to be a bad report from a country fighting for freedom' (867, quoting Gow). Levine's account goes on to identify the 'higher up' as the art historian Kenneth Clark, who had been Director of the National Gallery since 1933, but became (for a brief period) Director of the Film Division at the Ministry of Information between January and April in 1940. Clark discusses this period in his autobiography, *The Other Half – a Self-Portrait*.[9] Though neither Greenwood nor *Love on the Dole* are mentioned in the autobiography, Clark admitted to Ronald Gow in 1980 that he had initiated the instruction, following a strongly worded letter to *The Guardian* (26 February 1940) by Greenwood criticising the censorship of his film script in the light of the war against Nazi Germany and which argued that the Board had 'taken upon itself the powers of a Dr Goebbels' and that therefore 'all the talk of the freedom for which we are told we have been fighting [is] so much claptrap'.[10] In a footnote, Levine discusses the possibility that Greenwood was already 'in cahoots' with the MOI before writing this letter, but rejects this because there is no evidence and because the idea does not seem to make obvious sense. I do not necessarily want to argue that *Something in My Heart* was even indirectly an MOI-inspired project (though I wonder), but rather to suggest that Greenwood's experience of the *volte-face* about the film may have given him a sense that there was a cultural shift in which the MOI was playing a varying and sometimes inadvertent part, a cultural shift to which he, as the author of a famous novel which had pleaded for change, could make a further contribution.

The story of *Something in My Heart* opens in 1937 and initially concerns three main characters from Salford: Helen Oakroyd, who works in a textile mill, Harry Watson, and Taffy Lloyd, both of whom are on the dole. Harry, Helen and Taffy reproduce aspects of the roles of Sally, Harry and Larry in *Love on the Dole*, as well as re-using two names from that novel (Harry and Helen). Confusingly, however, the Harry here broadly corresponds to Larry, Helen to Sally, and Taffy to Harry Hardcastle. Harry Watson is clearly a self-educated and politically active working man, Taffy is also committed but consciously less articulate than Harry Watson ('I can't put it into words like Harry'[12]), while Helen is a 'beauty' on 'twenty-five bob a week' (8), who craves romance and feels a thus far unrequited love for Harry, but who, like her predecessor, Sally, is remarkably independent and tough-minded in many respects. The names themselves are, of course, pointing the reader back to *Love on the Dole*, but so too do many other allusions in the opening chapter. Thus, Taffy thinking about his situation not only echoes Mr Hardcastle's 'oh God, gimme a job!', but also summarises the sense which *Love on the Dole* gave so strongly of the impossibility of an ordinary life for the unemployed, and the resulting sense of hopelessness:

> Blimey! A job! A quid in your pocket and a decent suit of clothes to your back. Aye and married to a girl like Helen. Aw, but chuck it man. How many more mugs are there like you in Britain thinking the same thing? Millions of 'em and all signing on the dole like you and Harry. Most of 'em like you, too, young, strong and with the best part of their lives supposed to be in front of them. All being robbed of it, robbed of something that could never be replaced. (7)

Compare this to *Love on the Dole*'s Harry thinking about his similar lot:

> Nothing to do with time; nothing to spend; nothing to do tomorrow or the day after; nothing to wear; can't get married. A living corpse; a unit of the spectral army of three million lost men.[13]

Chris Hopkins

The themes of love and marriage on the dole raised by Taffy are also strongly picked up by the other two characters in the first few pages. Helen thinks about how much she likes Harry Watson, but also shows her independence by asserting that she does not necessarily need a conventional marriage relationship, 'If ever I fall in love with a fellow, I'll not ask him for a thing'.[14] She also observes that Harry does not seem to notice her and reprises some of the romance/class dynamic between Sally and Larry in the earlier novel:

> When, every Thursday, he was taking his class in economics at the Labour Club, she was among those present. Maybe he *did* guess how she felt and maybe this avoidance was his unspoken answer. No, no it wasn't that … He was too interested in his political activities; *that* was the reason. She found herself hating them and his other studious interests. Yet, it was partly because of these he was so different from the other fellows; this was the quality in him that was the mainspring of her love. (6)

In fact, Harry shortly afterwards articulates his own refusal to respond to her as stemming partly from political commitment, and partly from a somewhat retrograde assumption that romance and domestication will inevitably erode the single man's 'freedom' to engage with politics:

> You'll find yourself enmeshed … Instead of waiting for you at the street corner you'll find her at your house and, maybe, when you feel like studying … Romance? Love? Who's taking about these things? As well ask a soldier about those things when he's in the middle of a battle. You're in the same fix as a soldier – except that no battle can last long … Some of your fellow dole-birds have been out of work for ten years. A dreary, weary, spirit-breaking battle in the concentration camp of empty pockets. (10)

The comparison of unemployment with military service and, indeed, combat has a particular resonance of course, given that this is a wartime novel. Indeed, the first edition rear dust-jacket makes this very clear, referring to Harry and Taffy as 'two of that vast army of the unemployed' who have now joined the RAF. The meaning of unemployment is thus shifted towards something more heroic than the dominant hopelessness represented in *Love on the Dole* (though that is evoked too by the striking reference to 'the concentration camp').

Indeed, while the evocation of Greenwood's famous first novel is strong, there are also some notable differences between it and *Something in My Heart*. Where the 1933 novel often implies that the people of Hanky Park are in many respects trapped in a poverty very like that of the nineteenth-century, this novel suggests both a more modern England and also characters who are not quite so wholly stuck in the endlessly-reproducing system into which they are born. Thus aspects of consumer England and modern leisure seem to be more often referred to, even if they are no longer possible for most of the characters, and there is a greater knowledge of the wider world:

> Just look at 'em, patent leather and pointed toe: the only ones I've got left and what I used to go jazzing in. Aw! I'm no blooming Red. I'm an ordinary guy, a skilled mechanic out of a job ... But I can fix any blasted, broken-down car or machine with the next man (8).

There is also noticeably less use of Salford dialect and a greater use of contemporary idioms – often cinema or popular fiction derived Americanisms such as 'dough'. These are unemployed citizens, but citizens nevertheless of England rather than of just Hanky Park (indeed, the fact that Taffy is Welsh widens the picture of unemployment in itself, though this may also be an influence from the 1941 film of *Love on the Dole*, in which the politically-active Larry is played by the Welsh actor Cliff Evans with a clearly Welsh accent).[15] Though Taffy and Harry are trapped for the moment, there are even some possible ways out. Thus, Harry is, among other things, good at boxing:

> Lightweight champion of the Salford Lads' Club three times running ... You could have been British professional champion if you'd wanted and be walking about with a pocketful of dough just for poking somebody in the kisser. Turning the promoter's dough down like you did. (9)

However, Harry has 'other fish to fry', for he is studying through his union 'for the Ruskin College scholarship' (9). Both these escape routes, in their different ways, suggest a representation of unemployment in 1930s Salford as less isolating than the version depicted in *Love on the Dole*. Where in the earlier novel Larry seems to be in most respects the only political activist in Hanky Park, an odd exception whose origins and history are not revealed in the novel, and the unemployed youngster Harry Hardcastle has in the end only the street corners to go to, here Harry Watson is part of a society possessing some collective working-class institutions which can help the unemployed: boys' clubs, a Labour Club (6), a union which can fund study, and a national college for working people, to which some can aspire.[16] The contained stasis of Greenwood's earlier novel is to a degree opened up to a more national and even international culture here. The essentially ignorant and passive inhabitants of Hanky Park have been succeeded by much more politically-conscious beings; during a political discussion about how Hitler came to power in Germany on the back of unemployment and loss of hope, Harry reminds

Taffy of their joint attempts to do something: 'We've collected for the people of China and Spain and the Vienna workers. You were at the meeting for Sacco and Vanzetti' (21). The escape route through professional boxing is, of course, a more traditional one, and perhaps more like the 'escape' which Ned Narkey in *Love on the Dole* makes into the local police force through his physical strength and aggression, or, like the dream-vision of escape Sam Grundy offers in that novel through gambling on sports events.

Overall, then, this seems a slightly more hopeful Salford, even though the mass experience, as we are frequently reminded, is one of severe deprivation through joblessness. Another means of escape which is offered as a last resort in *Love on the Dole* is now seen as a focus of both mobility and, indeed, modernity. In a moment of desperation, Harry Hardcastle in *Love on the Dole* thinks his only course may be to join the army, but both Harry Watson and Taffy Lloyd share an obsession which is, if very marginally, contactable for unemployed men from Salford. At the very opening of the novel, Helen sees two ragged men and knows how they have spent their day: 'they had signed on at the dole late this afternoon and thence had walked to Barton aerodrome to watch those who could afford it take lessons in flying' (5).

Flying was deployed as a potent symbol of a number of things during the 1920s and 1930s – including escape, modern mobility, technological mastery of nature, the possibility of individual liberation from mass experience, and, particularly towards the end of the period, as a symbol of Fascist domination.[17] Here it certainly symbolises escape for Harry and Taffy, but is also associated with the modern, with resistance to Fascism and with individual and national recovery. Thus in due course the once desperate Taffy comes back to Salford to see Harry, who is still studying to get to Ruskin, having completed his (pre-war) RAF training as an Observer: 'Taffy Lloyd stood on the doorstep, sunburnt and grinning. A winged "O" was on the breast of his uniform … The same Taffy and yet – what a difference! Bright eyes, straight shoulders, a living air about him' (28). Where the civilian social order has failed him, the RAF has transformed him: 'I'm telling you … the way they never taught us *anything* at school…the education in the RAF … those instructors, they really *want* you to learn' (29). Harry, at the outbreak of war, joins Taffy in the RAF and qualifies as a pilot.

These transformations and modernisations of *Love on the Dole* are key to this wartime novel's message (and message does seem the right word in many ways). What was a call for help from the forgotten region of Hanky Park is here put into the larger perspective of 'Act 2' of the 1930s, the road to war and thence eventually to the hoped for post-war settlement for Britain. This perspective makes *Something in My Heart* precisely a progressive narrative in several senses, where *Love on the Dole* is within itself a largely circular one, except for the bitter progress for the Hardcastle family achieved through Sally's submission to Sam Grundy's 'patronage'. Just as the war led to a transformation of the context and meanings of *Love on the Dole*, and hence the possibility of a film version, so here the war, though immediately mainly through rearmament, can put an end to unemployment, poverty and loss of purpose. What was the identity-sapping nothingness of unemployment is here being written into a history – and a highly critical one – of pre-war government failure to manage this social and economic disaster and, prospectively, of what must replace such failures.

There is, though, some curious political ground to traverse in this process. Here is a novel expressing sympathy for the unemployed workers of the 1930s and which in many respects also makes clear its socialist and particularly Labour Party sympathies. The rather fluid, and sometimes opposed meanings attributed to 'flying' thus need to be made to serve the cause of democracy and to disseminate the idea that post-war Britain must be a very differently organised place from 1930s Britain. Though there has been no previous critical discussion of the novel in this light, *Something in My Heart* was not alone in either needing to transform the imagery of flying, or in its focus on the RAF as a symbol of the national and social unity created by the war effort. The novelist Rex Warner serves as an excellent illustration of how some pre-war images of flying had to be rapidly adjusted; his novel, *The Aerodrome*, which he was writing in 1939–40, was published in March 1941. It is about a patently Fascist and hyper-masculinist airforce, which takes over an equally obviously English village, in line with many pre-war leftist representations of flying (and even the RAF specifically) as inherently Fascist instruments of technological mass-destruction. But by the time the novel was published, the decisive Battle of Britain had taken place (between June and September 1940) and the RAF, in fact, in popular imagination and through the efforts of the Ministry of Information, had achieved an unassailably heroic role as the saviours of Britain from Nazi aggression and, indeed, occupation. Warner could not change a novel based on an entirely different premise, but did add the rather weak disclaimer:

> In this book my two worlds 'village' and 'aerodrome' are of course not intended to describe any village or airforce in existence. For the purpose of my story I have made both these worlds somewhat repulsive. Let the story, if it can, justify itself. But, in case it should be misunderstood, let me here assert that both for the airforce and for the villages of my own country I have the utmost affection and respect.[18]

A recent pioneering study by Martin Francis, *The Flyer – British Culture and the Royal Airforce 1939–1945*, has detailed just how important (and how variously representable) the RAF was to wartime British culture:

> Traditionally, debates about how far British society became more egalitarian (in both subjective and objective terms) between 1939 and 1945 focused on the home front, following the lead of Angus Calder's classic *The People's War* ... However, recently there has been more attention paid to the relationship between service life and social change in wartime ... With Colonel Blimp dead and buried, the military was no longer a safe haven for those who wished to escape the democratic and populist impulses of the modern world. *The Flyer* will include consideration of how these same issues of class and democracy were played out in the RAF. As the most junior of the three services, the RAF took pride in its lack of formality, and emphasised a technocratic and meritocratic vision of military life, appropriate to the supposed classlessness of the people's war. However, some flyers embodied old-style, public-school derived notions of martial masculinity. In both Bomber and Fighter Commands, moreover, social distinctions between officers and NCOs ... remained deeply entrenched. (5)

Greenwood's wartime sequel to *Love on the Dole* should certainly be approached very much in these kinds of terms. Its address to national unity and reform is made clear even by the first edition's rear dust-jacket 'blurb' which records how Harry and Taffy serve together with their 'RAF friend, Rupert Hardcastle, wealthy son of a great industrialist'.[20] In fact, this cross-class friendship is achieved only after considerable initial class hostility displayed by Rupert – resolved after Harry shows not only his superior judgement and flying skills but also knocks Rupert down in an impromptu bout of boxing.[21]

Social unity under the stress of war and in its comradeship is a strong theme throughout the rest of the novel, but this consensus is presented as a new, even revolutionary development: there is much criticism of the pre-war social order and much looking forward to a very different post-war society. This cluster of ideas is a frequent topic of thought and conversation across the class range of characters in the novel. Thus the indubitably upper-middle class Group Captain Donaldson reflects, 'Well, if Watson was an example of working class "ignorance" then the possessing classes had better do something about their own ignorance, for in the future they certainly wouldn't be able to patronise men like that' (109). And Rupert Hardcastle's father (who as well as being an industrialist has also been a major in the 1914–18 war and, moreover, a holder of the Victoria Cross) has a long discussion with his son about how much more efficient the wartime command-economy is: 'we're told what we've got to make and how much' (206). Surprisingly, Greenwood avoids what looks set to be an argument between the newly-enlightened Rupert (now father of Helen's child[22]) and his father as a pre-war style industrialist, instead moving what initially appears to be a complaint about wartime state-control into an acceptance by Major Hardcastle of the need for democratic change: 'We've accomplished all this upheaval in our own characteristic way – And its only a beginning. As for social reform. You haven't heard the last of the Beveridge Report.' (206). The now socially well-informed Rupert's only worry is that all the wartime reports on reform (he names in addition to Beveridge, the Scott Report, the Uthwatt Report and the Samuel Report[23]) will be forgotten, 'pigeon-holed' once the war is over. His anxiety is, in fact picked up and in principle addressed in one of the epigraphs to the novel (as in the case of *Love on the Dole*, there are multiple epigraphs, to some others of which I will return later) taken from *Hansard*:

> The Government welcome the fact that Parliament is ... at last facing this problem as a fundamental issue. We are indeed grappling with the problem which is uppermost in the minds of those who are defending the country today ... With my Right Hon. Friend the Prime Minister, I has an opportunity of visiting one of our ports and seeing the men of the 50th Division ... They were going off to face this terrific battle with great hearts and great courage. The only question they put to me ... was. 'Ernie, when we have done this job for you, are we going back to the dole?' ... Both the Prime Minister and I answered, 'No, you are not'.[24]

In short, the novel is dedicated (perhaps none too subtly, though the 'middlebrow' periodical *John O'London's* referred to it as 'an important novel of ideas'[25]) to supporting the war as a People's War, repeating and expanding the promise which A.V. Alexander had made at the end of the 1941 film of *Love on the Dole* that Britain would never go back to the 1930s: 'Their Reward must be a new Britain. Never again must the unemployed become forgotten men of the peace.'[26] The role of the film in marking a wartime political shift – or the promise of a shift – towards greater class consensus and the founding of the post-war Welfare State has been much discussed – but clearly this novel was another important, and more explicit, contribution by Greenwood at a later stage of the war towards this agreement on the need for major post-war social and political change.

I started discussion of *Something in My Heart* by suggesting that it might partly have been shaped, or influenced anyway, by Greenwood's wartime sense of a certain degree of 'democratic turn' in the Ministry of Information itself, and in the ways that the public began to make sense of the war. Given, of course, that Orwell's 'Ministry of Truth' is a satirical version of that government agency, the word 'propaganda' perhaps needs to be mentioned at this point. Clearly the novel is didactic (though also perfectly readable) and in a more explicit mode than *Love on the Dole*. Still, its ideas are firmly in line with Greenwood's established liking for social consensus and for social democratic change in a Labour-Party tradition, and it has been argued that the Ministry of Information did try to create and foster more broadly a propaganda which was more democratic or, paradoxically, a propaganda which was essentially 'true', while also sustaining morale and supporting the vital maintenance of the war effort.[27] It is also the case that the wartime services, as well as the general public, did contain many volunteers and conscripts with a considerable appetite for discussion of what they were fighting for, so that the novel's topics and represented conversations may not have struck contemporary readers as entirely unnatural or overly didactic[28] (though a review in the *Times Literary Supplement* complained that while the 'book is readable all the way through [it] would be more so if the author did not make his characters think aloud so often and at such great length').[29]

The precise relationship between the topics explored in the novel and Ministry of Information policy is complex, however. The MOI had a general policy of *not* indicating its sponsorship or patronage of publications, since it was felt that this would undermine authors' independence and suggest that there was a direct commissioning process to promote official views. Nevertheless, there was a very active Arts and Literature Division of the Ministry, just as there was a separate Film Division (which has been much more thoroughly studied). Moreover, the MOI had substantial control over a scarce resource – paper – and so inevitably had considerable influence on what was published and in what print runs. The Ministry often seems to have worked quite closely with particular publishing houses and may well informally have suggested the kinds of topic which might be viewed favourably as contribution to the war effort and therefore likely to be allocated a decent paper ration:

> A number of publishers benefitted from MOI policy, and for some, the links they forged proved financially rewarding ... Because ... the MOI continued with its strategy of invisibility, the full extent of its book, periodical and pamphlet programme has not yet been mapped ... [nor] the multifarious ways in which authors, agents, publishers printers, and distributors were, between 1939 and 1946, coopted – sometimes willingly, sometimes with great reluctance – into 'patriotic' government service.[30]

This quotation is from one of the few discussions of this relationship, in an excellent article by the publishing historian Valerie Holman, who, without mentioning Greenwood specifically, also interestingly notes that Hutchinson – who had become Greenwood's publisher after he parted company with Cape in 1938 and who published *Something in My Heart* – did seem to have a close relationship with the MOI, at least early in the war. Thus a report from April 1940, 'Book Activities of General Division',

> listed all work then under way for thirty-two books and a large number of pamphlets and leaflets. The publisher most frequently used was Hutchinson's, who, like many others, was persuaded to reduce the selling price of his books with a view to reaching a large readership. (206)

At any rate, Greenwood's novel with its project to both advance progress towards a more social democratic Britain and to record that this shift was already under way thanks to the exigencies of war, as well as showing some opening up of elite opportunities to working people and the benefits of central government planning, was certainly in tune with a good deal of public discussion in the last two years of the war. However, officially the MOI was, in fact, more or less forbidden to discuss post-war reconstruction and planning. Early in the war, in 1940, some figures within the MOI, including the Bloomsbury socialist Harold Nicholson, had argued that for the Ministry to carry out its function it had to be able to tell the British people clearly what the war was being fought for beyond survival, and thus what British war aims were.[31] The Prime Minister, Winston Churchill, who on occasion took a detailed interest in the work of the MOI, was very opposed to any such definition beyond the need to fight for national survival and the overcoming of the evils of Nazism, and remained wary for the rest of the war of discussion of post-war reconstruction and making what he felt were at best utopian and at worst positively socialist promises about the nature of post-war British society: 'Ministers should … be careful not to raise false hopes as was done last time by speeches about "Homes for Heroes" etc. … It is for this reason of not wishing to deceive the people by false hopes and airy visions of Utopia and Eldorado that I have refrained so far from making promises about the future.'[32] However, after the Beveridge Report was so well received by the British public on publication in December 1942, the MOI seems to have been put in an increasingly awkward position: 'How was it possible to buoy up the post-war aspirations of the nation while simultaneously bowing to the prime-minister's desire for silence on the subject?' (171). Brendan Bracken as Minister of Information in December 1942 (though a close associate of Churchill) is said to have at least briefly 'whipped all the horses of publicity' on the Beveridge Report:[33]

A large Press Conference was arranged for Sir William', writes Francis Williams, the Controller of Press and Censorship, 'a summarized version of the plan with diagrams was readily prepared and issued in large numbers ... as a result the Beveridge plan swept the country and indeed the world'.[34]

Nevertheless, the cabinet was, as Angus Calder points out, 'embarrassed rather than delighted by the Report's popular success'.[35] And 'after the first glare of limelight, the Government went to extraordinary lengths to stifle all official publicity for the report' (for example, suppressing – two days after it had been issued – an Army Bureau of Current Affairs pamphlet which summarised the report and was written by Sir William Beveridge himself).[36] However, it was impossible to put the lid back on the Report and, if the MOI did not encourage discussion of post-war reconstruction, there was the danger that the topic would anyway be discussed in print media and elsewhere without the Ministry being able to influence at all how it was presented. There was considerable awareness about this awkward situation in the Ministry itself, which received reports from Home Intelligence about public enthusiasm for the Beveridge Plan ('it is feared that the Government does not realise that it "has become a religion to some people"'), and recorded in the minutes of a meeting between the MOI and the Reconstruction Secretariat that there was a strong need to 'convince a suspicious and highly sceptical public opinion that the Government was in earnest [about] reconstruction' since a lack of public belief in the sincerity of government intentions 'was likely to have dangerous consequences'.[37] The curious and indirect relationship between publishers and the MOI may perhaps come into play here, though some speculation is necessary. Since it was MOI policy not to be seen directly to sponsor any publication, the Ministry's specific influence on publishers is often difficult to trace, but it seems plausible that publishers might want to catch public interest in reconstruction and that the MOI might not necessarily put up any obstacles (there was no direct censorship, at least, or only on specific security grounds[38]), since many of its own members were aware that it was a topic begging for discussion and closely linked to sustaining morale till the end of the war. Public interest in itself could not be simply disposed of:

> In June 1942 the Director of the Reference Division [of the MOI] informed the Director General of the steady increase in the "already constant demand" by Ministry speakers and others for material on the government's post-war plans ... The ban on the ventilation of post-war topics by Ministry speakers was ... extended to cover the Beveridge Report, although no way could be found of insulating speakers from audience questions in the

subject. Nor, indeed, could the ministry avoid preparing publicity on post-war topics for other departments and agencies.[39]

Ironically, as the last sentence of the quotation makes clear, other agencies were allowed to discuss post-war reconstruction more freely, and the topic seems to have been a particular favourite with the Army Bureau of Current Affairs. There had been books published on post-war reconstruction from quite early in the war, but there does seem to have been an increase in the popularity of this topic after 1942, and the period 1943–45 seems, perhaps not surprisingly, to have produced a positive crop of books about reconstruction, including J. Van Den Tempel's *Keep the Lamps Burning – an Analysis of Political and Social Problems in the Post-War World* (R. Hale, 1943), the Directorate of Army Education's *The British Way and Purpose, with Appendices of Documents of Post-War Reconstruction* (1944, a collated version of eighteen pamphlets which had been issued to army discussion groups by the ABCA), and a book which seems to have been published in large numbers, Donald Brook's *Writers' Gallery – Biographical Sketches of Britain's Greatest Writers and their Comments on Reconstruction* (Rockcliff, 1944, reprinted 1945).[40] The possibility that the MOI might have helped in one way or another with such kinds of publication despite its difficulties over reconstruction may be suggested by Valerie Holman's discussion of Ernest Barker's 'little book', *Britain and the British People* (Oxford University Press, 1942), which included the following statement: 'We have gained a new plan for liberty – liberty for ordinary men and women to live their lives in the freedom of educated minds, in freedom from ill-health, in freedom from want and from fear – the fear of unemployment and the fear of penniless old age.'[41] This clearly refers to the kinds of reform dealt with in the Beveridge Report and, as Holman makes clear, this particular publication was from beginning to end an MOI project (the book was printed in some 44,000 English language copies in total across two imprints in 1942 and 1944, with nearly 105,000 copies in translations into various languages by the end of the war) (215–6). Of course, this, though known as 'indirect propaganda', was one of the more direct MOI publishing projects and centred on a 'factual' rather than fiction work: where possible the Ministry preferred to work less directly through and with commercial publishers. Nevertheless, the case perhaps shows how complicated was the situation of official support for post-war reform and reconstruction:

> The need to present Britain as a forward-looking social democracy in the later stages of World War II informed not only the content of periodicals and selection of externally published books, but also how target audiences … were imagined and addressed. Increasingly, policymakers believed that

it was important to appeal to a mass readership ... The books selected showed a clear preference for 'middlebrow' authors such as J.B. Priestley. (220)

It might be that the MOI discouraged discussion of post-war reconstruction with one hand and encouraged it with the other. It might be that in many respects Greenwood's novel, which might very fairly be called 'middlebrow', is in line with many of the themes of MOI policy, while in other aspects critical of an apparent official grudgingness about post-war reform.

From looking at the contemporary reviews in 1944 of *Something in My Heart* in Greenwood's press-cuttings book in the Walter Greenwood Collection at Salford University Library, it is clear that the majority of reviewers certainly identified the novel as linking a critique of the 1930s to a discussion of wartime and post-war reconstruction. Firstly, they generally saw at once the link to *Love on the Dole*: 'Here is a warm-hearted story which may be ranked almost as a sequel to *Love on the Dole*'.[42] Secondly, across a wide range of newspapers there was sympathy with the view taken from the novel's discussions that state planning was the way to ensure that the social crisis of the 1930s could never return:

> Mr Greenwood has nothing good to say of the England in which such material [i.e. Harry, Taffy and Helen] was allowed to go to waste, but much hope of a post-war England which will make better use of its heritage of brains and character.[43]

> The situation obviously allows Mr Greenwood opportunity for sharp comment on the economic follies of the past and our hope for a more humane and rational system in the future.[44]

In one way or another, then, *Something in My Heart* seems to be Greenwood's follow-up to the wartime possibilities which the *Love on the Dole* film-case revealed, possibilities for the public promotion of the post-war reforms which would make the 1930s unrepeatable and which were so enthusiastically adopted in public discussion after 1942, despite various (though varied, uneven and complicated) levels of official unwillingness. Though so far I have stressed the novel's promotion of optimism and increasing social consensus, some of the epigraphs I have not thus far quoted suggest that it also has an awareness of considerable potential resistance to reform, and these epigraphs may suggest it is not just supporting what could be called the 'propaganda' of the People's War, but insisting that the idea itself becomes a post-war reality. Thus in juxtaposition to Ernie Bevin's post-war promise as recorded in *Hansard*, we have Dean Inge's extraordinary fears about post-war Britain in his *Evening Standard* column (4 January 1944):

> When I think of the horrors of revolution, of civil war, and of treasonable strikes and threats of strikes only bought off by unlimited blackmail and promises of more loot in future I am more afraid of what may come after the war than of the German army.[45]

And other different kinds of warning notes from Erasmus, George Dangerfield and a prolific British writer of Russian origins, George Sava:

> The people build cities and the Princes tear them down. The hard work of the citizens creates the wealth which the robber Barons plunder. Representatives of the people write good laws, only to have Kings break them. The people seek peace, but their rulers seize upon every opportunity for war.

> But history illustrates ... the eternal attempts of individual human beings to hasten or retard, to obscure or illuminate the inevitable.

> I had learnt that no triumph and no defeat is final.[46]

Some newspaper reviews of the novel also suggest a similar public awareness that there are some official barriers to discussion of the future and anxieties that hoped-for promises might not be fulfilled. Thus the *Irish Times* (perhaps distanced from some political undercurrents in Britain?) detects a difference between the hope and confidence of Greenwood's main characters and authorial uncertainty:

> This confidence seems not altogether shared by the author, who continually reminds one of their past, and occasionally hints that another slump might occur after the war. He quashes his bouts of pessimism, however, by a few references to the Beveridge Plan.[47]

In what seems to have been the longest review of *Something in My Heart*, in *John O'London's Weekly*, the novelist Pamela Hansford Johnson suggests that the issues it raises need to be more widely discussed, and also regards it as articulating views typical of those in the services:

> Let me say ... that this is an important novel of ideas, and that it ventilates a good many worries that are apt to fester in confinement. If future generations want to know what the fighting men were thinking during the

Nazi war, they will get a good deal of enlightenment from any copy of *Something in My Heart* ... that may remain extant.[48]

It may be that the novel is a specific intervention in the debate about post-war reconstruction, which voices the not uncommon suspicion that the government, or sections of it, might not follow through the radical reforms which it had somewhat inadvertently sponsored, and supplies its readers with a clear historical and personal narrative of why such reforms are necessary, possible, reasonable and deserved by the British people. The novel thus gives an insight into the extraordinary shift in public opinion about the responsibilities of the state which the People's War (including the MOI's general and specific sponsorship of that idea, despite its particular difficulties with post-war reconstruction[49]) helped bring about. In 1935 the British Board of Film Censors had considered a film of *Love on the Dole* to be out of the question because of its potential for stirring up discontent with the status quo: by 1940, this decision had been reversed (if only partly for a specific tactical reason in relation to US public opinion), allowing the 1941 film to be made, and by 1944 Greenwood was able to reconfirm and encourage this democratic turn by confidently publishing a novel which articulated a widely-shared vision, and cheerfully advocated not only the prospect but the actuality of sweeping changes to the nature of British government, and support for an already emerging egalitarian class-structure. The novel plays a part in what Ian Mclaine diagnoses as the 'most important single reason for the failure of [wartime] class resentment to assume threatening proportions ... its absorption into the public's post-war aspirations'.[54] It seems very odd that Greenwood's wartime novel has received no recent attention at all; certainly, it is a novel which may suggest how important *Love on the Dole* continued to be in the 1940s as a national reference point for an unacceptable past and a hoped for, planned future. Indeed, the novel and the tenor of most its reviews seem to have revived forcefully the very similar views which the film of *Love on the Dole* evoked in 1941, as exemplified by Nora Alexander of the *Sunday Pictorial*, who wrote:

> Time after time our Censors have waxed apoplectic at the suggestion that Walter Greenwood's *Love on the Dole* was fit subject for a film ... Now with unemployment a minor headache, the moralists have relaxed and the film has been made without a single change. The result is terrific ... but it is not depressing. On the contrary, it holds enormous promise for the future. If every man and woman in Britain could see this film, I don't think we would ever go back to the dreadful pre-war years when two million men

and women were allowed to rot in idleness. I don't think the censor meant us to feel that way about it. But Walter Greenwood did.[55]

Acknowledgements

I would like to thank colleagues in English at the University of Salford who invited me to give an early version of this research as a paper at their annual MA Day in 2011–12, and would particularly like to thank Dr Ben Harker who suggested that *Key Words* might be interested in an article on this topic. I would also like to thank Ian Johnston at the Walter Greenwood Archive, University of Salford Library, and my colleague at Sheffield Hallam, Dr Mary Grover, for invaluable assistance.

Notes

1. Walter Greenwood, *Love on the Dole* (London: Jonathan Cape, 1933), 249. All subsequent references are to this edition and will be given in the text.
2. See Paul W. Salmon's excellent concise article on Greenwood's career in George M. Johnson (ed.), *Dictionary of Literary Biography Vol. 191: British Novelists Between the Wars* (Detroit: Gale, 1998), 132–40.
3. For example, the *Times Literary Supplement* review of his comic novel *Standing Room Only or A Laugh in Every Line* (London: Jonathan Cape, 1936) is not uncharacteristic: 'A pity that he has been lured from Manchester and Salford; his previous books have made him a name as a chronicler of contemporary life … but in his new book he deserts reality and gives pictures of a world in which he is as little at home as his hero Henry Ormerod.' In fact, much of the novel is set in Salford and Manchester (though not in Hanky Park), with only a relatively brief interlude set in London. *TLS* 18/7/1936, 598. Article accessed via the *TLS Centenary Archive*, 17 November 2009.
4. *John O'London's Weekly*, 20 October 1934, review by Pamela Hansford Johnson (in the Walter Greenwood Collection (hereafter WGC) 3/2). See below for further discussion of this review.
5. I presume this is the James Park from Salford to whom Greenwood's 1950 book on *Lancashire* is dedicated and who by 1950 was, as that dedication makes clear, an Alderman of Salford.
6. Greenpark still exists as a company and since 1997 has been mainly a company marketing its film and picture archive under the title Greenpark Images. This history and the quotation are taken from the company website, http://greenparkimages.co.uk/history.html (accessed 11 June 2010).
7. Jeffrey Richards, *The Age of the Dream Palace – Cinema and Society in Britain 1930–1939* (London: Routledge, 1984), 119. The censors submitted individual reports rather than a collated report – the political worries in the first paragraph are those of the censor Colonel Hanna, while the issues of sexual morality are raised in the second quotation by the censor Miss Shortt. Both, however, use the word 'sordid' about the screenplay (it is Colonel Hanna who uses the word twice in his overall view of the script). For discussion of some of the issues about why this particular screen-play was so problematic and of how this

related to general film censorship practice in the 1930s, see both Richards, 108–52 and James C. Robertson's *The British Board of Film Censors: Film Censorship in Britain, 1896–1950* (Beckenham: Croom Helm, 1985), especially 83, 85, 132, 137, 140 and 167.

8   Caroline Levine, 'Propaganda for Democracy: The Curious Case of *Love on the Dole*', *Journal of British Studies* 45 (October 2006): 846–73.

9   Kenneth Clark, *The Other Half – a Self Portrait* (London: John Murray, 1977), 11–22.

10 See Levine, 'Propaganda for Democracy", 848.

12 Walter Greenwood, *Something in My Heart*, first edition (London: Hutchinson and Co., 1944), 8. All subsequent references are to this edition and will be given in brackets in the text (there is only one other edition – a Morley-Baker reprint, Leeds, 1969, which has the same pagination).

13 Greenwood, *Love on the Dole*, 25.

14 Greenwood, *Something in My Heart*, 5–6.

15 David Berry in his book, *Wales & Cinema: the First Hundred Years* (Cardiff: University of Wales Press, 1994) suggests that nothing is made of Evans' evident Welsh identity in the film of *Love on the Dole*: '[Larry] Meath is described as Welsh in studio publicity but no attempt is made to point up his origins'. I think this is not quite right: the film does not explicitly fill in the novel's apparent gap about Larry's origins, but merely by casting Evans with his Welsh accent as Larry it implicitly supplies an explanation. Larry in the film *is* an outsider – and brings to the apathy of Hanky Park some of the political radicalism and collective feeling which was in the 1930s so strongly associated with Wales. This meaning which the film adaptation adds to novel and play versions may interestingly influence Greenwood's rewriting of his novel here (for discussion of images of Wales in England in the 1930s see the opening discussion in chapter 5 'Depressed Pastorals? Documenting Wales in the 1930s' in my book, *English Fiction in the 1930s: Language, Genre, History*, London: Continuum, 2006).

16 Ruskin College, Oxford was founded in 1899 as a college where working-class people (men, originally) might have access to higher education. It still fulfils this function.

17 The meanings associated with flying in the period are discussed in a number of sources. See, for example, Valentine Cunningham's *British Writers of the 1930s*, (Oxford: Oxford University Press, 1988), 186–7, 203, Susan Ware's *Still Missing: Amelia Earhart and the Search for Modern Feminism* (New York: W.W. Norton, 1994), and my *English Fiction in the 1930s*, (ch. 10).

18 Taken here from the Penguin reprint of May 1941. There is much truth in Warner's statement in the opening paragraph of the disclaimer not quoted here that 'I do not even aim at realism': the novel is deliberately constructing a myth. Nevertheless, it ran up against a more potent national myth in 1940. Interestingly though, the novel was reprinted several times by Penguin during the war – in 1944, and January 1945 – so presumably publishers and readers found ways of making its topic not specifically unpatriotic (it is perfectly possible to read its narrative as a warning against excessive state power, a warning which might have had considerable resonances for readers even during this war for democracy. See my discussion in *English Fiction in the 1930s* and also N.H Reeve's discussion of the novel in his study *The Novels of Rex Warner* (London: Palgrave Macmillan, 1989). Martin Frances in *The Flyer – British Culture and the RAF 1939–1945* (Oxford: Oxford University Press, 2008) has an interesting discussion of the more faintly continuing association of the RAF with Fascism even during the war and briefly mentions Warner and his disclaimer (see 178).

19 Frances, *The Flyer*, 5.

20 Again, Greenwood re-uses a name from *Love on the Dole*, though somewhat oddly, given that it is transferred from the unemployed family to the rich industrialist.

21 Greenwood, *Something in My Heart*, 57.
22 One review objects strongly to the novel's several cross-class relationships, saying of Harry and his upper-class partner that 'they would both have been very unhappy' and that such a scenarios can only come from Greenwood's own 'social inexperience' (*National Review*, December 1944, WGC 3/2, 67).
23 The Uthwatt and Scott Reports (both from 1942) were concerned with different aspects of planning control for agricultural and rural land use (there was no wartime Samuel Report that I can locate: it seems slightly unlikely that Greenwood is referring to the 1925 Royal Commission Viscount Samuel chaired on the coal industry, the conclusions of which were welcomed neither by miners nor owners and which led to a lock-out and strike – although Beveridge also served in that Commission and it did recommend nationalisation of the mines: see entry for Samuel in the online *Oxford Dictionary of National Biography*, 2004). The Uthwatt and Scott Reports each concluded that there should be some state intervention and controls over rural land-ownership, but not the nationalisation which had been pre-war Labour Party policy – see Michael Tichelar's article 'The Labour Party, Agricultural Policy and the Retreat from Rural Land Nationalisation during the Second World War', available online at http://www.bahs.org.uk/51n2a6.pdf (accessed 23 February 2012; first published in *Agricultural History Review* 51, no. II (2003): 209–25). Angus Calder also briefly discusses both these reports, as well as the Beveridge Report, in the final chapter, 'Never Again? December 1942 to August 1945', *The People's War: Britain 1939–1945* (London: Jonathan Cape, 1969; London: Pimlico, 1992), 534. Subsequent references are to the 1992 edition.
24 Ernest Bevin, Debate on the Government's White Paper on Employment Policy, Hansard, 21 June 1944. Interestingly, the MOI charted carefully public views on the nature of post-war Britain and Ian Mclaine notes that 'Fear of unemployment was by far the most commonly reported phenomenon associated with people's expectations of post-war Britain: it was mentioned in almost every report and implicit in others' (*The Ministry of Morale: Home Front Morale and the Ministry of Information in World War II* (London: George Allen & Unwin, 1979), 179. Note that the epigraphs are unfortunately removed from the 1969 Morley-Baker reprint of the novel).
25 Quoted on the inside dust-jacket of the Morley-Baker 1969 reprint.
26 Closing title of the British National Film Ltd film of *Love on the Dole*, 1941, with A.V. Alexander's signature. A.V. Alexander, later Lord Alexander of Hillsborough, was a Co-operative Society MP and in 1941 was also First Lord of the Admiralty in the wartime Coalition (see his *Oxford Dictionary of National Biography* entry and also John Tilley's *Churchill's Favourite Socialist: a Life of A.V. Alexander* (Manchester: Holyoake Books, 1995)). The opening title also looks back to the depression as a thing of the past: 'This film recalls one of the darker pages of our industrial history.'
27 See Carole Levine, 'Propaganda for Democracy: The Curious Case of *Love on the Dole*', *Journal of British Studies* 45 (October 2006): 849–50.
28 Such tastes were not universal, but something of the atmosphere is given by the leftist children's writer Geoffrey Trease in his account of his wartime service in the Army Education Corps: 'It was accepted that the new conscript armies would fight better if they knew what they were fighting for. The Army Council had set up in 1941 the Army Bureau of Current Affairs to help the Corps and even the most red-necked Blimp paid lip-service to the value of talks and discussion groups.' Trease says that many men in the AEC were socialists and that 'it is now generally recognised that that the army vote in the 1945 election, which swept Labour into power, was a good deal influenced by those preceding years of discussion'. *Laughter at the Door – a Continued Autobiography* (London: Macmillan, 1974), 50 and 64.

29 11 November 1944. Press cutting in Walter Greenwood's press cutting's book (68), which was maintained for him by Durranty's Press Cuttings agency: this volume, covering 1938–46 is held in the Walter Greenwood Archive at Salford University as item WGC 3/2. My thanks to the university and especially to the archivist, Ian Johnstone, for facilitating my visit to the archive to explore this important and fascinating material.
30 Valerie Homan, 'Carefully Concealed Connections: the Ministry of Information and British Publishing 1939–1946', *Book History* 8 (2005): 199.
31 See Ian McLaine's still definitive study of the MOI *The Ministry of Morale* for discussion of the complexity of the MOI's position within government and its often difficult relationships with other government departments, the services and on occasion, the Prime-minister. See especially chapters 6 and 7: 'Morale and the Prospect of Reform' and 'Stealing the Thunder of the Left'. Nicholson's views of the role of the MOI and his disapproval of some of Churchill's attitudes are extensively discussed, but see, for example, 63 and 173.
32 McLaine, *The Ministry of Morale*, see, for example, 104–7, 181–5. The quotation is on 183 and is from 'Memorandum by Prime Minister, 12 January 1943, CAB 66/33.
33 Calder, *The People's War*, 528.
34 McLaine, *The Ministry of Morale*, 181. Mclaine suggests that Churchill did know about Bracken's publicity campaign, but that perhaps both regarded it as focused on impressing world opinion with Britain's democratic culture and that they were then completely taken aback by domestic enthusiasm and an appetite for actual political and social change. This might explain the striking gap between this initial MOI support and the subsequent ban on MOI involvement in public discussion or promotion.
35 Calder, *The People's War*, 531.
36 Both quotations and the information about the ABCA pamphlet are taken from Calder, *The People's War*, 531.
37 McLaine, *The Ministry of Morale*, 182 and 184.
38 'Of the publishers' worries, the least was censorship. Only security censorship applied to books' (Calder, *The People's War*, 511).
39 McLaine, *The Ministry of Morale*, 183.
40 There were (as of 23 February 2012), for example, thirty-two copies of the 1944 or 1945 editions on sale on AbeBooks UK, suggesting a reasonably large number of original imprints.
41 Holman, 'Carefully Concealed Connections', 214–5 (no page reference for the quotation from Barker's book is given).
42 *Daily Telegraph*, 20 October 1944, unsigned, WGC 3/2, 64.
43 Also 20 October 1944.
44 *Western Mail*, 31 October 1944, review by H.M. Dowling, WGC 3/2, 64. The *Western Mail* was (and is) a Cardiff-based newspaper, often regarded in the late nineteenth and early twentieth century as mainly supportive of the perspectives of mine and iron works owners.
45 There is one epigraph on the title page (from G.K. Chesterton's poem *The Secret People*) followed on the next page by five further prose epigraphs. Dean Inge's is the fourth (he was Dean of St Paul's and wrote a regular *Evening Standard* column from 1921 until 1946).
46 The Erasmus quotation is simply attributed by Greenwood to the author with no further details. The Dangerfield quotation is from the historian's work, *Victoria's Heir: The Education of a Prince* (New York: Harcourt, Brace and Company, 1941), while the George Sava quotation is from his autobiography about his life as a surgeon, *The Healing Knife* (New York: Harcourt, Brace and Company, 1938).
47 *Irish Times*, 28 October 1944, WGC 3/2, 65.
48 *John O'London's Weekly*, 20 October 1944, 32: WGC 3/2, 63.

49 Calder notes that 'several of the ministry of information's pamphlets which extolled the People and their war became best sellers', *The People's War*, 511.
50 Mclaine, *The Ministry of Morale*, 178.
51 Nora Alexander, *Sunday Pictorial*, 1 June 1941, quoted by Geoff Brown with Tony Aldgate, *The Common Touch – the Films of John Baxter* (London: BFI Publications, 1989), 1. There is some evidence from Mass Observation reports during the war that the novel continued to be widely read. Thus a commentary on a Mass Observation Literature Questionnaire from 1940 notes that: '[it] must be clearly realized that within fiction, too, there are a good many books which are in fact social and sociological documents, or serious works stimulating thought about present, past or future times. Books like "How Green was my Valley", "And Quiet Flows the Don", "Love on the Dole" and "The Grapes of Wrath", which are among the most popular fiction books for borrowing and buying[,] are works of fictions which really belong to the serious class.' This is part of File Report 13332, 'Books and the Public – a Study of Buying, Borrowing, Keeping, Selecting, Remembering, Giving and Reading Books' from July 1942 which also mentions (section XXXI) *Love on the Dole* as one of twenty-five fiction books borrowed from libraries which were 'most popular at the time of this investigation'. In Section XVII of the same report (about book buying habits), an observer notes that 'One of the waitresses at the snack counter is very keen to get a copy of *Love on the Dole*, but it seems difficult to get'. The Commentary on the Literature Questionnaire also notes that a film version of a novel may boost sales or library loan popularity and specifically mentions *Love on the Dole* among others: 'It will be seen that a very wide range is covered, naturally. If there is one notable characteristic, it is for people who buy fiction to buy books which have already been filmed. The most frequently bought fiction books, especially by C and D class people, are definitely those which have been filmed, like "Hatters Castle", "The Grapes of Wrath", "Love on the Dole", "Rebecca", "North West Passage", "Gone with the Wind", etc. Here again we come to the souvenir and permanent value of the book … Having seen a film, people like to keep [it] in some permanent form by buying the book' (from Mass Observation Archive online, Matthew Adams, http://www.massobs.org.uk/index.htm, accessed 15 February 2012). My own copy of the 1938 edition of the Samuel French Acting edition of the play of *Love on the Dole* is inscribed to a previous owner, 'With love and best wishes from Frances, Xmas 1941'. There was also the first radio adaptation of the play broadcast on BBC Radio's Saturday Night Theatre slot on 20 January 1945 (which, as Dr Ben Harker pointed out to me, may be a reasonably significant year for the play to have a new airing, with the end of the war in sight and political decisions about post-war reconstruction now needing to be made). See the Saturday Night Theatre – a Tribute to BBC Radio Drama website, which usefully lists all plays broadcast and their dates from the very beginning of the programme on 3 April 1943 onwards: http://www.saturday-night-theatre.co.uk/broadcasts.php (accessed 22 February 2012). There also seems to have been something of a revival of productions of the play on stage during 1945–46, both before and after the July 1945 Elections: WGC 3/2 has cuttings referring to at least four amateur productions, including one by the Bradford Co-operative Society's Education Committee (*Co-operative News*, Manchester, 13 April 46). There is also reference in the Glasgow *Evening Times* of 17 August 1945 to a political rally at the 'Cosmo Cinema' by the successful North Lanark Labour candidate, which was to include a screening of *Love on the Dole*.

Will Self and the Academics: Or, How to Write Satire
Alan Munton

The satiric fiction of Will Self (b. 1961) is notably divergent in content and method. This discussion is purposively limited to his satire upon academics and scholarship. Self's satire on psychiatry is carried by the character Dr Zach Busner, who appears in several novels and stories, and brings with him a range of academic material, including an imaginary academic journal and contradictory but recognizable intellectual practices. An episode from *Walking to Hollywood* (2010) is explored: this concerns a Los Angeles rap group called NWPhd [*sic*], an alternative version of the actual group NWA. The probable difficulty for readers of Self's wide range of cultural allusion is discussed. His approbation of Kant's transcendental idealism unexpectedly permits his fiction to perform a cultural critique, one partly consistent with Raymond Williams's account of consciousness in modernity.

*

> Oh yes, Stein is clever all right, but he just doesn't understand. He's an academic. ('Waiting')[1]

I

The challenge to writing about satire is that it is so various. Any art form can perform satirically, and any particular work of satire is likely to use a variety of means to carry through its acts of dissent: *divergence*, rather than order and control, is characteristic of satiric thought. The images of Bosch or Goya, the busy structure of Shakespeare's *Timon of Athens*, *The Beggar's Opera*, the fictions of Rabelais and Cervantes – all represent expansive rather than integrative modes of discourse. Conceptual dissent is often carried by disintegrated forms. In satiric fiction – here I limit the scope of the present discussion – such forms are often purposive. Annoyance, disgust or anger with immediate events may be a writer's first impulse, but satires have to possess only a minimum structure in order to function critically within culture: Gulliver travels in order that Swift may denounce the deplorable politics, religious triviality, misguided science and unacceptable violence that occurs at home. *Gulliver's Travels* is the predominant instance of a particular mode of satire – public, political, grounded in a recognizable consciousness – whose most significant purpose is to prevent the success of bad ideas. Such satire may also enable a significant statement about what is called 'human nature', as *Gulliver's Travels* does through the Houyhnhnms, Yahoos and Struldbrugs, but this occurs less frequently. At any period, the ideas under attack may be ones that are unreasonably dominant in a particular area of thought or action. Such satire will often identify the cultural means by which certain ideas become dominant, and may therefore be termed a form of ideology critique.

In contemporary fiction (to limit again), there exists, in the work of Will Self, a mode of satire directly related to Swift's practice, in that it is about ideas, is external in its approach, has a limited sense of character, and is written against the influence of dominant ideas. The primary concern of this discussion will be to explore Self's critique of culture, as it is enacted through texts that are *divergent* in kind. I want to introduce that critique by drawing attention to satire that tends in the opposite direction, being *integrative* in structure and outcome. Two examples are Deborah Levy's *Swimming Home* (2011), and Martin Amis's *The Pregnant Widow: Inside History* (2010). Each is a narrative of 'desire, and its inevitable flip-side, the death drive', to adopt Tom McCarthy's reading of *Swimming Home*.[2] Both fictions show desire at work, as a force at first delivering pleasure but then consistently destructive of life, love and happiness. *The Pregnant Widow* is, or wants to be, a novel about the early development of feminism, conceived as a revolution: 'the revolution was a velvet revolution, but it wasn't bloodless', because people were harmed.[3] The bulk of this 470–page work describes, often wittily, the sexual self-discoveries and misdirections of several young people on holiday in Italy in 1970, but their activities are intellectually weightless: how can it be a surprise that some people were harmed by these new possibilities? If the narrative is 'inside history', is it in any sense inside feminism? The emotional damage to Keith Nearing, the main figure, 'ruined him for twenty-five years', and this – in the words of Alexander Herzen used as an epigraph to the novel – is the 'long night of chaos and desolation' that is inseparable from revolutionary change. Amis's subtitle makes a large claim for the historical and cultural significance of the confused sexual activity of a few individuals that this fiction does not deliver.[4]

Literary culture is amusingly present in that Nearing is studying English Literature at Oxford, and reads a great deal of Jane Austen and the Brontës, about which Amis's characters make jokes that are witty and unrelentingly unserious. This unseriousness is consistent with the unserious sex, so that the literary allusions remain internal to the text and lack cultural leverage. Deborah Levy makes a related move in *Swimming Home*, where – in another novel about the cultured English on holiday in Europe – the main character, the depressed and disturbed Kitty Finch, writes a poem that has the same title as the novel itself, predicts events in it, and pushes forward the narrative (a poet, persuaded to read the poem, kills himself after adultery with its author). Again, a literary text is integrated into the novel. *The Pregnant Widow* and *Swimming Home* are what might be called integrative fictions of the psychology of bad behaviour. That is not what occurs in Will Self's fiction, where the texts of culture are made to be powerfully disruptive.

Self is a writer of fiction and journalism who defines himself as being on the libertarian left. In an interview (an inescapable form for understanding him), he sets out his position in an account that is divergent as to place and politics:

> Because I'm half American, when I started publishing I felt more on the cusp, an internationalist. I write with a lot of specific cultural references. Politically and culturally I regard myself as European, but Europe is influenced by America. I align myself with the utopian socialist libertarian tradition of English thought. I am fiercely anti-establishment …

Self pauses and then wryly adds, 'as you no doubt know. I regard myself as culturally English but politically completely disaffected'.[5]

The 'specific cultural references' that seem to intrude upon this political self-definition are in practice intrinsic to it. A characteristic journalistic instance of Self bringing together culture and politics is the occasion when the *Guardian* newspaper invited him in September 2010 to be one of four writers asked to attempt the General Paper by which All Souls College, Oxford partly chooses its Fellows. In the allotted hour each wrote on the question 'Is there something inherently coarsening about sport?' Self converts the moral term 'coarsening' into the experiential term 'stupefying', citing Montaigne, Lévy-Strauss and Richard Ford's novel *The Sportswriter* as he does so. 'Stupefying' implies 'stultification', Self goes on to say, and stasis and 'mindless repetition' are characteristics of a 'complex late capitalist society'. When he adds that 'most of us are stupefied anyway',[6] he directs us towards two causes of that: workplace conditions, and addiction.[7] This widely-referential, or divergent, argument invokes both the political and the personal.

The quasi-academic context of this journalistic incident suggests a way of delimiting, or controlling, the divergent tendencies of Self's fiction. I propose to discuss the fiction insofar as it concerns academic life because academics appear, with significant frequency, as the objects of satire in Self's fiction. A university 'don' appears as a narrator in *Cock and Bull* (1992), or academics from a variety of disciplines influence the action. In particular, the academic psychiatrist Dr Zack Busner appears in several works. It was both appropriate and an irony that early in 2012 Self should have been appointed Professor of Contemporary Thought at Brunel University, in a post established in both the School of Arts and the School of Social Sciences, where he will teach (as the university announced) courses on urban planning and human geography, and on Psychoanalysis and Contemporary Society.[8] Self's own account of his teaching interests shows how close they are to the fiction: 'I'm interested in [...] reading and memory in the digital age, the practice of pedestrianism as a form of urban study and political activism, the cultural supremacy of the so called psy professions, and that perennial sawhorse: whither the novel?'[9] With this situation in mind I shall proceed to a reading of Self's fiction through the ideas that are explicit or implicit in his satire upon academics and the academic life.

II

In September 2007 Self took part in a public discussion of contemporary fiction at the Centre for New Writing at the University of Manchester that was led by Martin Amis, who had recently been appointed Professor of Creative Writing there. Self showed himself more organized in his thinking than either Amis or John Banville (also present), and was able to work more confidently with recognizable academic concepts (the nineteenth-century novel and its culture, the white bourgeoisie, the politics of the National Health Service) than the others; that is, he wanted to be understood in this university-departmental context, and possessed the terminology and skills to achieve that.

Self also showed a knowledge of what undergraduate literature courses are like, even as he denied their significance for a contemporary reader not educated in the university. Such readers are unaware of 'the assumed centrality of the novel to our culture' he argued, and unlike students do not read successively *The Mill on the Floss*, *Tono-Bungay*, *Ulysses* and *Finnegans Wake*. Only academics conceive such periodicity: 'There is, to be blunt, a kind of "academicised" perspective about it that is understandable in people who spend their professional lives in university departments, about what the novel might mean in contemporary society or in contemporary culture.'[10] The culture, he said, is in practice much more fragmented, and novels compete with music and film for attention; indeed, even 'film has lost its position as a dominant cultural narrative medium, let alone the novel'.[11] (This remark points forward to the as yet unpublished *Walking to Hollywood*: '"I want to find out who killed film"' is the purpose of 'Self', its narrator.)[12] For this audience, the novel is not what academics conceive it to be; it is not 'central' to the wider culture, nor is it to be read historically in an agreed sequence or canon. As a contemporary cultural product it competes with, and stands in significant relation to, other cultural forms, notably music and film; this is a set of relationships that the university, with its departmental separations, cannot replicate in its teaching or research. In that respect, the university is not sufficiently flexible, or divergent, to respond to existing cultural conditions (I am not, of course, suggesting that the university should attempt to replicate the cultural marketplace). When Self comes to write *Walking to Hollywood*, he will associate satire on the academic with literature, music and film together: this episode is discussed below.

The most prominent academic in Self's fiction is the figure of Dr Zack Busner, a psychiatrist and clinician who makes his first appearance in two short stories in *The Quantity Theory of Insanity*, published in 1991; this was Self's first book. At his first appearance in 'Ward 9', Busner is 'a plump, fiftyish sort of man, with iron grey hair brushed back in a widow's peak', carrying a soft leather briefcase that contains 'too many files, too many instruments, too many journals, too many books and a couple of unwrapped, fresh, cream-cheese bagels'.[13] This no doubt characteristic academic behaviour is supplemented by a career as a 'pop psychologist' on television. Busner's publications appear in an academic journal invented by Self, the *British Journal of Ephemera*, which is first mentioned in the story entitled 'The Quantity Theory of Insanity'. Busner is both real and unreal. In the story 'Inclusion®' he moves from his clinical post at Heath Hospital in London to work for Cryborg, a large corporation that is testing, illegally, an anti-depressant called Inclusion that causes the user to become excessively 'interested'. Busner does not appear, but we read his diary: he takes the drug, and (like others on the research project) becomes closely interested by everything around him, including watching the game of curling on television, and a film based on John Betjeman's *Summoned by Bells*, so much so that he feels a suitable epitaph for himself 'would be "He had no interests but interest"'.[14] This is, first, a satire upon cultural production – what misfortune to be interested by such things! Second, it may be reflexive upon the author, for the phrase given to Busner stands also as the epigraph to the collection of stories, *Grey Area*, in which 'Inclusion®' appears, so that Self is not only telling us that interest is always preferable to uninterest, but is also glancing ironically at the breadth of his own concerns. These, when migrated into his texts, make considerable demands upon his readers, almost invariably testing their cultural interests (or their interest in culture); in this case, the culture around anti-depressant drugs (as in 'the cultural supremacy of the so called psy professions', to be taught at Brunel) mutates into the strange story of Busner becoming absorbed into the mind of an artist, Simon Dykes, who has been taking the drug. Busner writes of himself that 'I am free to roam the museum of grotesque ideas, images and objects' acquired by the artist's mind under the drug's influence. Many of Self's fictions are structured in this way: a narrative that is actual, or real, or credible will change course, perceptibly yet somehow persuasively, in order to speak truth out of unreality. In this case, the truth is spoken directly by the narrator in the story's closing words: 'You should stay interested in it [the drug's story] and not allow your thoughts to stray to unanswered letters, unreturned phone calls, unpaid bills, unfulfilled ambitions, wasted opportunities and people unloved and unmissed.'[15] This works in two ways: it affirms the dangerous premises of the story's interest in interest, but it is equally a moral truth situated in the real world: this is how you should behave.

Zack Busner appears in *Great Apes* of 1997, where human culture is converted into a world of chimpanzees. (One episode takes place at Exeter College, Oxford, where Self studied PPE as an undergraduate.) In this modified Swiftian setting Busner likes to think of himself as 'The radical psychoanalyst',[16] and indeed he has been given a plausible intellectual backstory. In the earlier 'The Quantity Theory of Insanity', Busner describes his intellectual rebellion against 'the narrow drive to reduce mental illness to a chemical formula':

> I sat up for night after night, reading Nietzsche, Schopenhauer, Dostoevsky and Sartre. I began to systematically doubt the principles on which I had based my career to date. I deconstructed the entire world that I had been inhabiting for the past thirty years.[17]

He sets up the democratically-run The Concept House. Nineteen years later it is still remembered, in *Walking to Hollywood*: '[H]e had started a "concept house" in Willesden, where therapists and patients had lived together communally with no distinctions between them'.[18] The antecedents of this lie in the work of R.D. Laing and David Cooper, specifically at Kingsley Hall, where in 1965 Laing and others set up a community 'for non-restraining, non-drug therapies for seriously affected schizophrenics'.[19] This is the British 'anti-psychiatry' movement, with which the American Thomas S. Szasz is frequently associated, although the beliefs of Laing and Cooper are 'ideas which Szasz detests'.[20] Self interviewed Szasz for *The Times* in 1992, and predicted that his work and thought 'will once again come to the fore'.[21] Szasz, like the other 'anti-psychiatrists', objects to the medicalization of mental illness, and is radically libertarian in that he opposes all forms of coercion of those defined as mentally ill by a medical bureaucracy. There is continuity between his beliefs – which were influentially set out in *The Myth of Mental Illness* in 1961 – and the views attributed by Self to Busner.

In *Great Apes* the chimpanzee version of Busner engages in grooming with his associate Jane Bowen (first seen in 'Ward 7'), and he finds 'medicaments' (drugs) in her fur. He remarks: '"I shall have to watch what I'm doing here, Jane, or I'll find myself sedated!", at which she heaved with soundless laughter.'[22] This is a complex and successful joke, not only about the use of drugs, but also about the use of language: he might be 'sedated' by the drugs in her fur, but if he were a patient, he might find himself sedated by a psychiatrist's prescription, contrary to Szasz's principle of non-coercion, one that Busner and Jane Bowen profess at this point. Yet Busner is also an absurd and inconsistent figure: although he has 'abandon[ed] his conviction that mental pathologies were in reality semantic confusions, he still counselled an inter-personal approach – even when liberally dishing out Largactil'.[23] The 'semantic confusion' refers to Szasz's criticism of the way in which language is brought to bear to define, and thereby invent, mental illness; in *A Lexicon of Lunacy* (1993) he has a thirty-one page list of synonyms for mental illness, both popular and technical; as Szasz points out, this language is not medical but metaphorical (a matter of some interest to literary studies).[24]

In the 1991 story, the Quantity Theory is the brainchild of Harold Ford, but in later fictions he is forgotten and Busner is treated as its effective originator. This theory is simply stated: there is only a limited amount of sanity in any society, and it moves about from group to group: 'What if there is only a fixed proportion of sanity available in any given society at any given time?' Ford asks. This question allows Self to project an intriguing set of possible consequences, such as the geographical: 'If you provide efficient medication for manic depressives in the Fens, there are perceptible variations in the numbers of agoraphobics on the South Coast.' The theory is published in the imaginary *British Journal of Ephemera*, as a 'Select Bibliography' at the end of the story shows: 'Ford, Hurst, Harley, Busner & Sikorski, "Some Aspects of Sanity Quotient Mechanisms in a Witless Shetland Commune", *British Journal of Ephemera*, September, 1974.' The story itself is narrated from a conference in Denver, where all the authors of this paper show up, some as members of a group calling itself 'the Radical Psychic Field Disruptionists', who are based on the practical street interventionists of the American 1960s and early 1970s, and are evidently academics who are no longer sane. Busner is there, 'nervously rolling and unrolling the end of his mohair tie', as he will continue to do in several fictions. Finally, Ford – the narrator – realizes that the theory has turned in on itself, and 'has been impacting on the sanity quotient itself'. There is one last possibility, for which he must find an equation: 'Namely that as more and more insanity is concentrated around educational institutions, so levels of mental illness in the rest of society ....'[25] The unwritten word is 'fall', and for 'educational institutions' read 'universities'.

What kind of satire is Self attempting here? Busner's ideas are made to vary so much that he is more an incoherent field of absurdities and truths than an intellectual holding to a specific but often pernicious point of view. The Quantity Theory is at the opposite extreme to libertarian 'antipsychiatry', since it is concerned to measure in order to understand and control, and in that respect is closer to Behaviourism as practiced by J.B. Watson and B.F. Skinner; Busner adheres to both.[26] The consistent aspect of Self's satire in this field is that it is directed against the generality of ideas that are used to exercise control over patients, and – by extension – the wider society. We may feel today that the discussion around 'anti-psychiatry', therapeutic communities and Behaviourist modes of gathering data is largely over; but it is an important part of the history of a number of disciplines, was more significant when Self wrote in the early 1990s, and has an unignorable presence in current debates about medication, the treatment of mental illness (or 'mental illness'), and scientific methodology. That is, the area identified by Self in what we may call the 'Busner' fictions is a complex cultural field which he identifies and then persuades to function, in that fiction, in a number of amusing, inconsistent, and often implausible ways. Self's fiction activates a cultural field in order to play with it, improvise around it, persuade the reader to feel differently about it, and then (very often) to abandon it, often to the reader's bafflement. Yet the major themes in Self are rarely abandoned altogether; once established in his early writing, they recur: the idea of the dead continuing to live among the living is one; the importance of psychosis in its various forms is another; the idea of 'scale' recurs as a satiric device; and the business of walking has turned into the body-mind collision of psychogeography.

When Busner turns up in Self's most recent fiction, *Walking to Hollywood*, he has become mixed up with the narrator of that text, who can only, with due regard to the differences between author and subject, be named 'Self'. Here, 'Self' describes his long history as Busner's patient, and concludes: 'For, just as I incorporated him – thinly veiled – into my novels and short stories, so he made use of me in the numerous articles and case studies he published.'[27] The 'Self' who narrates *Walking to Hollywood* is treating the originally fictional Busner as if Busner were real. Whether joined with 'Self' in this complex play upon narrative technique, Busner is throughout the imaginary academic who makes Self's anti-psychiatric satire possible.

III

I want to turn now from the recurrent or 'continuity' character Zack Busner to a single episode from *Walking to Hollywood*. My purpose is to show the way in which Self can concentrate a bewildering variety of cultural materials into a very few pages, and to ask what the resulting meanings might be. I have chosen the spectacularly aberrant moment when 'Self', walking through Los Angeles, passes at lunchtime along West Jefferson Boulevard towards the main campus of the University of Southern California (USC), and stops to listen to a rap group who are performing extracts from Marcus Aurelius's *Meditations* in the original Latin.

These five pages (180–185) allude successively to Gil Scott-Heron, Orlandus Lassus, Will Smith, the Modern Jazz Quartet, a Harry Potter film (probably *Harry Potter and the Order of the Phoenix* from 2007), Terrence Malick's film *The New World* (2005), a Chanel tie, Mike Leigh's film *Naked* (1993), Marcus Aurelius, Powerade Aqua (a sports drink), Marvin Gaye, the actors Jamie Foxx and Morgan Freeman, Tom Cruise as he appears in Michael Mann's crime thriller *Collateral* (2004), Scientology, actor Pete Postlethwaite, and finally an implied reference to the British actor David Thewlis. Most interesting – and most peculiar – is the invented name of the rap group: NWPhd (where the final lower-case d hints at a certain unfamiliarity with the academic actuality on the part of either Self or the copy-editors at Bloomsbury Publishing).

None of these allusions, taken separately (or even grouped as 'music' and 'film') is, in itself, particularly difficult to catch; it is the way each is brought into relation with the others that may persuade us to reconsider what cultural complexity has now become, and the ways in which Self is attempting to represent it in fiction, just as he outlined the problem at the 2007 Manchester University discussion mentioned above.

NWPhd has four members, who offer in Latin the second paragraph from the Liber Secundus (Book II) of the *Meditations* of Marcus Aurelius, beginning '*Hoc quicquid tandem sum, caruncula est et animula et animi principatus*'. One of the group performs this in Latin, and then a second raps a translation: 'Whatsoever I am, is either flesh, or life, or that which we commonly call the mistress and overruling part of man: reason.' (This expands the Latin by explaining that *reason* is meant; *ratio-* does not appear but can be inferred from the context.) Musical depth is added when deeper voices 'picked out a word or two and scatted with it [...] "*Quicquid-quicquid-principatus-quidipatus*"'. The translation of this also ends with 'reason': '"What-so-what-so-what-so-reason"' (181).[28] 'Self' plays the part of the critical scholar: '[E]ven a moderately competent Latinist [could] detect the incorporation into the English translation of later interpolations'. When he unwisely criticizes the English translation – 'Y'know your English translation doesn't exactly match up' – the rapper Howie is called over. Howie is Professor Howard Turner, who 'holds the chair in classics and comparative literature here at USC', and if there is any criticism '"you-gonna-be-answering to Howie, you fill me?"' These 'doctoral rappers' use the language and threats of the streets, but these are transposed to high-cultural practice: '"Don't come down this way again [...]. Unless you be confident you can parse a Latin sentence purr-fic'-lee".'[29]

This is comedy rather than satire, and it arises from bringing together, in one space, divergent modes of cultural discourse. Beyond this collision, the persistent element in these exchanges is the reference to reason. Self is not satirizing rap here, or the academic community, but asserting a value. Each of the three sections of *Walking to Hollywood* is marked by separate 'mental pathologies', and it is psychosis that underlies this section.[30] Reason stands against the incipient breakdown and confusion that 'Self' experiences in his travels; it may barely register with readers, but it is there, bearing significance.

The field of cultural reference is more complex than it may seem. The name 'NWPhd' is a play upon the name of the influential Los Angeles gangsta rap group NWA, or Niggaz Wit Attitude (active 1986–1991), which originated in the suburb of Compton and started the careers of Dr Dre, Ice Cube, Eazy-E and others. 'Niggaz Wit PhD' is a cultural joke which raises all kinds of questions that, characteristically, Self does not try to answer. Nor does he give the reader any guidance; you grasp the allusion, or you do not. Once it is understood that these are 'Niggaz Wit PhD', meanings develop. The violent and misogynistic lyrics of NWA are radically different from the ones given to NWPhd. I have chosen to quote from NWA's *Real Niggaz* because it is a song about Black self-definition which at the same time imagines, and projects, an anxiety about being Black that is as much about states of mind as are the struggles of 'Self' with psychosis in this section of *Walking to Hollywood*. Shortly before the stanza quoted below occur the lines: 'You can't harm me, alarm me / 'Cause we're the generals in this fucking hip-hop army / The niggaz wit [*sic*] attitudes if you didn't know'; and shortly after that Dr Dre raps: 'Real niggaz, straight off the streets of Compton', that suburb contrasting sharply with the streets around Southern California University. The song as a whole 'disses' (disrespects) Ice Cube, who had left the group after a dispute, but its meaning can be generalized beyond the immediate circumstances. The following stanza from *Real Niggaz*, by MC Ren, imagines the mental state of a black man who does not assert himself as the members of NWA do:

> You can run but you can't hide, you know I'm a find'cha
> 'Cause a nigga like Ren's only 2 steps behind'cha
> Don't look back, 'cause you're shaking and all scared
> A nigga in black can be your scariest nightmare
> So sleep wit the lights on, forget that the mic's on
> Don't step on my muthafucking stage without Nike's on
> Don't say it's psycho and then you just might go
> Mentally fucked up when I let the right blow.[31]

NWA are 'real niggaz' because they are not 'mentally fucked up', and because – despite the poverty, lack of employment, high crime levels and perceived police oppression in Compton – they possess a strong sense of self-identity.

When NWPhd rap Marcus Aurelius, Self chooses a passage that asserts the value of reason over the limitations of the physical body: 'Whatsoever I am', Marcus Aurelius asserts, 'is [...] reason', and reason should be dominant: 'suffer not that excellent part to be brought in subjection, and to become slavish'. Nor should reason be affected by 'unreasonable and unsociable lusts', which leads the group to their climactic phrase, 'Sla-vish luuuuuust!', hammered out at the end of their performance.[32] The aggression of NWA is a cultural fact whose origins in poverty and powerlessness we may go some way to accept as legitimating that aggression; but Self's variant is transformative in that it refuses to repeat or reconfigure any initiating aggression, as rap does. NWA and NWPhd both rap against mental and psychic subjection, but while NWA threaten members of their own group or community for their inadequacy, Self's version of the move away from dominance is located in the European tradition of rationality.

IV

An evident challenge of Self's fiction is the demands it makes upon the reader, my subject in this part of the discussion. The final chapter of *Walking to Hollywood* is entitled 'The Struldbrug' – 'Self' meets one while walking – but a readership that can recognize allusions to Swift may be less likely to identify the relationship between NWPhd and Niggaz Wit Attitude. Self's critique of Behaviourism requires specialist knowledge to understand fully, as do the debates about psychiatry and drug dependence in which Dr Zack Busner engages. *Cock and Bull* (1992) shows an informed knowledge of the debates around feminism, as Amis's *The Pregnant Widow* does not.[33] The reader's capacity for taking an interest – to return to an earlier theme – or his or her knowledge of contemporary culture, in both its 'high' and 'low' forms, is likely to be tested. Questions implicitly put to the reader might include: What do you know? How wide are your interests? What can you interpret? Can you interpret these texts at all?

At the Manchester event from which I have already quoted, Self was asked if he loved the reader. After Martin Amis had said that 'it's to have your work loved, your words loved, and that's the impulse [to write]', Self responded slowly:

> I hate the reader. I love the reader. I want to have sex with the reader. I want to stroke the reader. I want to pummel the reader. I want to tread on the reader's instep quite hard. And I want to embarrass the reader, cajole the reader.[34]

The reader who cannot read fully in Self's several cultures is the reader who is being hated, loved, pummelled, embarrassed or cajoled. At some point, this will include every reader. The text can still be read locally, for its immediate effects, or perversely – when meaning fails – for its non-effects; many readers will find immediate pleasure (or indeed disgust) in ways that may satisfy. Nevertheless, the wide 'interest' demanded of the reader, or (to put it another way) the absence of a readily identifiable overall meaning, can lead to reader dissatisfaction.[35]

Misreading is a possible consequence of this. A notable instance of misunderstanding occurred when Self was interviewed by the novelist and artist Tom McCarthy, and others, in 2001. *How the Dead Live* had been published in the previous year, and the interviewers knew the story of Lily Bloom, the vigorous but often dislikeable Jewish-American protagonist who, after her death from cancer, has been re-born into a distressing existence in 'Dulston', a decayed version of London's Dalston. This life was understood by McCarthy and his interview team as a material experience, which for Self it was not. There was a specific philosophical reason: 'But I'm not a materialist at all. I'm an idealist.' He argues – at first sight unexpectedly – against Western materialist concepts of reality, and in favour of a Buddhist understanding of process and karma: 'The novel is an unashamedly and openly Buddhist allegory, and that's just bad karma [for Lily]. Bad shit happens to you whether in this lifetime or the next if you do bad shit and have bad attitudes. So poor Lily gets hers.' She trails around 'Dulston' accompanied by a lithopaedion,[36] and her nine-year-old child (whom she had carelessly allowed to be killed by a car). McCarthy reads the text for its materiality: 'It [her post-death daily experience] manifests itself as matter', he asserts; but for Self 'this is her disintegrating psyche', and 'all of the London she sees, all the different layers of reality […] are produced from the furniture of her own mind'. What is represented in the text is not matter but 'an emanation of her own psyche'.[37] Her suffering is her punishment for lacking any sense of transcendence in her first, and truly material, life. Self's own reading of *How the Dead Live* describes his argument with the real, and this critique of material existence is the ground of his confident alteration of reality, and particularly contingent cultural reality, in his fiction. We are left with an apparent paradox: that one of the most prominent left-wing public intellectuals in Britain claims to be writing about culture from an idealist, and not a materialist, position.

What does 'idealist' mean in this context? Self uses it as a philosophical term, as part of the materialist/idealist antithesis, which means that it must refer to an account of reality where 'reality' is in some way a mental representation. Self specifies that he is 'a transcendental idealist',[38] meaning that he accepts Kant's distinction, in *The Critique of Pure Reason* (1781), between 'appearances or representations of perception and things-in-themselves'.[39] In philosophy, idealism is now largely abandoned because our sense organs are correctly understood to give us sensations of the thing encountered, but not also mental representations of that thing that we can (ourselves) make judgements about. If that were so, the act of perception would be double. This objection can be put aside if we return to the fiction and attend to Self's remark that Lily's 'bad karma' is 'an emanation of her own psyche'. In that case the post-death distortions in *How the Dead Live* are not reality ('things-in-themselves'), but a fictional account of Lily's consciousness (Kantian 'representation of perception') that enables Self to alter and distort for satirical or critical reasons. Self's claim to write as an idealist may therefore be justified, as long as the claim is limited to the work done in and by the fictional text. (He told Tom McCarthy that 'I don't wander around in an idealist world', so this presumably is the case.) Applied in this way in his fiction, Self's possibly idiosyncratic interpretation of transcendental idealism has the unexpected effect of making cultural criticism possible.

V

How, then, does Self write satire? He writes out of interest, meaning familiarity with a considerable range of cultural practices, with literature, film and music prominent among them. He writes out of a knowledge of addiction and its mental and physical effects, and develops from this a critique of the means of treating those consequences, which is psychiatry. He writes to alter the perceived world, or to change the consciousnesses found in it, and grounds that critique in Kant's philosophy. An advocacy of reason occurs. He writes, too, from a non-doctrinal position on the political left that often manifests itself in his journalism as an improvised response to immediate events, but is consistently libertarian in tendency. He also writes his fictions at a considerable speed, or so one infers from their improvisatory qualities, which do not leave much opportunity to develop character: this failure is frequently criticised.

There is a distinct sense in which Self's cultural and political position embodies what was for Raymond Williams a particular moment in the growth of consciousness as he describes it in a crucial summary in *The Country and the City*. 'What was once close, absorbing, accepted, familiar, internally experienced', Williams writes, 'becomes separate, distinguishable, critical, changing, externally observed'.[40] The latter part of that sentence describes the culture Self inhabits (along with the rest of us: it is modernity); but it also describes aspects of his practice as a satirist, although to make that transition, from describing the cultural situation to making a satiric response to it, it is necessary to alter or reapply the extended meanings of Williams's words for each case. A critical consciousness is not the same as a critical or satirical text; a culture that is changing is not the same as fictional satire that changes reality, as Self's does. To observe externally may well be a means of understanding, something that satire in the Swiftian mode often achieves. This adoption and adaptation of Williams's terms is meant as a tribute to their relevance even to satire, which he would not have had in mind here. Self's fiction may satirise academic processes and structures of thinking, but some of what has been said by academic criticism may adequately define him too.

Acknowledgement

This essay was written as part of a research project into satire, funded by the University of La Rioja, Logroño, Spain. Project no. API10/11. I am grateful for the advice of Dr Nathan Waddell.

Notes

1. 'Waiting', in *The Quantity Theory of Insanity* (1991; Harmondsworth: Penguin Books, 1994), 188.
2. Tom McCarthy, 'Introduction', in *Swimming Home* (High Wycombe: And Other Stories, 2011), viii.
3. Martin Amis, *The Pregnant Widow: Inside History* (London: Jonathan Cape, 2010), 393.
4. *Pregnant Widow*, 1, vii. This 'extreme privileging of the personal over the political' is for Ian Gregson evidence of Amis's 'ultimately conservative sensibility'. See Ian Gregson, *Character and Satire in Postwar Fiction* (New York and London: Continuum, 2006), 140.
5. Chris Mitchell, 'Will Self: Self Destruction' [interview] http://www.scribd.com/doc/57699214/Spike-Book May 1997, 463 (accessed 20 March 2012).
6. Anon, '"You May Now Turn Over Your Papers"', *The Guardian*, 25 September 2010, Review section, 2–4; Self at 3–4. Mary Beard, Mary Midgley and Geoff Dyer were the others invited to respond.
7. Any reader of Self's fiction who is also aware of aspects of his personal life will know of the extent of his engagement with drugs in his early adult life, and his present freedom from them. In 1993 Self was able to say of himself, in a discussion of how to write about drugs, 'I am a drug-addict writer in that way', that is, where writing method and experience meet. See 'Martin Amis', in *Junk Mail* (London: Bloomsbury, 1995), 384. For a public incident, see Chris Blackhurst, 'Self Admits Taking Heroin on PM's Jet', *Independent on Sunday* 20 April 1997, at http://www.independent.co.uk/news/self-admits-taking-heroin-on-pms-jet-1268111.html (accessed 21 October 2010).
8. 'Will Self Joins Brunel University as Professor of Contemporary Thought', http://www.brunel.ac.uk/news-and-events/news/news-items/ne_161686 (accessed 20 March 2012). See also Will Self, 'In the Spirit of Endeavour', *The Guardian*, 23 February 2012, 34, for his account of proposed courses. In 2009–10 he was a Visiting Fellow in the Department of English at University College London.

9 Self, 'In the Spirit of Endeavour', 34.
10 'Amis, Self and Banville Debate Contemporary Literature', http://www.arts.manchester.ac.uk/newwriting/news/C21Literature/ (accessed 17 October 2010). At 30′ 00″ and 31′ 02″ – 31′ 30″.
11 'Amis, Self and Banville', 32′ 08″ – 32′ 16″.
12 Will Self, *Walking to Hollywood: Memories of Before the Fall* (London: Bloomsbury, 2010), 122. Hereafter *Walking*.
13 Will Self, 'Ward 9', in *The Quantity Theory of Insanity* (1991; Harmondsworth: Penguin Books, 1994), 22. Busner also appears in *The Book of Dave* (2006), and elsewhere.
14 Will Self, 'Inclusion®', in *Grey Area* (London: Bloomsbury, 1994), 259.
15 *Grey Area*, 292, 293.
16 Will Self, *Great Apes* (1997; Harmondsworth: Penguin Books, 1998), 333.
17 Will Self, 'The Quantity Theory of Insanity', in *The Quantity Theory of Insanity*, 119.
18 Will Self, *Walking*, 116.
19 'R.D. Laing & Kingsley Hall', Kingsley Hall, http://www.kingsleyhall.co.uk/ (accessed 26 October 2010). In *Walking*, 'Self' arrives at Heath Hospital (probably the Royal Free Hospital), and is disillusioned by his fellow-outpatients: 'Were these [...] [t]he psychic insurgents I had fantasized joining' after reading Laing's *The Divided Self*? (112). This was Laing's first book, of case studies; psychiatric communities appear later in his work. In 2010 Self's selected stories appeared under the title *The Undivided Self*.
20 Jeffrey A. Schaler, 'Introduction', in ed. Jeffrey A. Schaler *Szasz Under Fire: The Psychiatric Abolitionist Faces His Critics* (Chicago and La Salle: Open Court, 2004), xiv.
21 Will Self, 'Thomas Szasz: Shrinking from Psychiatry', in *Junk Mail* (London: Bloomsbury, 1995), 284.
22 *Great Apes*, 196.
23 Will Self, *Walking*, 116. Largactil is one of the trade names for chlorpromazine, an important early anti-psychotic drug.
24 Thomas S. Szasz, *A Lexicon of Lunacy: Metaphoric Malady, Moral Responsibility, and Psychiatry* (New Brunswick, NJ and London: Transaction, 1993), 46–77.
25 'Quantity Theory', 126, 127, 149, 146, 147, 149.
26 J.B. Watson (1878–1958) gave his first definitive account of Behaviourism in 1913. He published *Behaviorism* [sic] in 1924. In a fiction antecedent to Self's, Wyndham Lewis satirised the theory in *Snooty Baronet* (1932). B.F. Skinner (1904–1990), theorist of 'reinforcement', published *Verbal Behavior* in 1957. Its reputation was seriously damaged by Noam Chomsky's 'A Review of B.F. Skinner's *Verbal Behavior*' [sic], *Language* 31, 1 (1959), 26–58.
27 Will Self, *Walking*, 118.
28 The translation used by Self is 'Marcus Aurelius Meditations' [sic], http://ancienthistory.about.com/library/bl/bl_aurelius_bki.htm (accessed 25 October 2010). The translated passage appears here as paragraph XVI of Book I.
29 Will Self, *Walking*, 182, 183, 182, 184.
30 'The mental pathologies that underlie the three memoirs – obsessive-compulsive disorder for "Very Little", psychosis for "Walking to Hollywood" and Alzheimer's for "Spurn Head" – are themselves displacements of a single phenomenon' (431–2). The displaced phenomenon is death.
31 'Real Niggaz', Songlyrics.com, http://www.songlyrics.com/n-w-a/real-niggaz-lyrics/ (accessed 30 October 2010). Slightly modified. A variant hearing of the final two lines is: 'Don't see a psycho, and then you just might go, / Mentally fucked up when I let the rifle blow.' The lyrics at this point are difficult to hear. 'Psycho' presumably refers to a psychiatrist. See http://www.metrolyrics.com/real-niggaz-lyrics-nwa.html (accessed 30 October 2010).

32. 'Marcus Aurelius Meditations', I, XVI and Will Self, *Walking*, 181. 'Slavish lust', 182.
33. See Emma Parker, 'Kicks Against the Pricks: Gender, Sex and Satire in Will Self's *Cock and Bull*', *English* 60, no. 230 (Autumn 2011), 229–250.
34. 'Amis, Self and Banville', Amis 20′ 55″ – 21′ 00″, Self 27′ 59″ – 28′ 19″.
35. The book-reviewer and novelist Adam Mars-Jones dislikes both the local and the general effects of Self's *How the Dead Live*. See 'Self, Where is thy Sting?', *The Observer*, 18 June 2000 for a dismissive review: http://www.guardian.co.uk/books/2000/jun/18/fiction.willself (accessed 20 March 2012). 'The tone is one of unvarying contempt [...] a dutiful nihilism'.
36. Lithop(a)edion: 'a fetus calcified in the body of the mother' (Webster's). Self: 'It's a calcified foetus that remains inside the body of a woman but has failed to lodge itself in the womb and often ends up somewhere like the perineal folds, so after death if you perform an autopsy, quite a lot of women will be found to have these calcified cadavers lodged inside them.' Will Self, in 'Interview with Will Self, writer', INS Interviews, conducted by Tom McCarthy, http://www.necronauts.org/interviews_will.htm (accessed 29 October 2010). The INS, or International Necronautical Society, is an association of artists and writers that specialises in examining death.
37. Self, 'Interview with Will Self, Writer'.
38. Chris Hall, 'Will Self: How the Dead Live: Dead Man Talking', http://www.spikemagazine.com/1000willself.php (accessed 20 March 2012).
39. D.W.H. [D.W. Hamlyn], 'Idealism, Philosophical', in ed. Ted Honderich *The Oxford Companion to Philosophy* (Oxford and New York: Oxford University Press, 1995), 387.
40. Raymond Williams, *The Country and the City* (London: Chatto and Windus, 1973), 297.

Recoveries

With the following presentations by Elinor Taylor and Joseph Pridmore of a number of working-class- and left-oriented novels from the 1930s, *Key Words* is inaugurating a new regular feature, aimed at the recovery and re-assessment of neglected, marginalised or forgotten figures and texts from radical, socialist and labour history. Readers are invited to propose suitable subjects for future issues, and to submit, should they wish, their own contributions for consideration. Should review copies of nominated books be required, please contact the reviews editor with full details of publication at stan.smith@ntu.ac.uk, and we shall endeavour to obtain them.

Recovering Thirties Fiction

Introduction

In 1989 Andy Croft outlined the prevailing myths about the literature of the 1930s, Auden's 'low dishonest decade'. In the wake of the renunciation by so many writers of their youthful commitment to the 'God that failed',[1] the period came to be seen as one characterised by 'a naïve, careless and treacherous literature of zealotry'.[2] Croft argued against the tendency to reduce 1930s writing to the work of a small group of familiar names – Auden, Spender, MacNeice, Day Lewis, Orwell and Isherwood – and against over-dependence on their subsequent recantations, which had created the image of the 1930s as 'politically gutted, imaginatively emptied' (Croft, 169). Croft wondered what version of the 1930s might take the public imagination from a different selection of texts and authors: instead of A.J. Cronin, Lewis Jones; instead of Winifred Holtby, Storm Jameson (154).

A survey of recently reissued novels of the 1930s suggests that the political and imaginative possibilities of the decade are being recovered. The Library of Wales has republished Lewis Jones's *Cwmardy* and *We Live*, and Jack Jones's *Black Parade*. New editions of John Sommerfield's *May Day* and Simon Blumenfeld's *Jew Boy* have recently reappeared from London Books. The list could also include Storm Jameson's *In the Second Year* (Trent Editions,

---

1 See Arthur Koestler et al., *The God that Failed: Six Studies in Communism* (London: Hamish Hamilton, 1950).
2 Andy Croft, 'Forward to the 1930s: The Literary Politics of Anamnesis', in ed. Christopher Shaw and Malcolm Chase, *The Imagined Past: History and Nostalgia* (Manchester: Manchester University Press, 1989), 151.

2004) and the *New York Review of Books Classics* edition of Sylvia Townsend Warner's *Summer Will Show* (2009). A long out-of-print novel of the Battle of Cable Street, Frank Griffin's *October Day*, has also recently been republished with an introduction by Croft to coincide with the seventy-fifth anniversary of that event. Meanwhile the Association for Scottish Literary Studies has produced a volume of two novels by the Glasgow writer Dot Allan, including her distinctive 1934 work *Hunger March*.

The reappearance of such texts as Sommerfield's and Lewis Jones's is indicative of the ambiguous presence of the 1930s in the popular imagination. In one way, their appearance might be a sign of the decline of Communism as an ideological bête noire. The kind of fervent renunciation of Communism that shaped the 1930s myth in the postwar era has begun to seem remote. In another way, the recovery of these texts might be seen as an affirmation of the renewed relevance of that decade. Since 2008 the 1930s has become the standard reference point for discussing the current economic crisis.[3] The restaging of the Jarrow March in late 2011, the seventy-fifth anniversary of the original event, suggests the continuing resonance of that decade as a by-word for crisis.

The ambiguities of our present relation to the 1930s can be found in the way the republished texts are presented. Take, for example, John Sommerfield's *May Day*.[4] The novelist John King's introduction to the book seems at points to be offering a kind of apology for Sommerfield's politics, while still asserting that 'Idealistic literature, whether naïve or not, is more important than ever' (16). King presents Sommerfield as an optimistic and sociable man whose 'belief in the individual' underpinned his strategy in the novel (12). It is not easy to concur on this second point. The strategy of the text can just as easily be read as working very deliberately against the over-valuation of the individual in an attempt to shift its emphasis on to specifically social relations. Sam Jordison's *Guardian* review of the republished novel amounted to a denunciation of its ('spectacularly wrong') political premises, while acknowledging clear parallels to the present-day. The novel, Jordison suggested, was a failure because it did not depict problems in an 'individual' enough manner.[5] It is apparent that the myth of the 'red decade', in which writers naively aligned themselves with Communism to the detriment of their art, still persists. The cliché is only bolstered by the reprinting of Sommerfield's own reappraisal of his text,

---

3   See, for example, Jon Hilsenrath, Serena Ng and Damian Paletta, 'Worst Crisis Since '30s, With No End Yet In Sight', *Wall Street Journal* (18 September 2008): online edition.
4   John Sommerfield, *May Day* (1936; London: London Books, 2010). Introduction by John King.
5   Sam Jordison, 'A Misplaced May Day Dream for the Masses', at guardian.co.uk, 29 April 2011.

written for its republication in 1984, which, while not quite a declaration of apostasy, expresses the author's rather predictable assessment of it as 'early '30s Communist romanticism' ('Postscript', Sommerfield, 243).

Hywel Francis's foreword to the Library of Wales volume of Lewis Jones's two novels *Cwmardy* and *We Live* expresses a comparable set of anxieties.[6] Francis almost seems to want to detach Jones from his role in the Communist Party. Jones, Francis writes, was 'a maverick in the best sense of the word', and certainly not a party 'apparatchik' (x). It might be nearer the mark to say that Jones was both these things. It is disingenuous to overlook the fact that he was a major organisational force in the Party. That Francis wants to paint Jones as a rambunctious and mischievous character is to reprise the assumption that there was a clear distinction between those Communists who were puppets of the Party and those who, for well-meaning but mistaken reasons, aligned themselves with it. Francis's reasons for characterising Jones like this are, of course, not difficult to grasp, nor should they be dismissed. It may well be necessary to bring the author to life this way at a time when ideological commitment is viewed with great suspicion. Jones, like Sommerfield, is presented as the antithesis of the ideologue: he is remembered for his 'love of the people and compassion' (xi). These reservations about presentation are minor, and outweighed by the value of the novels themselves in helping to recover, albeit in a mediated way, another view of the 1930s: of possibility as well as failure. I shall discuss at greater length below two writers whose work provides the opportunity for a rather different vision of the era.

Frank Griffin: *October Day*[7]

The recent republication of Frank Griffin's 1939 novel of the Battle of Cable Street, *October Day*, is another sign of this more positive attitude to the decade. Republished by New London Editions to coincide with the seventy-fifth anniversary of that event, when the British Union of Fascists were prevented by popular opposition, organised by the Communist Party and others, from marching through the East End of London, the novel follows a cast of Londoners brought together, more of less accidentally, by a groundswell of popular outrage at the BUF's intentions. Griffin uses a comparable technical strategy to that of Sommerfield: a group of characters whose narratives crisscross the political action taking shape in the city. The bus conductor Bert, 'a picture of progressive youth' (59), forms a relationship with the homeless and unhappy Elsie, recently released from prison; the unemployed and harassed

---

6   Lewis Jones, *Cwmardy; & We Live* (1937; 1939. Cardigan: Parthian: Library of Wales, 2006). Foreword by Hywel Francis.
7   Frank Griffin, *October Day* (1939; Nottingham: Five Leaves Publications, 2011).

Joe Slesser escapes the irritations of his impoverished domestic situation to go to the march, where he strikes up a friendship with a Communist couple, Claire and Calvin. Meanwhile a policeman, Harold Thurgood, who has been conducting an affair with the dissipated widow Lady Stroud, who is also Elsie's former employer, is on duty at the march. Griffin was a Communist Party member, and the text has its didactic moments. Claire and Calvin function mainly to provide a political commentary for the benefit of the other characters, often in a long-winded and rather unrealistic manner. This is odd, since elsewhere in the text Griffin demonstrates an excellent ear for dialogue. Perhaps deliberately, however, Calvin's sermonising tendencies can also appear comic. The manic intensity with which he accosts the hapless and initially apolitical Joe does seem humorously overblown: "'Of course it's right!' Calvin exclaimed, and turned again to Slesser, seizing him by the lapels of his coat' (95).

October Day's vision of political action is a vision of a community in carnival mode, of a 'mighty and glorious festival' (125). Occasionally it becomes cartoonish: "'But just wait till there's t'revolution,'" declares an old woman, "'Then there'll be sights, there won't 'arf!'", before throwing a rock at Lady Stroud's car, "'The thin-gutted, staring cow!'"(110). Apparently anticipating these objections, the 'Author's Note' assures the reader that the scenes contained are based on the facts as recorded by the cameramen of the newspaper, 'to which any doubting reader is referred' (13). There are moments where the propagandist line seems a little too strong, as, for example, when Lady Stroud declares that "'What we need in England is a strong man at the top, someone like Hitler, to keep these people in order'" (175). It is a commonplace that such views were held in such circles, but the dialogue nonetheless feels forced.

Griffin's Joe emerges as a human being: contrary, often naïve, drily humorous in spite of his circumstances. His eventual politicisation, which amounts to nothing more radical than a decision to join a union, comes as a consequence of discovering that both fascism and the state are, in the novel, indiscriminate in the targets of their violence. He is more indignant than furious: '*He* hadn't caused the rotten trouble. *He* was neither a Red nor a Black. *He* hadn't charged at the van and tried to bash up the fascists, but they'd tried to get him for it just the same as if he had' (78). He ends up in a fight with a group of Fascists who mistake him for a Jew, in spite of his indignant protestations to the contrary (165).

However, this is above all a novel of human relationships forged, intensified and transformed by the experience of collective action, and demonstrates that, in spite of contemporary scepticism, explorations of political development need not negate the credible depiction of individual lives and struggles. At the novel's end, Elsie has moved into Bert's flat, and Joe has made things up with his wife, whom he realises is as much a victim of circumstances as he is: 'It's this being on the dole, her having to worry about the food and the rent and the kids, that does it' (218). Thurgood's affair with Lady Stroud has turned sour, and, after nearly strangling her to death, he commits suicide. Griffin's novel lacks the experimental reach of Sommerfield's, and works from less theoretically-involved premises. *May Day* begins with an epigraph from Marx, and is overt about its attempt to fashion a narrative method out of dialectical materialism: '*In this whirlpool of matter-in-motion, forces are at work creating history ... Every true story of today is the story of this struggle.*'[8] Griffin, though a Communist, starts and ends with a simpler proposition: 'If you stood together you could win; you were invincible. There were so many of you that no power on earth could resist you, once you stood together.'[9] Griffin's community, united in anti-fascist action, is likely to be less 'spectacularly wrong' for contemporary readers than Sommerfield's jarring 'Demonstrate for a free Soviet Britain!'[10] It is a fast-paced, funny and human account of an event now disappearing from living memory, supported by Croft's detailed introduction that frames the text with biographical detail and original reviews.

Dot Allan: *Makeshift* and *Hunger March*[11]

Questions of authorial politics in the depiction of social upheaval are unavoidably raised when reading the republished edition of two novels about interwar Glasgow life, Dot Allan's *Makeshift* and *Hunger March*, originally published in 1928 and 1934 respectively. Allan was a middle-class woman who made a career as a journalist, novelist, and short story writer at a time when it was still unusual for a woman of her background to do so. The introductory essay by Moira Burgess is enlightening: a thoroughly researched and informative background to a writer who is no longer well known. Biographical information about Allan is scant. Burgess draws attention to her involvement with Scottish PEN, though the details of the duration and extent of her participation are too sparse to support any conclusions about its relevance to the novels presented here, as Burgess acknowledges. However, her comments on Allan's involvement are suggestive. She reports that in 1950, along with several other significant women writers, including Marion Lochhead and Elisabeth Kyle, Allan undertook fundraising work for PEN. Of this activity, Burgess makes the rather odd comment that, 'In the interests of Scottish literature one would rather have seen these considerable writers getting on with their

---

8   Sommerfield, *May Day*, 26.
9   Griffin, *October Day*, 162.
10   Sommerfield, *May Day*, 26.
11   Dot Allan, *Makeshift and Hunger March* (1928; 1934). Introduction by Moira Burgess (Glasgow: Association for Scottish Literary Studies, 2010).

writing, as, it appears, all the men were doing' (xi). There is perhaps something of a throwaway tone to this comment, but it does indicate a critical tendency to assume that a writer's best interests are served by a refusal to engage with political activity, and that such engagements can only be to the detriment of the writer's work. The *Glasgow Herald* considered Allan's involvement with the organisation significant enough to describe her as 'a strong supporter' in its obituary,[12] which might suggest a more sustained and principled commitment than Burgess's characterisation allows for.

The lack of information available would be less problematic if Allan had not written, in *Hunger March*, an intensely, but very elusively, political work. This novel raises considerable problems with the terms in which Allan is presented. Burgess acknowledges the weaknesses of her writing, chiefly its melodramatic tendencies and its faltering attempts to construct credible working-class characters. Both these are genuine problems with her work. Burgess's tone is in one way apologetic, but there is also an excusatory note: 'Perhaps, as a West End lady and a dutiful daughter, she was shackled by the inhibiting influence of the very conventions she depicts, and felt she could not go so far' (xxii). This may well be a reasonable speculation, but it casts a particular light on the novels themselves. The two novels are strikingly different from one another. *Makeshift*, originally published in 1928, concerns an aspiring middle-class poet, Jacqueline Thayer, and her negotiation of the demands of family and romance with her quest for self-expression. It contains some striking phrases, but is overall a quite conventional novel, bound to a rather Victorian plot in which freedom comes from an unexpected inheritance, allowing Jacqueline both to escape the prospect of an unsatisfactory marriage and to pursue artistic self-fulfilment. The naïve Jacqueline finds herself at the mercy of men, and of 'the cruel snobbery of the servant class' in her pursuit of escape from a life in which she is always expected to 'make shift' and be content with 'second best' (143).

Alongside the work of contemporaries such as Sylvia Townsend Warner and Rosamond Lehmann, Allan's *Makeshift* seems conservative. It does little to prepare the reader for the second novel republished here, *Hunger March*. This novel, which originally appeared in 1934, is a deeply strange and unsettling piece of work. At the level of structure, it resembles both Sommerfield's *May Day* and Griffin's *October Day*. It is a narrative of short scenes confined to a single day, featuring a range of characters all linked in some way by the hunger march about to convene in Glasgow's George Square. Like *May Day* and *October Day*, *Hunger March* features no single main protagonist, moving instead between several clusters of characters. One group is comprised of a

---

12 'Obituary: Dot Allan, Novelist and Journalist', *The Glasgow Herald*, 4 December 1964, 17.

middle-class woman, Mrs MacGregor, her employee, Mrs Humphry, and Mrs Humphry's unemployed son, Joe. Another cluster involves Arthur Joyce, a businessman grieving for his son, lost in the First World War, and Joyce's two clerks, Charlie Wren and Celia. Another, looser narrative thread brings together Jimmy, a journalist, Adèle Elberstein, a singer in Glasgow for a concert, and Carlo, an Italian hotel worker fleeing Mussolini's regime. A Communist leader, Hamish Nimrod, makes several brief appearances. The narrative, like Sommerfield's, shifts between these characters, sketching out the connections and intersections of their lives.

But where Sommerfield announces his intent with the words of Marx and with a meditation on the forces of history, Allan's novel begins with a long, strange 'Proem' that establishes *Hunger March*'s unsettling premise:

> The first hunger march took place in Egypt. Joseph's sons, the ten brethren of Joseph, come to seek corn when the famine was in their own land, the land of Canaan, were the first hunger marchers. They marched, not as our ex-servicemen, our neo-pagans, our paid incendiaries, our honest men and our Communists do, brandishing crude weapons, shouting defiance, but in the peaceful manner of a pastoral people whose faith in neighbourly charity is undefiled. (195)

This image, taken from the Book of *Genesis*, reveals the moralising tendency of the novel as a whole. Hunger marches for Allan seem to have a metaphysical aspect as instances of a perpetual injustice. These opening phrases reveal a troubling belief in an orderly, moral kind of suffering. The 'peaceful manner of a pastoral people' seems to be preferable to the modern hunger march, with its threatening, disorderly tones. This characterisation of modern urban protest continues: 'So, centuries later, modern hunger marches, bearing rude weapons, blaring harsh music, were to encircles our cities' squares, our Government buildings, voicing the prayer of Joseph's brethren: Give Us Bread!' (198). This is written from the point of view of the disturbed spectator. Allan's phrasing suggests that history is something that *happens* to people, apparently without reason or agency: 'Paris awoke to the cry one wet October morning in the early days of the French Revolution' (198). The novel seems to abhor the untidiness and inconvenience the march brings, lamenting that, far from being 'a splendid outpouring of humanity knit together by a common cause', the march becomes 'a shuffling mob trailing half-heartedly at the heels of their leaders; a mob wasting its strength in shouts of imprecation, in paroxysms of passion as objectless as they are pitiful to behold' (203). This distaste is coupled with an anti-technological streak running through the text. The generation marching now are 'made outcast, one half, by the machine' (200). Man still asserts his 'right to live' above the din of the machines, but the integrity of this entreaty seems to have been lost and corrupted: 'His brain, addled by confused justice, by the jargon of diverse politicians, and stupefied by the incessant din of clattering machinery, works only in spurts' (201).

The narrator of the 'Proem' declares that there is a moral and spiritual obligation to assist, but this appears as a philanthropic, not a political impulse. Throughout the text the march appears as a kind of memento mori: 'There but for the grace of God, go I!' (201). A mixture of presumption and indifference tends to characterise Allan's treatment of the poor. This is apparent when Arthur Joyce's clerk, Celia, tries 'to imagine what it would feel like to be unemployed, to go from day to day weighted by a sense of failure' (237). Celia has already decided exactly what unemployment must be like: she assumes it is attended by a debilitating sense of failure. Thus the empathetic effort she is making is superfluous. Mrs Humphry's employer, Mrs MacGregor, looks upon the marchers with the kind of baffled pity that is the novel's dominant reaction. She wonders: 'had they assembled here of their own free will with the object of displaying, as Eastern beggars do, their sores to the world?' (370). *Hunger March* is not insensitive to the indignity of unemployment, but its expressions of that apprehension are troubling. The cub reporter Jimmy, whose own class position is far from secure, wonders about the unemployed man drawing his dole: 'Did it ever occur to him he was an unwelcome guest of the white-collar brigade, that his needs were draining its resources, choking like a heap of filth a strong clear stream?' (322). It occurs to Jimmy that perhaps the 'white collar brigade' has not made such a good job of things, but he too lapses into the anti-technological assumptions made elsewhere. The problem, he thinks, is that the 'workshops were so cluttered' and thus there are not enough 'clear spaces open to the sky' (323). The novel's insights into social injustice, to which it is certainly not blind, break down because they continually dissolve into such anti-modern generality.

A generalised preference for order over disorder emerges clearly and troublingly in the plotline concerning the Italian hotel employee, Carlo, a refugee from Mussolini's regime. On hearing of the march, Carlo is so frightened by the prospect of unrest and disorder that he commits suicide. It is 'a dread of political meddlers, of Fascists, of all who dare authority and dabble in affairs of state' that disturbs the balance of Carlo's mind and provokes him to suicide (253). His body is glimpsed by the singer Adèle Elberstein, who interprets it as a sign of the horrors that lurk in the attic rooms of the servant class from which, thanks to her sexual manipulation of men, she has escaped: 'Top floor, typical top floor' (318).

Carlo's violent death, however, resonates ironically. In spite of his terror of unrest, at no point in the novel does the hunger march present any threat to order beyond a temporary disturbance. This ironic undermining of the march's significance is most clear in the treatment of the unemployed character, Joe, son of the long-suffering Mrs Humphry. Joe's limited experience of the world, occasioned by his inability to find work and consequent complete dependence on his mother, leads him to a naïve commitment to Communism. His inexperience conspires with his reading of Marxist writers to condition a Pavlovian kind of response: 'any stray orator had only to utter the words "tyrants", "capitalists", to touch the little live switch which lit up the boy's brain' (246). Joe's mother thinks he has 'some dark strain of his blood which rebelled against life as it was. Joe wanted to destroy things, to smash them for all the world like a wee laddie who has no more sense that to break up its toys' (342). One plotline in the novel follows Joe as he assaults one of Joyce's clerks, and, believing that he has killed him, flees: 'He hadn't struck intentionally at a human being, alive and palpitating like himself. He had only hit out at Capitalism, at cruelty. And they would hang him for that' (313). Temporarily, he feels surrounded by 'an air of importance' (311). But it is no surprise to discover that the clerk recovers fully; in *Hunger March* it seems impossible that Joe could ever do anything of any consequence. His belief that he has struck a blow in the class war is ridiculed as simply the fantasy of a young, workless man. The association of the march with young male impulses is reiterated by Arthur Joyce, the businessman, who sees the procession as 'boys, boys of all nations, a host of pink-cheeked, confiding youths like [his son] Jerry, ready for the sake of the wingéd dream conceived by their ardent minds to run their breasts upon a spear' (332). In Joyce's eyes, the demonstration is no different from the First World War: an expression of young men's willingness to die for a cause.

Ultimately, what is offered is a decidedly individualist set of solutions. The technocratic order – bringing with it the loud noise and chaos that is so abhorred in the novel – has produced an overcrowded world from which escape must be made. Charlie Wren has an extraordinary vision of the hunger march eventually encircling the whole world: a great protest against 'a God who had put them into the world and then left them to fend in it for themselves' and in which each was 'fighting neither for nation nor for party; he was fighting neither for supremacy nor for riches, but simply to gain a foothold in an overcrowded world' (409). For Charlie, as for Celia, the only way through this vision of total war is through marriage, the 'protection of man and woman from that terrible loneliness inseparable from life in an overcrowded realm', a partial release from the 'struggle to communicate' (406). For Jimmy, the resolution is a full spiritual conversion. He decides to follow his father and grandfather into the Church, believing, at the novel's close, that 'freedom of the spirit has nothing to do with one's way of living' (421). He believes that 'no kind of political adjustment, no state of Communism, or of perfervid Nationalism was going to save the country' (421).

Hunger March is an extraordinary piece of imaginative work, unsettling not because its grasp of politics is slight, but because it is written with the full force of moral and ideological conviction. The terms in which this republished text is presented, as the work of a middle-class woman, rather inexperienced and inept at dealing with the realities of social injustice, seem inadequate for interpreting the strength of its assertions. The novel's ironic structures serve to deprive its working-class characters of agency to an extent that is difficult to attribute to simple lack of familiarity. A more thorough analysis would pursue the ironic currents of the text, to give a fuller account of its complex configurings of the relation between individuals and the impersonal forces on which the novel is premised. Moreover to construct an account of 1930s writing that is not, in Croft's phrase, 'politically gutted, imaginatively emptied' demands an appraisal of such texts as Allan's alongside the more politically clear-cut work of Sommerfield, Griffin and Jones. Historical distance, and the profound alteration of the political landscape, has meant that the work of these three writers may be read in a less hostile light than they would have encountered in earlier decades. The same distance should enable a re-evaluation of works such as Allan's, which resounds with political messages no less alien and radical.

Elinor Taylor
University of Salford

Walter Brierley: *Means-Test Man*

Raymond Williams's lifelong involvement with working-class life and history pervades all his extensive body of sociocultural studies, novels and literary engagements, while his pioneering of recovery research for neglected and overlooked working-class writing helped shape this field of study as we know it today. *Key Words* is therefore an appropriate forum in which to talk about *Means-Test Man,* Walter Brierley's superior working-class novel of 1935, reprinted in a new edition by Spokesman in 2011.[1] This reappearance might strike a note more ominous than celebratory, however, in the light of that novel's publication history. As with its mid-1930s first edition and the previous Spokesman reprint of 1983, a worsening economic climate has made Brierley's account of the damaging effects of long-term unemployment all too topical. The latest edition's back-cover copy is quick to remind us of this, and Andy

---

1 Walter Brierley, *Means-Test Man* (1935); Nottingham: Spokesman, 2011.

Recoveries

Croft's introduction to the 1983 version, also reproduced here, has taken on the same relevance now that it had then.

Croft's name will be familiar to readers of *Key Words*, and his *Red Letter Days: British Fiction in the 1930s* remains the authoritative text on the literary moment to which Brierley belongs.[2] In his introduction he contends that *Means-Test Man* is 'one of the most powerful and original English novels of the 1930s'.[3] Croft argues that its especial strength comes from Brierley's focus on the implications of joblessness and dependency on state relief entirely within the individual experience of one small family, as they spend a week waiting for the visit of the eponymous government inspector. This approach eschews a much more common tendency in 1930s working-class writing, which was to adopt socialist-inflected themes of mass resistance and collective action. These are all but absent from *Means-Test Man*, a silence that has proved both controversial and provocative for those tackling the novel.

Methuen, the original publishers, boasted in 1935 that 'It is almost the duty of every intelligent British man and woman to read this book [...] and to face up to the facts in it'.[4] Many favourable early reviews agreed: Croft describes in his introduction glowing write-ups from the *Economist* and *TLS*, and adds Oliver Baldwin's remark that 'every MP should read it'.[5] Croft also notes one dissenting voice, however, that 'was to set the tone for subsequent responses from the Left to the novel' (xiii). It belonged to Ernie Wooley, who wrote in the *Daily Worker:*

> The weakness of the book, recognizable, perhaps, only to those who have experienced long periods of unemployment is that the unemployed worker who sits timidly at home waiting for the investigator is not the rule, but the exception [...] A book which brought out this fighting spirit of the unemployed would have been a much greater use to the working-class'.[6]

Wooley's militant tone is more than just bluster. The 'fighting spirit of the unemployed' he refers to had been demonstrated in the decade and a half leading up to *Means-Test Man*'s year of publication, by which time five of the six National Unemployed Workers' Movement hunger marches on London had taken place, as too had two of the three Jarrow Marches. Though these achieved only little in terms of immediate state assistance, they succeeded in galvanising unemployed workers into repeated political action on a nationwide

---

2   Andy Croft, *Red Letter Days: British Fiction in the 1930s* (London: Lawrence & Wishart, 1990).
3   Brierley, *Means-Test Man*, xv.
4   Christopher Hilliard, *To Exercise our Talents: The Democratization of Writing in Britain* (Cambridge, MA and London: Harvard University Press, 2006), 148.
5   Brierley, *Means-Test Man*, xii.
6   *The Daily Worker*, 22 May 1935; cited in Brierley, xiii.

level.[7] This is not even to mention the General Strike of 1926, the Great Lockout of 1921, or such earlier events as the transport strikes of 1911–12 which occurred during Brierley's childhood. In an earlier issue of *Key Words* I wrote, with an unknowing echo of Wooley that has become appropriate here, that by the mid-1930s 'Collective social protest was the historical norm rather than the exception'.[8]

In working-class writing published around the same time as *Means-Test Man* this 'fighting spirit' is more starkly evident than in Brierley's novel. Walter Greenwood, Lewis Jones and James Hanley, for example, all wrote novels in the 1930s that feature strikes or collective mass action, and not merely in the spirit of passively reflecting contemporary social conditions of the time. Rather, these social conditions have a decisive bearing on plot and character development. In Greenwood's *Love on the Dole* (1933), for example, the agitator Larry Meath dies as a result of injuries inflicted by police batons during a demonstration.[9] Hanley's *The Furys*, published in the same year as *Means-Test Man*, contains a mass gathering to protest such institutionalised brutality and also a strike which, according to one of the characters, is in support of coal miners: '"They want us to support the miners. Poor bastards! They always do it dirty on the miners".'[10]

We might reasonably expect *Means-Test Man's* Jack Cook, who is an unemployed miner, to take more than a passing interest in such matters while they are occurring up and down the country. Instead, though, Brierley shows us a world where it's next to impossible to imagine anyone in the village of Wingrove (a slightly fictionalised version of Waingroves in Derbyshire, the author's birthplace) rising up in industrial action or organised protest. The closest Jack ever comes to engaging with such debates is in Chapter Two, 'Sunday', for him 'The worst day of the week, the most trying, the most deadening',[11] and 'a dangerous day, too, when a moment's weakness might lead to the very core of domestic accord being poisoned or ripped away' (66). His interior monologue continues:

> But there was no danger of that from his side, his hate was general, not based on envy of another. He softened as he came down to particulars, his wife, his child, another out-of-work; he did not feel like breaking shop

---

7   For a full account, see Peter Kingsford, *The Hunger Marchers in Britain* (London: Lawrence & Wishart, 1982).
8   See my article 'Gender and Community in Working-Class Writing', *Key Words* 5 (2007–8), 44.
9   Walter Greenwood, *Love on the Dole* (London: Jonathan Cape, 1933).
10 James Hanley, *The Furys* (1935; Harmondsworth: Penguin, 1985), 106.
11 Brierley, *Means-Test Man*, 64.

windows for their sakes or chivvying Members of Parliament; it was just a sorrow, just a sadness because things were as they were. (66–7)

Jack's perspective on violent protest is simply to dismiss the concept, in generalising terms, as something that exists outside his experience. Conflicts in the personal and domestic spheres, meanwhile, are far more important and take precedence. This is symptomatic of the novel as a whole. Jane's attitudes, by contrast, are somewhat more complex. There are four separate instances in the novel's week-long span where Jane displays accord, albeit of the crudest possible kind, with radical ideologies. These politicised moments are sudden flashes and often occur as a direct response to external stimuli – one, for example, happens when Jane is jolted out of a pleasant reverie by a woman who barges past her in the street, and another when her infant son John comes home crying after being hit by their loutish neighbour Mr. Jinks. For all that these incidents fill her with ire, Jane remains politically ill-informed. She grasps basic notions of inequality, as is revealed by such internal reflections as 'Thousands of harassed men, women and children were penned in with them, beings with no independence, no freedom, underfed, underclothed, not trusted' (55), but although we are told 'behind her hate and anger was a strong activity reaching out towards something definite' (102), she never arrives at it. In her rage over Jinks's behaviour, Jane almost immediately conflates the man with a cabinet minister whose picture she remembers seeing in the paper: 'In that moment she had felt near her enemy somehow. [...] A suggestion of wildness had swept her' (102). The connections Jane draws to relate lived experience to a wider external politics are arbitrary, and as with her husband (albeit via a somewhat different route) any attempt to do so inevitably leads her back to her personal and private sufferings: the difficulty of running a household on state benefits, her material deprivations, and the impending humiliation of the Means-Test man's visit.

One can see how the character of Jane might have been turned to comic effect by an author seeking to trivialise the growing trend towards violent political protest in 1930s Britain. Brierley, however, takes care to never reduce her to a twentieth-century Mrs. Malaprop, generating mere humour by putting her own flawed interpretations onto matters which the reader understands far better. The resultant impression of Jane is far darker and more disturbing. Her incipient socialism grants her only a means of indulging the self-destructive anger and hatred engendered by her circumstances, not a productive outlet for those emotions. Although we may not be able to picture her joining a picket line or participating in a riot, Brierley illustrates plainly that her 'strong moods' (101), to use Jane's own phrase, are a damaging force to her personal happiness and the fragile domestic harmony of the Cook household.

Here, as elsewhere in the novel, Brierley might be heard to sound a cautionary note about the extreme forms of political activism. Such elements of *Means-Test Man* may have influenced the conclusion of critics such as Wooley and, more recently, Roy Johnson, that the author appeared not radical enough for his radical era, too much of an establishment figure, somehow not quite authentically working-class. Andy Croft cites in his introduction Johnson's assertion that Brierley, 'in every possible way [...] represents the working man as the middle-class would like him to be; but not, fortunately, as he often is' (xiv).[12] In this interpretation, Jack Cook and his creator become a conciliatory voice in a world steadily descending into unrest, crying out for good old-fashioned working-class endurance, constancy and above all, calm, in the face of increasingly uncertain times.

Such assessments of *Means-Test Man* not only fail to give due consideration to Brierley's project of articulating the Cook family crisis only in the terms that they themselves understood, but also overlook a fundamental characteristic of the world he depicts. There is simply little potential for unrest in Wingrove, as there is hardly any unemployment. What we see is a pit village that is getting by more or less as well as it has ever done, in which Jack and the handful of other out-of-work characters are very much in a small minority. On each of the five weekday mornings of the novel, Jack listens to a veritable parade of hobnailed-booted workers tramping past his home along the one high street:

> Some were close, just on the other side of the hedge, others were on the far side of the road; men's voices and steps were slow, dragging at times, boys and young men seemed more cheerful, laughs passed among them and happy banter about girls and sport. Salutes, invariably 'Mornin'', were exchanged as the miners going up to the Pirley and Pentland pits met those going down the hill to Tenby, Blackley, and the mines in the little valley below Pinton.[13]

With five different locales boasting operational pits, all within walking distance, this small corner of Derbyshire seems to be positively booming. As Croft reminds us, Brierley is writing of the Notts-Derby coalfield, where employment figures were comparatively high (xv), while the mass unemployment and consequent organised working-class protest that lies behind Wooley's invocation of a 'fighting spirit' was much more characteristic

---

12 Croft calls our attention to Johnson's 'The Proletarian Novel', *Literature and History* 2 (October 1975), 84–95, and 'Walter Brierley: Proletarian Writing', *Red Letters* 2 (Summer 1976), 5–8.
13 Brierley, *Means-Test Man*, 94.

of urban centres, particularly Liverpool and Manchester.[14] The nearest city to Wingrove is Derby, ten miles away, which in the 1930s as now was a relatively small and rural county seat with 'little tradition of trade-union militancy or political activity'.[15] Brierley is aware, more than many of his detractors, of the determining influence of local milieu on personal and collective working-class experience.

From the beginning to the end of the novel Jack wrestles ceaselessly with feelings of angst, ostracism, restlessness and shame, not so much because he has no job but because most of the other men he knows do. This turmoil is played out to such an extent that some readers may lose patience before the conclusion. But Brierley means us to understand that any frustration or exasperation we may feel is more than shared by his hero. Jack's feelings are drawn wholly from Brierley's personal experience. In an early published piece he wrote of how 'the dependence on the state for money without having honestly earned it has made me creep within myself, losing faith in everything except my own capabilities, closely examining, sometimes even suspecting, friendly gestures' (xv). Much the same is what faces Jack in *Means-Test Man*. He refuses to be seen in the street when the pits let out and colliers returning home might meet him, and takes his Sunday walks in a neighbouring village where nobody knows him by sight. His reason for this is simply that he is receiving Public Assistance, and believes that in Wingrove 'The villagers knew all this and some pitied, some looked the other way, fearing pauperism to be infectious or as a state incompatible with their own' (80). On buying a concessionary ticket for a cricket match, 'Anger, hate, bitterness coursed through him, he burned with some kind of shame' (28), while even accepting a cigarette from a man who happens to be in work prompts a paragraph of agonising. When Jack is queueing in the Labour Exchange waiting to sign on, his thoughts express the extent of the abjection and outcast status he attaches to those in his condition:

> One thing was common to all the different types in the queue without a name – to every member of every type: in some it was stronger than in others, but the consciousness of being below was there – being below the normal level of living in other senses than the economic. This fact was patent when the men were in the Exchange, more so than when they were in the street, for the very presence of the manager or supervisor brought

---

14 See Harold Hikins (ed.), *Building the Union: Studies on the Growth of the Workers' Movement, Merseyside 1756–1967* (Liverpool: Toulouse Press, 1973) and *Strike: The Liverpool Transport Workers' Strike 1911* (Liverpool: Toulouse Press, 1980); and Bob Holton, *British Syndicalism 1900–1914: Myths and Realities* (London: Pluto Press, 1976).

15 Brierley, *Means-Test Man*, xv.

a silence about the rank, there was a kind of fear that a word might bring official eyes on them to their detriment. (168–9)

For many readers this may chime discordantly with George Orwell's words in *The Road to Wigan Pier*.[16] Writing of how he met unemployed workers on his return from Burma in 1928, Orwell states: 'the thing that horrified and amazed me was to find that many of them were ashamed of being unemployed [...] the attitude towards unemployment in those days [was that] it was a disaster which happened to you as an individual and for which you were to blame' (78–9). However, Orwell charted a decided shift in working-class attitudes over the nine years between that time and the publication of *Wigan Pier*. In an oft-quoted exemplum, he imagines two fictitious coal-miners and asserts that ten years ago, it was the case that 'So long as Bert Jones across the street is still at work, Alf Smith is bound to feel himself dishonoured and a failure. Hence that frightful feeling of impotence and despair which is almost the worst evil of unemployment' (79). This, however, had changed by 1937:

> When people live on the dole for years at a time they grow used to it, and drawing the dole, though it remains unpleasant, ceases to be shameful. Thus the old, independent, workhouse-fearing tradition is undermined, just as the ancient fear of debt is undermined by the hire-purchase system. In the back streets of Wigan and Barnsley I saw every kind of privation, but I probably saw much less *conscious* misery than I should have seen ten years ago. The people have at any rate grasped that unemployment is a thing they cannot help. It is not only Alf Smith who is out of work now; Bert Jones is out of work as well, and both of them have been 'out' for years. It makes a great deal of difference when things are the same for everybody. (80–1)

There's a danger in setting too much store by the sweeping statements of George Orwell – *Wigan Pier* in particular contains some famously dubious ones – but even if we take his words to reflect a broad reality, Jack Cook becomes an anachronistic figure. Just two years before Orwell's book, so close to the end of the decade of change he identifies, and after three years of unemployment, Jack's feelings remain identical to those of Alf Smith in the first instance. There's no fellow-feeling with the Bert Joneses, and certainly no sense that joblessness in Jack's community is tolerable because everybody's in the same boat. The examples from Brierley's novel above, especially the sequence in the Labour Exchange, illustrate clearly enough that in Wingrove drawing the dole is still both unpleasant and shameful.

---

16   George Orwell, *The Road to Wigan Pier* (1937; London: Secker & Warburg, 1997).

Recoveries

The village can appear an anachronism in other ways too. Combined with the frequent sumptuous invocations of the Derbyshire countryside (the author admired Hazlitt, and in 1930 submitted a homage to him as his application for a National Miners' Welfare Scholarship), the cricket matches on the green, Sunday school, Jack's roguish friend Kirton who enjoys poaching, and a long tradition of coal mining that's still by and large healthy, the picture of Wingrove can seem more like a fantasised rural idyll than a realistic portrayal of Britain during the rapid social and technological changes of the mid-1930s (x). It is the threat to that idea of a happy and timeless rural existence, a threat posed in part by rising unemployment and the clinical depersonalisation of state responses, that concerns Brierley the most.

All these ideas converge in the looming figure of the Means-Test man himself. What he stands for, rather than what he is, allows Brierley to turn his uneventful visit into a truly dramatic climax, in which the reader suffers as the Cooks do and understands completely their suffering. The Means-Test man, who is relatively young, walks with a 'faint swagger', rides a motorcycle, slicks back his hair and wears a 'thick gold-coloured ring'[17] announces even in his physical appearance a grounding in contemporary mid-1930s fashions and attitudes, all of which look strikingly vulgar in the more genteel and homely Wingrove. His coolly officious manner, businesslike rather than friendly – 'callous' is Jane's word (263) – represents a government whose approach to helping those in need has become less and less compassionate. Jack and Jane dread having such a man in their home because decent, respectable working-class people of their generation simply do not throw open their private financial troubles to prying strangers, nor should ever be reduced to going cap-in-hand to those strangers for the money they need to live on. While the Means-Test man is inspecting their Co-op book, the couple looks on in mute outrage at the indignity:

> Jack glanced at Jane. He was tired of standing here and she looked tired too. But he couldn't have sat down, and he was sure Jane couldn't; that would seem as if they felt a certain amount of comfort, which they certainly did not. They were wanting him to get it over with and go quickly. The master and mistress of a household – the two heads of a home – husband and wife in their castle – English. And this man sat here at the table where grace used to be said, where friends used to come and laugh over tea, always on the first Sunday of the year, that nearest John's birthday. And this man sat where those friends had sat, he was like a lord and they stood trembling before him. (262–3)

---

17 Brierley, *Means-Test Man*, 257.

It's that concept of an old, working-class Englishness, one of unspoken customs, expectations and values, which Brierley fears so deeply for. The castles he speaks of are under siege, by the nation's leaders on the one hand with their Means-Test and their prowling investigators, and on the other, tacitly expressed through Jane and her angry politicised moments, by a new working class that chooses organised and sometimes violent resistance over a stoical bearing-down. *Means-Test Man* is one of the last novels recording the strengths as well as the vulnerabilities of this traditional working-class *mentalité*, increasingly eroded by the bureaucratic and disciplinary regimen of an indifferent state, only fleetingly aware of the impending catastrophe which was to close this low dishonest decade.

Joseph Pridmore
Heilongjiang International University

Keywords

The two following contributions to a revived 'Keywords' section seek to extend the project initiated by Raymond Williams in *Keywords* in 1976, continued with his revised edition in 1983, and more recently carried forward by Tony Bennett, Lawrence Grossberg and Meaghan Morris in *New Keywords: A Revised Vocabulary of Culture and Society* from 2005. Perhaps 'historical semantics' is the definition which best covers Williams's work in this area, but since this work was at the heart of his intellectual project (it is the starting point of *Culture and Society*) even this description is inadequate. In the following pieces, Hywel Dix traces some of the contexts, military and technological especially, in which transitive verbs have come to be used intransitively, and how these semantic and grammatical changes tend to occlude social relationships. Debra Rae Cohen and Michael Coyle, meanwhile, offer a witty account of the word 'wireless', which, as in its contemporary instantiation as wifi, once carried utopian promises; yet social forms then and now have remained stubbornly resistant to the transformative possibilities imbedded in these terms.. The editors of *Key Words* would welcome further contributions to this revived section, which was formerly a regular feature of the journal, initiated by Deborah Cameron.

The Death of the Transitive Verb: Some Effects of Computing and the Internet on Linguistic Evolution

Given Raymond Williams's interest in making active a series of competing and oppositional meanings within the language in which capitalist society is expounded, there is a rather striking characteristic of his *Keywords*. Out of a total of 131 entries in the critical vocabulary, only five are entries for verbs. These are *determine, improve, interest, reform* and *work*. Naturally, a much greater number of entries are dedicated to nouns derived from verbs or related to them.

Both with the terms for kinds of activity, and the terms for particular kinds of person, however, the overall emphasis is on the nouns, not on the verbs. It is as though Williams is more interested in either the product of a particular activity, or in the person carrying it out, than in the process of carrying out the activity itself. For a study devoted to analysing the social and historical processes whereby certain terms gain hegemonic recognition within a political order and devoted also to contesting the interpretation both of those terms and of the order to which they refer this is a significant limitation.

In the thirty years or more since Williams's work, large advances have been made in the study of social linguistics. We now know much more about the relationship between language and power, or between language and gender or language and social class. Similarly, we have a much more nuanced understanding of how perceived differences in prestige related to the languages of different social groups give rise to distinct forms of linguistic evolution. Just as the study of languages has developed greatly, so language itself has continued to evolve. This is both a natural process in a human world, and a historical development with causes and roots which are, although complex, traceable.

This paper will examine a number of verbs currently used to refer to political relationships within the dominant ideology of our time. It will draw on a suggestion made by Williams in *Keywords* that subtle shifts in the use of particular linguistic structures come about more rapidly in certain periods than in others to argue that in a period of communications technology via the internet and home computing on a large scale, a particular shift in linguistic practice has become apparent. That shift is more than simply an expansion of meaning in one or two individual words. Rather, it is the gradual development of a new linguistic structure, which can be characterised as the use of transitive verbs in a series of intransitive senses.

The effect of this comparatively new usage is that the grammatical object of the sentence becomes detached from the grammatical subject of the sentence, so that the sentence presents the appearance of a subject without an object. The person carrying out an action becomes separated off from the carrying out of that action, so that the agent of the action is linguistically concealed from view. Reading such grammatical constructions alongside the earlier, transitive uses of the verbs in question enables the reader to resist that act of linguistic concealment, reconnect subject to object and hence to question the social and political structures to which language refers.

Deploy

The *Oxford English Dictionary* (*OED*) defines *deploy* as a verb with an object: to move (troops) into position for military action. The dictionary gives an example sentence: forces were deployed at strategic locations. It then goes on to give a secondary meaning for *deploy* as a verb without an object: to move into position for military action. This is illustrated by the exemplar sentence: the air force began to deploy forward.

For almost a decade, the economies of Britain and America have existed on a perpetual war footing, and this historical experience has brought a particular degree of prominence and regularity of usage for the concept of troop deployment. During the same period, in online and broadcast and print media coverage relating to warfare in Afghanistan and Iraq, a gradual shift has come about in usage of the verb *to deploy*, from the former to the latter. Thus at a speech to the United States Military Academy at West Point, Virginia, in 2009, President Obama told military recruits, 'As cadets, you volunteered for service during this time of danger. Some of you have fought in Afghanistan. Many will deploy there'.[1] He did not say 'you will be deployed' and he certainly did not say which military commander would be responsible for deploying the soldiers.

Instead, he went on to say, 'The 30,000 additional troops that I am announcing tonight will deploy in the first part of 2010 – the fastest pace possible – so that they target the insurgency and secure key population centers'.[2] By talking about the troops *deploying* (noun in the intransitive) rather than *him* deploying *them*, President Obama in effect divorced himself from the consequences of the action that he was announcing, linguistically separating himself from the action in question and avoiding the need to name any agent within the American military who would be responsible for the deployment. This might have been a militarily expedient avoidance, generating a level of secrecy for the names of the people involved in leading the deployment even while making a public announcement about it. It was also politically expedient, enabling the president to separate himself from the commitment of troops that he was announcing. Arguably, this is a grammatical structure appropriate to a war economy, in which mass communications provide access only to carefully selected and approved information and in which there is little public access to the names and roles played by leading decision makers.

Dispatch

According to the *OED*, the verb *to dispatch* can only be used as a transitive verb, that is, a verb with an object. The dictionary gives the meaning: 'To send off to a destination or for a purpose', as in the example sentence, 'he dispatched messages back to base'. The dictionary gives related meanings for the word ranging from *deal with* or *address* to *kill* (as in the example phrase, 'the executioner's merciful dispatch of his victims'). All of these are transitive uses of the verb; they require a grammatical subject and a grammatical object. It is interesting to note that the example sentences provided are of an essentially militaristic nature, referring to the dispatching of messages to base, through the euphemistic use of the word to refer to execution and killing, and up to a final use of the word as a noun: the battle dispatch as an official report from a battlefield.

1 *Telegraph*, 2 December 2009.
2 *Telegraph*, 2 December 2009.

Although it has not yet come to the attention of the *OED*, the word *dispatch* has recently started to be used in an intransitive way. Yet the fact that a particular change has not yet found its way into the dictionary does not mean that it is not starting to occur. For example, the online retail company Amazon routinely sends out a message to its customers to inform them when a particular order has been fulfilled. This message is normally entitled: 'Your Amazon.co.uk order has dispatched.'

The use of the verb in the intransitive in this case separates the process of dispatching an order from the person carrying it out. Such separation also occurred in a slightly older usage of the verb, which would have retained the transitive but placed the verb in the passive voice, as in the expression, 'Your order has been dispatched'. However the passive-transitive construct retained some implication of a human agency carrying out the action, implying as it does an unspoken refrain, 'Your order has been shipped *by our delivery team*' or simply '*by us*'. By contrast, the intransitive construct, which is so recent as to not yet have made its way into the *OED*, retains an active voice but renders that voice disembodied – as if the item being dispatched has placed itself in a parcel and taken itself to the post office for delivery. Human contact and human relationships are bleached out of the process through this grammatical structure.

The clouding of relationships implicit in the new use of the intransitive verb hints at a new kind of relationship between the people involved, that is, between customer and supplier. It is significant that 'Consumer' was one of the nouns that Raymond Williams originally analysed in *Keywords*, exploring a gradual transition in how the verb *to consume* was understood across Europe. Williams identified a 'relative decline' in the use of the word 'customer' in favour of 'consumer' to describe 'a buyer or purchaser' from the early modern period onwards. This transition from 'customer' to 'consumer' was significant because, Williams suggests, '*customer* had always implied some degree of regular and continuing relationship to a supplier, whereas *consumer* indicates the more abstract figure in a more abstract market'.[3]

The shift from *customer* to *consumer* seems to be related to a changing social history in which expanding networks of transport, gradual urbanisation, the onset of a market economy and longer trading routes each contributed to a gradual situation in which people gradually ceased to purchase food, clothing and basic materials from one supplier who was individually known to them, and instead found themselves meeting and trading with people with whom they were not directly acquainted more and more often. In other words, the social and historical changes implicit in the shift from *customer* to *consumer*

---

3   Raymond Williams, *Keywords*, rev. edn (London: Flamingo, 1983), 79.

are changes of human relationship. In turn they are in the process of being replaced by a different historical process, wherein the purchase of consumer goods from large multinational corporations via the internet renders the figure of the retailer not just unknown from the perspective of the consumer, but also fundamentally unknowable. The recent usage of a sentence such as 'Your order has dispatched' hints at the latest stage of a much longer and more complicated social history, inscribed within the evolution of the words themselves.

Ship

Like *dispatch,* the verb *to ship* is commonly used by internet-based retail companies to inform its customers of the likely delivery date of a particular item that they have ordered. Indeed, Amazon itself uses *dispatch* and *ship* interchangeably and is as likely to use the phrase 'Your Amazon.co.uk order has shipped' as 'Your Amazon.co.uk order has dispatched'. As with *dispatch*, this replaces the passive-transitive construct 'has been shipped' which still retained a residual implication of the agent by whom the action had been carried out, and filters human agency out of the transaction.

This time the *OED* recognises both a transitive and an intransitive usage for the verb. The sequence in which different uses have come into common practice is particularly instructive. The initial definition is listed as *to transport goods or people on a ship*. This is then extended by metaphorical implication to mean 'send by some other means of transportation or by rail' so that even in the transitive sense it was already a verb of abstraction.

The gradual onset of intransitive uses of the verb dates from the late eighteenth century, when *shipping* was no longer understood as the process of sending particular goods or people on a ship, but instead became something that the sender simply did – with no object. Thus the new definitions *to go to sea from a home port*; *to embark on a ship*; and *to take service on a ship* came into usage. This was during a period in which Britain was establishing naval supremacy over the world and the slightly more active use of the term *to ship* changed from referring mainly to objects and how they were handled to actions which people directly carried out – possibly reflecting a growing active confidence with regard to the world's oceans in the imperial period. Interestingly, as with both *deploy* and *dispatch* many of the example sentences given in the *OED* are militaristic in usage: 'Jack shipped with the Admiral'.

The third stage in the history of the verb *to ship* is appropriate to the internet age. At this stage, the verb is used in the intransitive and although in the active voice it has become used in a highly abstract and metaphorical manner. The definition provided for this more recent intransitive usage by the

OED is 'to be made available for purchase', with the example sentence, 'the cellular phone is expected to ship at about $500 sometime this summer'. It is a new commercial application equating *to ship* with *to sell*, or more accurately, *to be sold*. The different stages of common usage of the word correspond to different grammatical structures in which it has been used. They represent a transition from the imperial era when *shipping* was something that was actively done to other goods and peoples, through a mainly militaristic usage in the twentieth century to a period since the end of the Cold War when the principal determinant of global relationships is no longer imperialism or warfare on a worldwide scale, but global capitalism. As Raymond Williams notes, this is a linguistic history that is 'saturated with the experience of a society based on money relationships'.[4]

Launch

Just as *to ship* can mean both *to go to sea by ship* and *to send something or someone else to sea in a ship*, *to launch* also combines usages that sometimes require an object (transitive uses) and sometimes do not require an object (intransitive). Perhaps the most prominent example of both kinds of usage in 2011 was the final mission of America's space shuttle programme. Linguistically speaking, it is possible to say both that the shuttle Atlantis launched on 28 June, and that it *was* launched *by* NASA. The former (intransitive) example is the more recent of the two usages, detaching the verb from an outside agency as if the shuttle actively launched itself. The older, transitive usage would require, in grammatical terms, that the shuttle be launched by an outside agency. The confusion and almost equally common usage that exists between the two constructs possibly refers to a period in which space travel has become globally recognised, but when very few people really understand either the technical processes required or the political and institutional hierarchies behind those processes. Does the shuttle launch itself or is it launched by someone – and if so, who? The knowledge that it [was] launched exists in parallel with a lack of knowledge about how precisely that launch was caused to take place.

As with *to ship*, there is also a more recent usage for the term *launch* and it is again more abstract, referring not to transportation as such but to capitalist relationships within the consumer economy. In a prominent advertising campaign in 2010, for example, the automobile manufacturer Alfa Romeo proclaimed that the new model, the Giulietta, 'launches at Geneva'. Similarly, the computing and telecommunications company Apple proudly announced in March 2011 that its new iPad 2 would launch later in the year.

4   Williams, *Keywords*, 173.

Keywords

The *OED* lists no meaning for *to launch* in this recent, intransitive and metaphorical sense. In very recent usage, the 'launch' event is a staged spectacle which large companies use to render natural, or even seasonal and hence expected and anticipated what is really a carefully planned marketing strategy, contingent upon a developed global market for high-level consumer goods. It creates a sense of momentum and perhaps excitement, building up in advance a market for the new product being launched. This sense of anticipation is not only reflected but positively fostered by the new linguistic usage of the verb, creating the impression not that Alfa is launching a new car, or that Apple is launching a new product, but that the Giulietta model and the iPad 2 simply launch themselves in a spontaneous burst of creativity and fashionable design. The fact that this usage has not yet entered the *OED* despite its common application, especially in web-based communications, underlines the extent to which linguistic evolution in general and the loss of transitivity in particular are processes that are still occurring, and that such evolution is a manifestation of particular human practices.

Install

Just as the intransitive metaphorical usage of *launch* has been accelerated by mass communication via the internet, *install* is a further example of a verb that has come to be used in an intransitive sense during the process of computerised communications. In the case of *install*, the use of the intransitive can seem to describe an almost magical process whereby things happen without anyone making them happen.

A pop-up box on the computer screen announces: 'Your new version of BT Broadband desktop help is now installing' – rather than, 'BT is now installing your new version of desktop help'. The impression created is one that frustrates understanding. Something is happening, but who is causing it to happen, or how, is less clear. This example is striking because it contains an abstract 'you' at the receiving end of the action (as in 'your new version') without containing a corresponding sense of the 'I' or 'we' carrying it out. Clearly there is nobody inside the machine carrying out the action and this might be one reason why the use of a first-person subject appears inappropriate. Possibly this can be related to the more general fact that many more people use home computers than really understand the technical process of their operation so that in the almost magical sense described it really does appear as though computers operate themselves.

The *OED* does not provide a definition for *install* in the intransitive. The two definitions offered are *to place equipment or machinery in position for use* and *to place someone in a new position of authority*. In other words, like *deploy* and *dispatch* it is a word that speaks of a particular relationship to political and military power. The change in grammatical usage from the transitive to the intransitive is in this case so recent as to be happening before our very eyes. This could be said to reflect an age of uncertainty; an age in which military action is widely reported but rarely explained; in which political decisions are made without us knowing how or by whom; and in which technology informs our lives without us really necessarily understanding how it works. Or as Raymond Williams puts it in *Keywords*, an age in which 'the problems of information are severe'.[5]

Complete

To complete is a further example of a word like *install* which, primarily through computerised messaging, has started to be used in the intransitive sense. In general, *complete* remains a verb in need of an object, for example, *the student completed his assignment* or *the child is trying to complete her stamp collection*. As with *install*, however, there has started to be a specific, intransitive application of the verb relating to the installation of new software updates on computer desktops. During the installation process of new updates, it is common for computer screens to display a pre-programmed message from Microsoft Windows: '2 out of 3 updates have completed successfully'. As with *install*, this linguistically cuts off any sense of the corporation providing the updates by categorically refusing to state, 'Microsoft is completing updates'. *Upgrade* and *upload* have come into similar intransitive usage through the communications of very common websites such as Yahoo and Google.

In all of the cases discussed, the development of intransitive uses of certain verbs is in contrast both to the use of the passive voice, and to an earlier transitive use. There are sufficient examples to suggest that at issue is more than just a variation in how we understand a few individual words, and that what is occurring is the generation of a new set of relationships expressed by a correspondingly new and developing linguistic structure.

The shift from transitive to passive already had built into it an account of the social history of certain commercial or political relationships in which it was either not possible to state who was causing certain actions to occur, or positively desirable that such attribution be concealed. The intransitive usage of *deploy, dispatch, ship, launch, install* and *complete* has been greatly accelerated by communications technology, home computing and the internet. The linguistic development in question describes a series of relationships in which the communicator and the recipient of communication do not know each other and in which perhaps they cannot know each other. For in a real sense, in all of the web-based communications analysed here, there is no individual at the end

5   Williams, *Keywords*, 18.

Keywords

of the line. There is rather a corporation, a conglomerate or an organisation whose communiqués exist often in the form of prescribed messages, which can easily be addressed to an individual at one end but which nevertheless cannot truly be said to have been addressed by an individual at the other. Thus, the death of the transitive verb is a process that makes possible in language an entire set of social relationships on a global scale, in which the relationship between agent and recipient of particular actions is fundamentally unknowable from the perspective of the recipient and in which it appears that the technology of communication itself has become the agent of the communication.

Hywel Dix
Bournemouth University

Wireless

Resonant with utopian promise in the late nineteenth century, the term 'wireless' became a site both of paradoxical signification and of ideological struggle in early twentieth-century Britain before fading from use after the Second World War. It had already declined in importance decades earlier in the US, where it eventually came to conjure comic or archaic images of geeks with headphones and crystal sets. Today in the early twenty-first century it has once again become part of a new and globalized collective dream of universal information exchange.

At the dawn of the twentieth century, 'wireless' — first as an adjective attached to Marconi's experiments in wireless radiotelegraphy, then as a noun in its own right — inspired the same kind of utopian thinking that the beginnings of telegraphy had half a century earlier. As magic and mechanism, wireless harked back to the excitement surrounding the idea of a resonant universe crackling with electricity and pulsing with vibration. It offered the promise of the prosthesis, extending the reach of Man, with the added magic of the prosthesis being invisible. The term 'wireless', evoking the unboundedness and mystery of the ether, held out the hope of universal connectivity across space, across time and even, as Jeffrey Sconce has detailed, across the barrier between life and death: the restoration of the absent.[1] Marconi himself envisioned that his invention would be used by 'men on lonely lightships and isolated lighthouses … to send messages of a daily private character … to render less painful their isolation'. The very wirelessness of his technique implied that it

---

1 *Haunted Media: Electronic Presence from Telegraphy to Television* (Durham: Duke University Press, 2000).

recognized 'no frontiers' and thus, he said, could 'fulfil what has always been an essentially human need'.[2]

This kind of utopianism became, before the First World War, both political and aesthetic. For Modernist revolutionaries like Filippo Tomaso Marinetti, wireless served as an emblem of the liberation of imagination and language in the new technological age. In his 'Technical Manifesto' (May 1912), he first evoked what he called the 'wireless imagination' (*immaginazione senza fili*): 'the absolute freedom of images or analogies expressed by liberated words, without the conducting wires of syntax and *without any punctuation*'. But the changing grammatical usage of the term 'wireless' itself ironically mirrors the gradual foreclosure of Marinetti's imagined freedom; the burgeoning institutional structures of wireless broadcasting imposed a new 'syntax' on the wireless imagination.[3]

Even at the time of Marconi's first experiments the term was already being shorthanded into a noun: the *OED* cites the first appearance of 'wireless' in noun form as occurring in November 1899, in the *Times*: 'we were transcribing many telegrams for many parts of England and France, which had been sent 50, 45, 40 miles by "wireless"'. This usage did not become customary, however, until after the First World War, with the establishment of broadcast stations – despite the fact that the shift to broadcast 'wireless' entails a fundamental reformulation of information flow, being, by its very nature, one-way rather than multidirectional.

The irony of the word's retention is heightened by the echoes in the rhetoric of John Reith, the first Director General of the BBC, of the earlier language of etheric unboundedness. Even with the establishment of the BBC as a controlling apparatus, and the birth of the broadcasting system, Reith was still harking back to the promise of universal communication: 'Wireless ignores the puny and often artificial barriers which have estranged men from their fellows. It will soon take continents in its stride, outstripping the winds; the divisions of oceans, mountain-ranges, and deserts will be passed unheeded. It will cast a girdle around the earth with bands that are all the stronger because invisible.'[4]

But as a noun, 'wireless' became a flexible portmanteau term that migrates to cover, all at the same time, the medium of broadcast radio, the content that rides in on the carrier wave, the set on which one receives that content (a marketed and licensed commodity), and, by extension, the BBC corporate monopoly itself.

2 Quoted in Orrin J. Dunlap, *Marconi, the Man and his Wireless* (New York: MacMillan & Co., 1937), 289.
3 'Futurist Sensibility and Wireless Imagination', in *Selected Poems and Related Prose* (New Haven: Yale University Press, 2002), 87.
4 *Broadcast Over Britain* (London: Hodder & Stoughton, 1924), 219.

Keywords

Today's renewed use of the word 'wireless' recapitulates this drift between product and system, between markers of an ideal and the signs of its commodification – although the direction of this drift has actually reversed that of the previous century. As before, the term was revived in 1980s and 1990s public usage in relation to various kinds of information transfer – initially short-distance devices such as garage door openers and TV remotes, then through consumer products of Bluetooth technology associated with data reception and transmission: wireless headset, wireless keyboard, wireless mouse.

Yet the word 'wireless' itself, especially in relation to internet usage, is often implied rather than stated, taken as read because it has become so incorporated into other language (as earlier 'wireless' itself absorbed the words 'telegraphy' and 'telephony') as a prefix or acronym. The term 'wi-fi', which stands in for a local area network, implies the words 'wireless fidelity' without using them, coined as it is to echo and one-up the obsolete audio technology of 'hi-fi'. But the almost universal use of the term largely occurs without cognizance of the fact that it actually originated as, and remains, a trademark. A much more obvious example of the subsuming of the ideal of 'wireless' into trademark is the popular Nintendo game console, the Wii, which – despite the company's insistence that the name is meant to look like two people standing side by side, and the fact that it is pronounced as 'we' – clearly seeks to borrow the resonances of the wi-for-wireless prefix.

In fact, as 'wi-fi' comes to stand in for 'wireless internet' itself – for the medium to which one gains access as well as the modality of such access – the abbreviated term not only carries with it the echoes of the historical tension within the term 'wireless', but also becomes the site on which current struggles for the internet itself are played out. Although 'Wi-Fi' is a commodity which can be 'piggybacked' or 'pirated', 'wi-fi' as medium, and as sign of democratic access to that medium, is increasingly seen as an essential service, a universal right.

Debra Rae Cohen
University of South Carolina

Michael Coyle
Colgate University

Review Article: Education and Value: Grasping the Real Nature of Our Society

Jennifer Birkett

Jonathan Bate (ed.), *The Public Value of the Humanities.* London and New York: Bloomsbury Academic, 2011. xv + 319 pp. hb. ISBN 978-1-8496-6471-4; pb. ISBN 978-1-8496-6062-4; ebook ISBN 978-1-8496-6063-1.

Thomas Docherty, *For the University. Democracy and the Future of the Institution.* London and New York: Bloomsbury Academic, 2011. ix + 198 pp. pb. ISBN 978-1-84966-615-2; ebook ISBN 978-1-84966-631-2.

Raymond Williams's chapter on 'Education and British Society', in *The Long Revolution* in 1961, rejecting the concept of education as an ahistorical 'fixed abstraction', set out an analysis that has lost none of its sharpness and relevance:

> There are clear and obvious connexions between the quality of a culture and the quality of its system of education. [...] [W]e speak sometimes as if education were a fixed abstraction, a settled body of teaching and learning, and as if the only problem it presents to us is that of distribution: this amount, for this period of time, to this or that group. The business of organizing education [...] is certainly important. Yet to conduct this business as if it were the distribution of a simple product is wholly misleading. It is not only that the way in which education is organized can be seen to express, consciously or unconsciously, the wider organization of a culture and a society, so that what has been thought of as simple distribution is in fact an active shaping to particular social ends. It is also that the content of education, which is subject to great historical variation, again expresses, again both consciously and unconsciously, certain basic elements in the culture, what is thought of as 'an education' being in fact a particular selection, a particular set of emphases and omissions.[1]

The books presently under review are worth reading in tandem, in the perspective Williams affords. Jonathan Bate's edited collection, *The Public Value of the Humanities*, is important for the understanding of the research material from the humanities currently entering public awareness and attitudes through teaching and the media, and in some cases helping directly to shape social policy and economic development. As Onora O'Neill, a previous President of the British Academy, explains in her Foreword, the collection was initiated

---

[1] Raymond Williams, *The Long Revolution* (1961; Harmondsworth: Penguin, 1965), 145.

by the Arts and Humanities Research Council, in the context of the 'partly phony' war about the value of research to taxpayers (v). One of its jobs is to set out why it is impossible to show direct economic benefits to society from humanities or indeed much other important research, and it does that job well, setting out some of the interesting mediations which can take research results to the community at large. It is less good at showing why such questions are asked in the first place, which was never merely, as O'Neill suggests, the wish to protect research funding for the sciences. There are issues of selection here which raise much larger political questions, which Bate's collection has not been formulated to tackle.

The wearing of blinkers is a necessary adjunct to the publication of subsidised projects, not just when the subsidies come from the MoD, drug companies, or Imperial Tobacco; and the teeth of the academic establishment are not notorious for biting the hand of the State that feeds them. Defences of the humanities (and the social sciences) in the mid-1980s, conducted within a university system where individual academics were still protected by codes of academic freedom, pulled fewer punches. Indeed, for the generation facing the first heavy swings of Margaret Thatcher and Sir Keith Joseph against disciplines and institutions, punching back was the primary aim. That first moment of extreme anger also had the benefit of a context in which the energy and experience of the 1960s were still working out through communities across the board, trade unions were still organising and organised, subject disciplines and faculties still had a sense of identities to be protected, and Labour, which had just provided working people with a raft of protective and progressive employment legislation, was not yet New. Since then, a long war of attrition has seen that 1980s generation replaced by younger scholars who know only what it is to live in an occupied state, trained to the self-monitoring template and all the instruments of tick-box culture, too burdened by heavy workloads to have time or energy for resistance, and no organisations left through which to organise it. Twenty-five years on, fury has been stirred up again by the Coalition government that allowed student fees to rise to astronomical levels – not so much pricing students out of the market, as underlining for them that the education they are about to receive is truly of the market, a market-embedding experience. At the same time, State support for teaching in the humanities and social sciences has been completely cut, underlining for the universities that for them too, life or death is to be a matter of markets. The question remains: what means do academics have left to challenge the attack?

Jonathan Bate's collection is a shop-window for current humanities research. His Introduction lists reasons for the taxpayer to cough up cheerfully. Humanities researchers interpret the signs of past and present, and help shape the future; they explore and advise on society's ideas of value; they teach the art of disinterested thinking; they make an economic contribution to the country; they teach critical thinking (this latter point is made very briefly: blink, and you'll miss it). Bate presses the notion of modern scholars as a Coleridgean clerisy, whose task is to preserve the heritage of the past, disseminate knowledge throughout the realm, and with it heightened understanding of the individual's rights and duties, and by their activities raise a nation's profile and power. This, in the lengthy quotation from Coleridge selected by Bate, is crucially an order with an elite at the fountainhead, and lesser ranks spread nationwide. If this mode of organisation seems familiar, it's because it is, and it is a point to be pondered in the context of the quotation from Williams with which I began.[2]

Twenty-four discrete essays on current research in the various disciplinary areas of the humanities are gathered under four headings which echo AHRC funding 'themes' (themselves, though we're not told this, trailing in the wake of ERA – European Research Area – research priorities): 'Learning from the Past', 'Looking Around Us', 'Informing Policy', and 'Using Words, Thinking Hard'. These are not gripping headings, and they invite the question of what readers they are meant to attract. The great and the good, from Vice-Chancellors to Michael Gove, supportive Members of Parliament, educational journalists, and a few other friends in the culture sections of the media, have presumably all had their free copies. The Amazon website will not crash under excited enquiries from the public at large, but these readers are not directly addressed. This is a pity, because if they could get through the Introduction and the headings to the substance of the essays, there is much to catch a general reader's imagination. There is one reference to the difficulty of persuading your taxi driver to appreciate the value of humanities research, and one extended attempt to interest an Australian sheep farmer, encountered on a train. Realistically, it's other humanities researchers who will be taking out the book from the reference shelves in their university libraries, to find out what other people in other disciplines are doing, and to check out how their own research stands up against those selected here for official approval.

Such readers will not be disappointed. Today's researchers are a lively and diverse breed, and they are doing some very interesting work, which for the most part, in its content and methodology, reflects their own progressive and enlightened social choices. As Mrs Thatcher's ministers often complained, academics are adept at getting round the obstacles placed in their way by their State funders (I paraphrase). Section 1, 'Learning from the Past', opens with

2   Williams was the first to revive discussion of Coleridge's concept for mid-twentieth-century purposes, in the seminal chapter, 'Mill on Bentham and Coleridge', in *Culture and Society* (1958; Harmondsworth: Penguin, 1961), 65–84. See in particular the claim that, irrespective of Coleridge's specific definitions, 'for Mill, as for us, the importance [of the concept] lies in the principle' (78–9).

Reviews

Mary Beard's account of modern revivals of Classical drama, showing how discussion of the hard political and social issues of the present day benefits from painstaking archival research and new linguistic discoveries. In Tony Harrison's play *Fram*, one of the minor heroes is Gilbert Murray, Professor of Greek at Oxford in the early twentieth century, populariser of Classical drama and champion of liberal values, whose work supplied material for the feminist and peace movements. This section closes on Vanessa Toulmin's description of the rediscovery in 1994 of the films shot by the Blackburn film company Mitchell & Kenyon between 1900 and 1913, the making of the archive, the creation of the BBC documentary fronted by Dan Cruickshank, and the involvement of the local communities who figured in the original films as contributors to as well as consumers of the research. In Section 2, 'Looking Around Us', Stephen Daniels and Ben Cowell report on the AHRC programme in Landscape and Environment, a collaboration between Nottingham University and the National Trust: 'A central theme of the programme is exploring the range of values, including aesthetic, commercial, spiritual, scientific, social, historical and ethical values, which are expressed in the way landscape is seen, designed, made and managed. The programme has examined the cultural complexities, and power relations, of such values, both combining and competing: landscape as both common ground and contested terrain' (105). Particularly interesting is their account of a project on the upland commons ('Contested Common Land'), still surviving as a collective resource, now claimed by the 'intersecting demands and values of farming, recreation and conservation' (113). Historians and legal scholars have been brought together to study the implications of the 2006 Commons Act, which gave commoners 'powers to enter into binding agreements with government agencies promoting sustainable management' (112). Evidence was gathered from conversations with farmers, landowners, and land managers – which prompts this reviewer to wonder what this means for the definition and interpretation of values, and what that in its turn means for the wider concept of public ownership. The precedent set by Williams's 1973 study *The Country and the City* is evident here, and Matthew Johnson's essay, 'Making a Home: English Culture and English Landscape', makes specific allusion to the Williams tradition in showing how recent academic research into landscape seeks to be accessible to a modern, multicultural society, to evoke 'a social landscape that is inclusive of the poor, the marginalised, and of different faiths and cultures' (124):

> In the 1970s, the literary and cultural critic Raymond Williams was opening our eyes to the construction of the English countryside through the eyes of the 'outsider' in the form of the city dweller. Williams' academic point was that to understand Romantic and other views of the English landscape,

you had to understand first the Industrial Revolution. [...] Williams' thinking [...] reiterated the fact that different groups of people read the countryside in different ways and turn these readings into cultural capital in literature as well as art and cultural practice. He and his students – political and cultural critics like Stuart Hall – went on to develop his ideas of social class and apply them to questions of colonial and ethnic divisions. Their work opened up new and exciting questions such as: to what extent does the English landscape exclude as well as include? (126)

An important essay by Mike Press on research in art and design lists the range of contributions that this fairly new research field is making to a variety of other disciplines, as well as to practical innovations in craft and manufacturing, and in the exploration and application of digital imaging techniques to healthcare, forensics, and marine recovery.

The collection's third section, 'Informing Policy', includes contributions from Law, Genocide Studies, and History. Simon Szreter describes the History and Policy network, which began as a Cambridge-based website in 2002, and has fed its research into, for example, a practitioners' forum with Trade Unions, and policy discussions by Third World governments (the impact here of Szreter's own work on the early development of the English Poor Law is fascinating reading). The essay points to two well-argued papers on the History and Policy website from Spring 2003, which offered clear warnings about the unrealistic approach of the 'coalition of the willing' to the war in Iraq, spelling out from past political experience the impossibility of 'creating democracy' in other countries without putting in money and effort. These two essays are, of course, an example of the lack of 'impact' research can have when politicians have already decided their goals, but their presence on the website makes an important statement.

Richard Howells, explaining to his sheep farmer and fellow traveller the limits of instrumentalism as a justification for the practice and study of the arts and humanities ('Sorting the Sheep from the Sheep'), argues that the humanities are indeed of great economic and social benefit, but they are more than that:

> In a truly liberal democracy, we must be prepared to allow both the arts and education to flourish regardless of what specific enrichment or enlightenment they proceed to provide. We must be unafraid to let the population be exposed to ideas and reach conclusions with which we may not necessarily agree. (239)

Reviews

As he points out, citing Adorno and Horkheimer, 'the expression "the culture industry" was originally coined as a derogatory term' (239). Such flashes of anger are few in the collection, so it's worth adding to them Nicholas Davey's comments, in the essay which closes Section 4, and the whole collection, on the capacity of philosophical research

> to enrich wider debates about community, society, individual responsibility and legitimate aspirations, questions which the 'unacceptable face' of capitalism, as a former Conservative Prime Minister (Edward Heath) once described it, has now made so urgent. [...] In the ability to think in ways that refuse the current ideology or belief, and in the power to speculate about the different and the otherwise, lie the seeds of political freedom, the seeds of a belief in the possibility of real and significant individual engagement and intervention and, most important, the seeds of a faith in the future where things can indeed be made otherwise. (309)

Anger is writ large in Thomas Docherty's monograph, *For the University*, which is a box of fireworks. Addressing not just the case of the humanities but the whole university sector, it is unlikely to be offered as a gift to many high-ranking University administrators, not least those mentioned by name for collusion with the enemy (Steve Smith, Sally Brown, Julia King, and David Eastwood). Active in the sector since the 1970s, Docherty is well placed to point out the question mark now being placed over the whole future of the University as an institution: 'an attack on the fundamental principle that the University exists as a key constituent in a public sphere' (viii). Politicians, he argues, are no longer satisfied with simply encouraging mistrust of the University as a site of class privilege. More important now is their wish to establish 'the right of a government to manage things in a society without fearing contradiction from another source of potentially critical authority' (1). He establishes the context of this operation: the attack on trades unions, and on the professions at large, with crisis management used as a cloak for ditching principles, and the installation of monitoring and quality assurance, bureaucratisation and tick-box control of all activities as signs of mutual mistrust. He sets out his own position: the first principle of the University must not be thought of as a single agreed aim, but as the agreement to pursue the free search for principles. This is a flexible and continuing process, where primacy does not go to the preservation of the familiar and the known, but the quest for the true, the good and the beautiful. Docherty's rhetoric does not serve his argument well, and his aspirations are Utopian, but his enthusiasm is contagious. He has a good ear for the vacuity of establishment rhetoric, and engages in some entertaining balloon pricking. 'The student experience' as currently constituted, organised by template, plays to 'a logic of consumerist conformity' (5), and in practice precludes real student learning, which is that which comes by individual experience and risk-taking. It's as though the university gives the student the brochure for Italy, as a substitute for the experience of travelling and living the difference of Italian life and culture (53).

With May 1968 as his starting point, he argues that the university can no longer be thought of simply as the site for the struggle between ideas, but must provide the ground for a different and refreshing kind of 'impact': 'a form of impact that brings education, the body and politics together in a rather explosive fashion' (10). As his subtitle suggests, he wants to argue for an institution which will restore to society 'a sense of the possibilities of historical change and of personal autonomy […] central to ideas of freedom and justice' (11). Bate's Coleridgean clerisy has no place here. Instead, Docherty invokes a diverse team of philosophers, writers, and critics to explore what this new space of learning might involve: Martha Nussbaum, John Dewey, Edward Said, Alain Badiou, Giorgio Agamben, Charles Dickens (whose fictive Gradgrind is ubiquitous throughout both books), F.R. Leavis, E.M. Forster, Hegel and Hannah Arendt, Pascal, John Donne, and (never nowadays knowingly omitted from academic lists) Slavoj Žižek. This is, he seems to be showing, how the heritage of accrued knowledge should be used, not to circumscribe thinking, but to provide a plethora of signposts to ways of performing acts of transformation and risk.

Docherty's chapters move across the various sore spots of today's university experience, the familiar lamentations of staff in corridors and common rooms, in a vigorous and lively style. There are many moments which fellow-academics will greet with delighted recognition. Universities experiencing the rapid expansion of the 1960s, Docherty says, like Billy Butlin's post-war holiday camps, turned to quality control under pressure from the market, to create consistency across the patch (58–9). The result has been the homogenisation of 'excellence' (60). The chapter on research, working the motif of 'space', starts with the excitement of blue skies space research in the United States in the 1960s, and the concepts of expansion and new frontiers that characterised Jack Kennedy's vision, together with the visionary ideas of Harold Wilson and Jennie Lee, pushing boundaries, promoting 'the white heat of technology', and launching the paradigm-shifting innovation of the Open University. These are compared to academia's present-day treatment of 'space' as a cost heading. University space nowadays is committed to limits. So-called centres of excellence reduce the number of spaces where research can happen; the auditing of research requires the limitation of thought to conformity with pre-established themes. A furious chapter on leadership in the academy, or rather, the lack of it at all levels, denounces the training patterns imposed on university teachers, the mechanisation of the teaching process, and the special-skills training nowadays offered to potential managerial leaders. Vice-chancellors, Docherty notes, now prefer to see themselves as Chief Executive Officers.

Good leadership encourages dissent, but such leaders have overseen the demise of academic freedom, in every sense, including the ability to criticise government – and one's own institution. Stalinist practices, he argues, have become 'everyday' (112), and he offers an astute discussion of how these practices work, encouraging pre-emptive acts of conformity and self-censorship, and the internalisation of dominant values (or codes, or protocols). The chapter on assessment unpicks the difficulties and value judgements involved in different kinds of assessment processes, and exposes the politics of all forms of assessment. Currently, he asserts, the preferred templates reward the student for collecting and repeating information, not for the exercise of critical judgement. The last chapter, on Finance, challenges the current funding model not simply for allegiance to business models, but to ones that are outdated: models of the production line that are no longer relevant, and are aimed at producing a kind of nineteenth-century conformity. No-one concerned with university finance, he says, understands how the University actually operates in society. The Browne Review on student fees was argued entirely in terms of what individual graduates gain from their education, with no sense of the wider contribution the whole system brings to public goods. The Vice-Chancellor of Birmingham University, a key contributor to the Browne Review, is attacked for his deployment of a rhetoric of student choice, which takes no note of the rigged market in education created by high fees, or the consequences of inadequate funding at all levels of the whole educational system.

The argument builds to a crescendo, and the discussion stops. There is not much breath left for a solution, but Docherty provides one in his Afterword. It is worthy, but flat. Higher education should be funded by a progressive tax system, which should be used to fund a range of different types of institution (academic, and also craft, vocational, technical, and so on). The Scottish degree model is the one to adopt, where a period of common generalised education, allowing students to take risks and work through various lines of curiosity, is followed by a period of specialisation. To make all this work, we need to revive a sense of politics, and especially to create political discourse round the question of the value of the University. Whether Docherty has managed to create such a discourse is a moot point, and whether all his assertions can be sustained is open to question. He has certainly formulated key issues, with energy. Whether energy and discourse are enough by themselves to revive a politics, and a polis, gone moribund, is even more moot.

We are living now in the aftermath of the situation identified by Raymond Williams at the end of 'Education and British Society':

> It is a question of whether we can grasp the real nature of our society, or whether we persist in social and educational patterns based on a limited ruling class, a middle professional class, a large operative class, cemented by forces that cannot be challenged and will not be changed. The privileges and barriers, of an inherited kind, will in any case go down. It is only a question of whether we replace them by the free play of the market, or by a public education designed to express and create the values of an educated democracy and a common culture. (176)

The barriers have gone down, and up again, the education market, where values may fall as well as rise, plays freely, but with the help of state subsidies, and key words remain undefined ('values', 'educated', 'democracy', 'common culture'), though hardly unassailed. Against the idea of education as 'a fixed abstraction', Williams in *The Long Revolution* insisted on the dynamic, continuous nature of that struggle for values – not acquiescence in a fixed abstraction but an active grasping which can never let go or give up. Bate's collection and Docherty's polemic, between them, show some of the gains and losses made in that contestation – and underline, too, the growing complexity of the question that Williams, in a more hopeful but equally embattled time, could still pose as a simple binary.

University of Birmingham

Reviews

Raymond Williams, *The Long Revolution*. Foreword by Anthony Barnett. Cardigan: Parthian, 2011. xxiv + 422 pp. £10.99 pb. ISBN 978-1-908069-71-9.

'The key to any description is its starting-point: the particular experience that is seized as determining.' For anyone reading or rereading Raymond Williams, it is striking how the complex simplicity of this and other such formulations still retain an unsurpassed capacity for provoking the engaged thinking we all need to defend. Readers of *Key Words* are all likely to welcome the decision by the Welsh publishing house Parthian to reissue *The Long Revolution* to coincide with the fiftieth anniversary of the book's original publication in 1961, and to renew access to Williams's highly specific mode of argument and address. In this edition, Williams's seminal work (from which the quoted sentence above is taken) is supplemented with a fascinating Foreword by Anthony Barnett, a former 'backroom boy with the New Left Review' (xx), and someone for whom reading Williams's later book, *Modern Tragedy*, was he says a life-changing experience (xxi).

Barnett's approach to Williams is rooted in and grows out of the rich soil of his own experience of Britain's New Left politics, and particularly the internal politicking of the influential journal *New Left Review*, where he acted on the editorial board for a number of years. His opening question, 'After half a century, why should we still read *The Long Revolution*?' (vii), is one well worth considering, and perhaps especially so by readers of this journal.

His own immediate answer is that since 'we live in revolutionary times' – a period inevitably recalling the outbreak of revolutions across Europe in 1848, but now encompassing Africa and the Middle East as well as the growing resistance of the anti-capitalism of the Occupy Wall Street protesters – Williams's careful probing of the idea of revolution remains a critical and necessary resource for contemporary thinking and activism. *The Long Revolution* is best read today, in part at least, as a reminder of the need to resist 'naïve hopes of fast, real change', argues Barnett (vii), and to accept the set of challenges posed by any attempt to create a viable and ongoing participatory democracy, and the necessary transformation of passive subjects into active, engaged citizens.

The Foreword usefully places *The Long Revolution* in the wider context of Williams's work, not only as part of the second trilogy which also includes *Culture and Society* and *Communications*, but also indicating how it looks ahead to the now often neglected *Modern Tragedy* (1965), and the later study, *Towards 2000* (1983). In so doing, he casts useful light on Williams's relations with the British Left, and, in particular, on the complex relations with Britain's premier leftist intellectual journal, Perry Anderson's *New Left Review*.

For Williams *aficionados*, and for historians of Marxist theory, the Foreword is most interesting in the light it casts on the deeply ambivalent reaction to Williams's work in *New Left Review* circles. On the one hand, the journal did much to acknowledge and promote Williams's work, regularly publishing (and now reissuing) his essays and interventions and, in its related publishing arm, Verso books, making available important studies and collections such as *Problems in Materialism and Culture* (1980) and *The Politics of Modernism: Against the New Conformists* (1989). On the other, it published the single most scathing attack on it: Terry Eagleton's 1976 essay, 'Criticism and Politics: The Work of Raymond Williams'.

'Were I to read something like this now', writes Barnett, 'I'd laugh and chuck it in the bin' (xxi). At the time, he responded to what he now describes as Eagleton's 'vacuous Trotskyite posturing' (xxii) by reading more of Williams (including the life-changing *Modern Tragedy*), and writing 'a massive response' to him. This was rejected by the editorial board (though they did publish a shorter version of this later that year), but, recognizing that something more was necessary 'to integrate Williams back as a contributor', the idea of a 'book of interviews' was conceived (xxii), and this became the celebrated volume, *Politics and Letters: Interviews with New Left Review*, published in 1979.

This may still serve as perhaps the single best introduction to Williams's work as a whole, but is also important as a classic staging of the complexities of the Marxist 'base and superstructure' theory that Williams worried at throughout his life. Indeed, *The Long Revolution* itself, with its central claim that 'the isolation of economics as the key to change has led [...] to simplification and abstraction' (146), constantly though only ever implicitly addresses that central question and problematic. And, not surprisingly, the *Politics and Letters* interviews single out *The Long Revolution*, with its critique of any too simple an idea of the economic determination of culture and society, for the most sustained questioning and interrogation. Just how bitter and ambivalent a process this was, though barely breaking the surface of the polite and scholarly exchanges that constitute the volume, is evident in how it left Williams (so he later recorded in letters to two of the interviewers, Anderson and Mulhern), in 'a condition of almost overwhelming anxiety' and, very uncharacteristically, with a feeling that 'the only really productive thing I can now do is garden' (cited in Fred Inglis's *Raymond Williams* (1995), 261).

Nonetheless, Barnett for one took strength from Williams's arguments, and came to realise just how much he had been 'in thrall to the *Review* and Anderson'. Reading Williams (and particularly *Modern Tragedy*, as we noted above) enabled him (and undoubtedly many others both at the time and since) to 'break free from that subservience' (xxii). Looking back, the most striking feature of the book, and indeed of Williams's work as a whole, is now, argues Barnett, its assertion of a humanism which was 'not a liberal or individual humanism', but rather one in which 'the liberty of others is essential to our own' (x).

With this emphasis and qualification, Williams's humanism sets itself against both traditional liberal theory, and the willed subjection to the dictates of the Party characteristic of Stalinist Communism. And it is this more complex humanism that, argues Barnett, makes *The Long Revolution* such necessary reading today. Only such a complex humanism can serve as the basis for successful resistance to what Williams later labelled, in *Towards 2000* (1983), the 'Plan X' we now recognize more familiarly as neo-liberalism, understood here as 'the emerging rationality of self-conscious elites' (Williams 1983: 247) which in seeking to calculate 'relative advantage, in what is accepted from the beginning as an unending and unavoidable struggle' (245) necessarily works to implant 'a deep assent to capitalism even in a period of its most evident economic failures' (245). *The Long Revolution* is, above all, perhaps best read as a part of the necessarily ongoing attempt to resist all forms of that assent.

In the fact of this resistance (and as I suggest in more detail in an essay in this issue of the journal), I find that the strongest and most connecting points for us in rereading *The Long Revolution* are to be found in the deep connections the book posits between education and democracy. For Williams, the long revolution was above all the 'cultural revolution', 'the most difficult of all to interpret', and best understood as 'the aspiration to extend the active process of learning, with the skills of literacy and other advanced communication, to all people rather than limited groups'. This extension, he asserted, was 'comparable in importance to the growth of democracy and the rise of scientific industry' (11). Calling to mind such assertions is all the more necessary at a moment when the purposes of higher education, which is tasked with a significant role in the reproduction of the social totality as a whole, are, in practice, being restricted to the furtherance of the STEM disciplines, and the forgetting or sidelining of the conflictual social order in which they are embedded. Against the grain of most social thinking at the time, *The Long Revolution* suggested there were no grounds for complacency in the increasingly prosperous period of the late 1950s. There are, alas, all the more reasons to attend to its arguments and formulations in today's more visibly desperate and disturbed world.

John Higgins
University of Cape Town

Raymond Williams, *The Country and the City*. Foreword by Stan Smith. Nottingham: Spokesman, 2011. xvi + 336 pp. £19.95 pb. ISBN 978-0-85124-799-1.

This new edition of Raymond Williams's major historical work, *The Country and the City*, is timely. The book will startle many new readers by its apparent relevance to today's struggles. Dedicated to the 'country workers who were my grandparents', Williams's book stakes his personal claim, and makes the inflection of the work, together with his commitment, plain on the first page. This is a wholeheartedly political work in which, as Stan Smith observes in his new introduction, 'Williams insists on the actively political nature of the act of perception'. Published in 1973, *The Country and the City* immediately joined the radical canon of the time, alongside E.P. Thompson's *The Making of the English Working Class* (first published in 1963, and again in a revised edition in 1968), and John Berger's book on the visual arts, *Ways of Seeing* (1972). These works popularised a way of looking at history in which the experience of everyday life, and the position and circumstance of the observer, were central to what was seen. Whether it was the hauteur of models in high-end fashion magazines, or a family painted by Gainsborough looking out over the head of the viewer from the well-planted grounds of their country house, we are invited to see evidence of the class relations they contain; we are urged to see a lively connection between the way things are now, and the way they have come about, through an historical process which was both contrived and contested. Thompson, Berger and Williams wanted to unsettle their readers with a new historical synthesis. We are invited to see what is hidden within older, more authoritative accounts of the past. We are invited to see, perhaps for the first time, that labouring men and women made their own world, made their own institutions, and had their own perceptions, despite their manifest absence from the work of Jane Austen or of most historical writing.

In the forty-odd years since *The Country and the City* first appeared it might seem that the battle had been won, but after an hour with the amusing deceptions of *Downton Abbey*, or a visit to a stately home, in which the well-preserved kitchens, or even the servants' quarters, have been opened to the public, we can see how well a resolutely conventional way of seeing can incorporate what were once radical insights into a new bourgeois historical synthesis, in which the essential passivity of the great majority of men and women is restored and reasserted.

It is here that the continuing relevance of *The Country and the City* comes to the fore. In ways that it is hard to dismiss or incorporate, Williams has written a difficult book in which the emergence of capitalism is traced through criticism of literary works. He maintains a strict counterpoint throughout the book, not simply between town and country, but between the pastoral and the counter-pastoral, between improvement and ruin, between plenty and exploitation, between knowable and unknowable communities, between bucolic charm and a five per cent return on investment in sugar from the Indies, or wheat ploughed, planted, and harvested in Dorset. Throughout, we are brought face to face with literary work, with 'views' and 'prospects', that efface the labour that actively produces the world, or which incorporate it only to marginalise the continuous creativity and effort of labouring people. Williams then insists upon presenting us with the challenge of William Cobbett, John Clare or Thomas Hardy, who demand a different kind of attention from us. Williams has produced a history in which lacunae are revealed, looked at anew, and a too easy acceptance of the received wisdom that creativity is the product of a rarefied elite is angrily confronted with a radically different reading.

It is a reading that, after forty years, retains its sharpness. 'What oil companies do, what the mining companies do, is what landlords did, what plantation owners did and do', and continue to haunt us. Williams reminds us that 'many have gone along with them, seeing the land and its people and its properties as available for profitable exploitation: so clear a profit that the quite different needs of local settlement and community are overridden, often ruthlessly' (293). He could be writing about the Niger Delta and the depredations of big oil; or about the struggle of India's Dalits and tribal peoples against the dams and water-management schemes envisaged by the powers-that-be in the Narmada Valley Development Plan, which will despoil the lands, drown the villages, and destroy the way of life of the country people who live there. The contemporary relevance of *The Country and the City*'s angry criticism is apparent throughout, whether Williams is writing about the 'Morality of Improvement' or the novelty of George Eliot's efforts to wrest multiple voices from different social strata in the flow and flux of capitalist development. This is of a piece with the complexity of Williams's reading. Even as he discusses colonial domination, he attempts to grasp, as he did in his own fiction, the often subtle and surreptitious ways that communities are penetrated by pressures which will ultimately unravel a cherished way of life. When discussing Chinua Achebe he says:

> What is impressive about *Things Fall Apart* is that as in some English literature of rural change, as late as Hardy, the internal tensions of the society are made clear, so that we can understand the modes of penetration which would in any case, in its process of expansion, have come. [...] The alien law and religion are bitterly resented and resisted, but the trading-station, in palm-oil, is welcomed, as an addition to the slash-and-burn subsistence farming of yams. (286)

It is a 'very complicated process' in which 'external invasion' provokes 'internal contradictions' that in turn destroy the strongest personalities and institutions of the old society.

In this way Williams makes clear the difficulties inherent in artistic representation of a whole way of life in which the growth of trade and cities, of industrialisation, and development of all sorts, put the apparently 'knowable' rural community of the country, of the village, and of the small country town, more or less beyond the reach of artistic representation. Indeed Alan O'Connor has noted a kind of irony in Williams's deployment of the idea of 'knowability', because what was always being shown in his criticism (and in his own fiction) was how much of society, and even the individuals of which it is composed, are in fact, radically 'unknowable'.[1] However, Williams did detect an attenuation of social consciousness in literary modernism, which he associated with the growing density of urban life: 'The historically variable problem of "the individual and society" acquires a sharp and particular definition, in that

---

1 Alan O'Connor, *Raymond Williams: Writing, Culture, Politics* (London: Blackwell, 1989), 69.

"society" becomes an abstraction, and the collective flows only through the most inward channels' (246). In *The Country and the City* it sometimes seems that Williams regarded the country, and the life lived there, as in some sense more authentic, more genuinely collective, than the discordant ruptures produced by the urban: 'Out of the cities, in fact, came these two great and transforming modern ideas: myth, in its variable forms; revolution, in its variable forms. Each, under pressure, offers to convert the other to its own terms. But they are better seen as alternative responses, for in a thousand cities, if in confused forms, they are in sharp, direct and necessary conflict' (247).

The conflict alluded to here is that which Williams imagined existed between the internalisation of collective consciousness, as a kind of subjective or psychological myth, and the feeling within modernist work that 'actual' social collectivities are abstract, superficial, or ephemeral. He identifies this conflict in the work of James Joyce and other modernists, and it is an observation that reveals his belief in what he called 'historical realities' or 'real history' and, as a matter of course, in a whole way of rural life, destroyed by the capitalist class, figured in this regard, as a 'pitiless crew'. Williams is aware of the difficulty here. He is the scourge of idealised notions of an idealised past – he knows and acknowledges that ownership and control of land and equipment are decisive factors – but he is unable to recognise the progressive character of capitalism. This point of view put him at some distance from the work of E.P. Thompson and other Marxists who were always prepared to accept the progressive character of capitalism as merely the latest (perhaps, the last) and most effective form of class rule. In contrast Williams always regarded with suspicion the idea that capitalism was in any sense 'progressive'. Consequently, in *The Country and the City* he describes enclosure and agricultural innovation in terms similar to those of William Cobbett, in flagrant disregard of the growth in population and of rural employment that such developments promoted; it meant largely ignoring the way in which changes in animal husbandry, land use, and productivity rendered the fears of Thomas Malthus entirely redundant.

Williams's moral outrage at the misery of the agricultural labourer as commons were enclosed, cottages pulled down, wastes drained, and woodlands fenced, is as visceral as his hatred of the 'stately home' and its occupants. In *The Country and the City* this animus leads him to a reflection on the manner in which the Marxist tradition, in opposing 'rural idiocy' and positing the dissolution of the boundaries between town and country, became complicit in the oppression of the rural poor to such a degree that he detected a connection between Leon Trotsky's *Platform of the Left Opposition* of 1927,[2] and Stalin's brutal 'victory'

2   See 'Chapter 3: The Agrarian Question and Socialist Construction', in Leon Trotsky, *The Platform of the Joint Opposition* (1927), at: http://www.marxists.org/archive/trotsky/1927/opposition/ch03.htm.

over the peasants in the forced collectivisation of agriculture a few years later (302–3). Williams wanted to give prominence to an alternative emphasis in the outlook of Marx and Engels in which socialism is conceived as abolishing the contrast between town and country, which they thought had been brought to its most extreme expression by capitalist development.

In the early 1970s these commitments led Williams to welcome the peculiarly radical aspects of the Chinese Revolution, in which rural life and the peasantry were brought back to the centre of things. He welcomed the way in which, in 'the famous Chinese phrase about world revolution, the "countryside" was surrounding the "cities". Thus the "rural idiots" and the "barbarians and semi-barbarians" have been, for the last forty years, the main revolutionary force in the world' (304). It is unlikely that Williams knew very much about the Great Famine that killed in excess of thirty million peasants during the Great Leap Forward, or that he knew very much about China at all, yet he could welcome the restoration of '"the intimate connection between industrial and agricultural production"' (304) which he quotes Marx and Engels calling for, as akin to the outlook of utopian socialists and of William Morris. Williams endorsed the reassertion of the intimacy between industry and agriculture with reference to Mao Zedong's thought: 'The utopian socialists had made many proposals for new kinds of balanced communities and societies'; their 'phrases were remembered, but as an old, impractical, childish dream. Yet it is an emphasis that is now being revived. It has been stated as a direction of policy in the Chinese Revolution. And it has been significantly revived, among Western revolutionary socialists, as a response to the crisis of industrial civilisation and what is seen as megalopolis' (304).

Things turned out differently of course. The emancipation of the Chinese peasantry from communes and collectivisation following the death of Mao and the defeat of the Gang of Four resulted in spectacular increases in agricultural yields and household incomes, which in turn initiated, and have funded, thirty-odd years of rapid city building and industrialisation. Indeed, this is the sort of development that has resulted in the extraordinary fact that just over half of the world's seven billion people now live in cities.

Raymond Williams's teaching sometimes took him into thoroughly urban settings. He also lived for some years in the small town of Hastings, but the only city he ever lived in was Cambridge, which is a 'city' by ecclesiastical rather than by any social, demographic, or economic criterion. Williams always chose to live in or near the countryside. His view of the 'border country' in which he grew up, his father's occupation as a railwayman, and his own life as a teacher and writer, led him to understand that he lived inescapably within the matrix of urban relationships produced by capitalist development, but he was uneasy and conflicted about it. He liked to view himself as a countryman, and he viewed the bourgeois society in which he lived in largely negative terms. It is never clear what 'community' means; it is, rather like 'real history', elusive and radically untheorised. Consequently, although *The Country and the City* is a work saturated with these personal tensions between the individual and society, between town and country, and between the life of a professional intellectual and the working class, Williams comes down on the side of the essentially rural community, which he regards as intrinsically antipathetic to capitalism, and to the despoliation of the environment. Many new readers, I am sure, will welcome this 'structure of feeling', and learn a great deal from the critical interplay between literature and social change. However, Williams's history must be treated with caution; his sophisticated qualifications, and the often labyrinthine conditionality of his clauses, not to mention his ellipses, will favour only the most vigilant readers.

Don Milligan
Studies in Anti-Capitalism

Raymond Williams, *The Volunteers*. Cardigan: Parthian, Library of Wales, 2011. 240 pp. £8.99 pb. ISBN 978–1–90699–826–4.

In general, with the possible exception of *Border Country*, which was published in a fairly generous print-run by Penguin in its first paperback edition in 1964, the seven novels which make up Raymond Williams's fictional writing have not been all that readily available throughout the twenty-four years since his death. Mostly out of print – again the exception would be *Border Country*, which was republished by Parthian in 2006, and is one of their 'best-sellers' – only rarely are his novels to be found in second-hand bookshops, no doubt reflecting their somewhat limited original print-runs.

This new edition of Williams's political thriller, *The Volunteers*, published by Parthian Books in its Library of Wales series, is therefore particularly welcome and will, one hopes, help to introduce a new generation of readers to Williams's fiction, though to do that effectively may now require the novel to be available electronically, for the increasing numbers of people using 'Kindles' or other electronic means of reading.

The Volunteers was originally published in 1978, before the final volume of what has become known as Williams's Welsh trilogy, and was therefore his third published novel. In subject matter it may seem at first far away from both *Border Country* and *Second Generation*, set as it is in a future almost a decade ahead of the time at which it was written, and following the pursuit of would-be ministerial assassins by radical journalist – 'consultant analyst' – Lewis Redfern, for his global media corporation employer.

However, the geographical centre of much of the action of the novel is South Wales – running back in time from the apparent attempted assassination of a government minister at St Fagans National History Museum near Cardiff to the occupation – and shooting dead of a worker – at a coal yard in one of the Welsh mining valleys, and then forward, along the track of Redfern's pursuit of the truth about the assassination attempt, to, finally, the official inquiry into the shooting, at which Redfern comes to play a central role. Though much of the other action – Redfern's investigative journalism – takes place in London, several of the central characters – Redfern himself, the political radical turned career politician turned community trust executive Mark Evans, and his librarian son David – all have strong Welsh connections, though we only learn of Redfern's towards the end of the novel.

The pace of the novel is certainly something to appeal to a new generation of readers, as is the apparent 'cool' of Redfern, the first-person narrator, though Williams himself was surprised, according to the discussion of the novel in *Politics and Letters*, that it should have been described, as it was by its original publishers Eyre Methuen, as a 'political thriller'.

It is that, but it is also, as one would expect from a writer of Williams's range and perception, a considered exploration of some of the underlying political realities of what was then and is now contemporary Britain, and the ways in which it is or is not possible to oppose and challenge the established order. Redfern has chosen a solitary and ultimately compromised path; the established political figure Mark Evans another, potentially more influential strategy which is about to be publicly exposed as the novel ends; his son David a species of terrorism; and the loaders in the coal yard a more traditional form of class struggle. In the end, Redfern, who is increasingly confronted by the isolation and inadequacy of his own position, returns to something approaching solidarity with the loaders and, it transpires, his own more distant roots, but it is unclear quite where this leaves him. As so often in Williams's fiction, there are no final answers and the reader is encouraged to take the analysis forward for him- or herself.

Ian Gasse

Jeff Wallace, ***Beginning Modernism.*** Manchester: Manchester University Press, 2011. xii + 314 pp. 20 illustrations. £9.99 pb. ISBN 978-0-7190-6789-1.

What does a student need to 'begin' modernism? According to Jeff Wallace's substantial book, a lot of information, but also the opportunity to practise readings and responses to a number of texts, verbal and visual, in the intermittent exercises where the author dialogues with the beginner and encourages active participation. Like other guides this is both information pack and 'how to' manual, and the two functions not unexpectedly jar with each other at times. The regular injunction, in sub-headed sections called 'STOP and THINK', might imply that thinking can be suspended elsewhere in the book, where the reader's implied function might appear to be the transcription of the copious lists of names and dates of writers, artists, and movements from Europe and beyond with which the book is packed.

The range of knowledge on show is certainly impressive. There is a deft initial overview of recent scholarly debates about modernism, and some excellent summaries of the paradoxes and antitheses that lie at the heart of it. Rational/irrational, progressive/reactionary, elitist/popular, 'the often contradictory relationship between modernity and modernism' (20), these contribute to the ethos of 'creative destruction' which can also be seen as 'the replacement of an "either/or" with a "both/and" epistemology in modernism' (126). The beginner will certainly understand from this book that modernism is not easy, and further that it involves acquainting oneself with art, architecture, sculpture, music, film, dance, literature and so on. The book's appropriate emphasis on the internationalism and multidisciplinary nature of the phenomenon raises again the question of what is the best type of guidance through such a complex field. In chapter 4, 'Modernist Ideas', Wallace gives excellent potted summaries of key thinkers such as Marx, Darwin, Nietzsche, Freud, Einstein, Saussure, Bergson and several others, though elsewhere the summarising is less happy and arguably somewhat redundant. For example, in chapter 6, on 'Modernist Poetry', it is not really clear what use the one paragraph on Yeats – including the assertion that his later poetry 'combined a delicate beauty with a compressed density of meaning' (197) – really serves, nor the paragraph on Pound's *Cantos*. Here the book becomes something of a gazetteer, concerned to say a bit about everything, making one wonder whether the reader would be better served by a more focused case-studies approach.

This chapter, along with the following chapter on 'Modernist Fiction', is a little perfunctory, with meagre references to outdated secondary criticism and with a few moments of inattention, such as the dating of the *Pisan Cantos* to 1925-62, or the declaration that *Four Quartets* was 'largely written among the ruins of a blitzed London during the Second World War' (210). More telling is a sense that the overall architecture of the book gets a bit lost. For example, the discussion of Imagism (198–203), tends to be sealed off from the visual arts context Wallace has worked so assiduously to provide thus far, so that there's no follow-up to the movement's own declared affiliation with sculpture. There is a sense that Wallace's heart isn't altogether in these chapters, and that he's much happier on the terrain of European art, architecture, performance and 'modernist spaces', together with the theorising that informs these. Thus he

Reviews

has a whole ten pages discussing Rosalind Krauss's observations on modern sculpture, which is arguably self-indulgent given his glancing treatment of subjects elsewhere.

'Modernism and the Visual Arts' are certainly for Wallace the portal into the subject, as the weighty second chapter – the longest in the book – indicates. The detailed survey becomes a conventional art history at times, with the reader-orientation promised at the outset of the book – the aim to 'carefully "talk" you into, and through, certain issues in modernism' (2) – not always maintained. The 'emphasis on the close reading of texts' (2) does come back in the 'STOP and THINK' exercise on a Jackson Pollack painting (54–5), but whether the student can really think about any visual 're-enchantment' the painting might offer, on the basis of the small black-and-white reproduction included here, is a question that seems not to occur to the author. As well as 'thinking' I wish there had been more emphasis on the student doing some reading, looking and visiting galleries and buildings where some of the original art is on offer. At times the beginner is directed to other introductory guides on modernism rather than to the primary texts, as if mastering the subject is all about steeping oneself in secondary discourse: a dangerous message to students I believe. Thus the 'STOP and THINK' section on Strindberg's *A Dream Play* asks the student to consider several questions based on Wallace's paraphrase of the play. Nowhere is there a reminder that all this won't be of much use unless students first read the play itself. The section on music (273ff) announces itself as 'the most interactive of the book', in that it 'asks you first to seek out and listen to some examples of modernist composition'. Why the beginner isn't instructed to first seek out examples of textual and visual composition is something of a mystery.

In summary, this book is nicely produced, industriously assembled, earnest and sincere in its pedagogical intent. Apart from a lack of attention to late modernism (the one reference to Auden as a 'later British modernist poet' (198) begs the question about what happens to some aspects of modernism in the 1930s), the historical and theoretical contexts are meticulously provided. I don't think, however, Wallace fully carries his project through. The grasp on the 'you', the beginner, is uncertain and submerged at times, and I'm not sure some readers won't founder on what might seem a mass of disheartening and on occasion indigestible material. The alternative, of course, would have been to aim at a less saturated coverage and spend more time on fewer case studies that could open out to the wider issues. But only the beginner can really assess how helpful this book is, or which might be the better method of approaching the extremely challenging task of introducing modernism. Of Wallace's professional competence, his impressive range of knowledge and interests, there can be no doubt. Even this, though, raises the question of how far the academic proprietorship of modernism isn't itself a somewhat disheartening spectacle, a question Lionel Trilling once famously raised and which Wallace's self-awareness doesn't extend to. One of the things this book made me think is that we need recurrent reminders that Eliot didn't write *The Waste Land* for students to sit exams on, though the endless succession and mutually acknowledging circulation of student guides might suggest otherwise.

Steve Ellis
University of Birmingham

Deaglán Ó Donghaile, *Blasted Literature: Victorian Political Fiction and the Shock of Modernism*. Edinburgh: Edinburgh University Press, 2011. xii + 260 pp. £65.00 hb. ISBN 978-0-7486-4067-6.

It is 1891, and a city street explodes. The newspaper headlines read: 'Anarchists Bomb Strasbourg' and 'Tensions Sweep Across Europe'. This is fiction, however, from the opening of Guy Ritchie's 2011 film *Sherlock Holmes: A Game of Shadows*, itself sufficient evidence of the continuing narrative impulse offered by the politically-motivated bomb outrages of the 1880s, 1890s and 1900s. Deaglán Ó Donghaile's subject is the fictions written in immediate response to the reporting of anarchist and Fenian violence in these years. James's *The Princess Casamassima* (1886) and Conrad's *The Secret Agent* (1907) are the most prominent examples of the response to such events as the assassination of Alexander II of Russia in 1881, the Phoenix Park murders in Dublin in 1882, the Chicago Haymarket affair of 1886, the bombing of the Liceo Theatre in Barcelona in 1894, and the Greenwich Observatory bomb of the same year, the 'relatively undistinguished event' (98) that so interested Conrad.

The achievement of Ó Donghaile's discussion is to retrieve a body of fiction known as 'the dynamite novel', of which the Stevensons' *The Dynamiter* (1885) is an early example. This is 'a uniquely "lowbrow" piece' (28), and there were many others, notably John Coulson Kernahan's *Captain Shannon* (1897), 'a chaotic and unstructured novel' (67), and Richard Henry Savage's *The Anarchist* (1894), which – though politically conservative, as all these works are – does notice that capitalism in the United States is 'ungrounded, unstable and unanswerable to any centralised authority' (100). Also recovered is a remarkable quantity of contemporaneous journalism about Fenian and anarchist violence, whether from *The Times* or, more usefully, from *The Irish World and American Industrial Liberator*, *The Alarm*, *Freedom* (all from the USA), or *The Torch*, *The Anarchist* and *Freedom: A Journal of Anarchist Communism* (all London). This performs a real service for researchers.

The conservative texts that Ó Donghaile necessarily confronts do not offer ready opportunities for a critique from the left. That a W.H. Smith bookstall should survive a bomb concealed within popular library books hardly justifies the invocation of Raymond Williams on mass literacy and democracy (69). The author's unrelenting emphasis on Fenian violence, in act and word, leaves the impression that Irish republicanism had no other rationale than unmotivated aggression; this is precisely the position taken by most of the fiction under discussion. Nevertheless, he is acute on the ways in which writers and publishers rapidly converted extreme experience into a commodified object, the 'dynamite novel'.

A final chapter, 'Shock Modernism', is argued differently. Ó Donghaile recognises that Wyndham Lewis's *Blast* magazine (1914–15), promoting the art movement Vorticism, was written from an anarchist perspective; but he is unable to develop this. It is correct that Lewis was influenced by the French anarchist philosopher Pierre-Joseph Proudhon (here, 'Joseph Pierre': there are numerous such errors), but that occurred in the 1920s. Alex Houen's *Terrorism and Modern Literature* (2002) is invoked to argue that the culture of *Blast* resembled French syndicalist strike action, an implausible argument that one regrets finding repeated here. Ó Donghaile's most astonishing assertion is that 'Vorticism […] is marked by its tendency to commodify terrorism as a form of aesthetic practice' (185). This derives from a wider argument, the idea that to distribute an anarchist pamphlet could be an act of terrorism.

That argument emerges in the discussion of *The Torch* (1891–97), a periodical edited by Helen and Olivia Rossetti, aged thirteen and sixteen respectively when publication began. They rapidly became radicalized towards anarchist violence. Ó Donghaile writes: 'Copying the methods of Christian pamphleteers, distributors left copies in public places such as railway carriages, waiting rooms, tramcars and cafés, a practice that, given some of its more shocking content, amounted to a form of literary terrorism' (146). No evidence is given that anyone actually felt terrorised by these texts; nor indeed what it might mean to be terrorized by a text.

I was myself bombed by the Front pour la Libération du Québec while teaching an evening class in Montréal in 1969. We were discussing *As You Like It* when the end of the building was blown off, the lights went out and smoke entered the room as my students helped me find my coat and get out. I have never thought of that experience as 'terrorism', but rather as politics, and I find the discussion of the term here and in Houen's book both unreal and overstated. This difficulty with the word derives from the author's decision, announced in the Introduction, that since the term 'terrorism' is 'notoriously pejorative', he will 'not enter the definitional debates that surround it, other than to draw attention to its historical usage' (19). For Ó Donghaile to apply the term to *The Torch* and to *Blast* is itself a contemporary intervention, and consistently pejorative. Repeatedly, the author argues from actual political violence to textual violence, or 'shock', a term egregiously over-used as a substitute for theorization: 'Vorticist avant-gardism promised to reproduce the sensational impact of political violence by offering itself as a form of textual shock' (192). Ó Donghaile tries to align Wyndham Lewis's *Blast* with an advertising scam from 1894, when two men from Tamworth sent hoax bombs (detonators only) through the post in an attempt to win a £250 prize offered by the popular weekly *Answers*. *Blast* was 'an aggressive, modernist version of the explosive advertising strategy' (185) used by the Tamworth bombers. After correctly identifying the political tendency of *Blast* and Vorticism, Ó Donghaile's argument becomes eccentric. This final chapter undermines what is valuable in the earlier ones.

Alan Munton
Exeter University

John Nolan and Carroll Ann Friedmann (eds), *The Person I Am: The Literary Memoirs of Laura (Riding) Jackson*. Nottingham: Trent Editions, 2011. 2 vols, 372 pp. & 354 pp. £15 each, pb. Laura (Riding) Jackson Series: General Editor, Mark Jacobs. ISBN 978-1-84233-1439 and 978-1-84233-1446.

Literary memoirs can be of interest to readers for many reasons. They may offer new insights into the conditions under which important literary works were conceived or created; they may generate a new and richer historical understanding of the time and the contexts of that literary creativity; or they may respond to a rather baser fascination with literary gossip. These two volumes of memoirs by Laura (Riding) Jackson offer something, but perhaps not quite enough, of each of these reading pleasures.

Laura (Riding) Jackson is an intriguing and important figure for a number of reasons. She was a prominent poet in the 1920s, closely associated with the Fugitives, and frequently published in *The Fugitive* magazine. She moved from the USA to England in 1925, and formed a close relationship with Robert Graves, subsequently living with him in Majorca, where they welcomed many writers and intellectuals to their home, until 1936. She co-authored with Graves the very influential *A Survey of Modernist Poetry*, which was published in 1927. Riding continued to publish poetry throughout the 1930s, but in the early 1940s she completely and emphatically renounced poetry as a cultural form, declaring the 'impossibility of poetry fulfilling in any degree of humanly livable practicality the human need and hope of a speech – a verbal expression-mode – of self-sustaining truth' (I: 228). Thereafter, she dedicated herself, in close collaboration with her second husband, to a major project on the relations between language and truth under the broad rubric of 'rational meaning'. This major, and never fully completed, intellectual project sought to challenge what she saw as 'the predominating feature of twentieth-century intellectual activity […] the dwindling away, in its general inspiring force, of a naturally restless will to know the knowable utmost, to achieve the totality of the possible in knowledge' (I: 299).

Both (Riding) Jackson's life and her work are thus of considerable interest to scholars and readers of modernist literature. Across the two volumes of these literary memoirs the key issues outlined above are presented and debated at considerable length. The first volume contains material that was arranged for publication by (Riding) Jackson herself, while the second was arranged by the editors and consists of texts that had mostly been previously unpublished. The organization of the two substantial volumes thus inevitably follows slightly different principles, and also involves a degree of repetition as the same literary and philosophical questions are explored across a range of texts. This does pose some challenges for the reader simply in terms of the scale of what is offered, and also makes it at times difficult to discern the significant historical developments of (Riding) Jackson's thinking and writing from the 1920s to the 1980s.

(Riding) Jackson presents her memoirs both as a corrective to the mistaken critical judgments and literary histories of others, and also as an exposition of her own philosophical and literary values. She writes with a significant degree of consciousness that her world-view has not always been readily accepted: 'I have believed in the veridicality of my vision, lived by a faith in its intrinsic strength that contradicted the actualities of failure' (I: 15). This rather admirable, and even generous, recognition that her own deeply held views are not always shared by others does not, however, characterise the memoirs as a whole. She writes at times with a kind of obsessive disdain, and an insistent sense of being wronged and undervalued, that are difficult for the reader to engage with. When she writes, 'to return, for a little, to the subject of myself' (I: 55), one is not necessarily overjoyed.

The most interesting and original parts of these memoirs lie in (Riding) Jackson's attempts to articulate the importance and originality of her engagement with the philosophy of language and the nature of truth: 'the task of exploring the nature of language as the adequate apparatus of truth' (I: 26). This is more consistently present in the first volume, but aspects of her commitment to these issues can be found across both. She defends, repeatedly and often effectively, her view of the ethical and cultural importance of 'a special literary world, viewed as representing to the other world its consciousness of itself' (I: 31). But — and this seems to me to be a significant issue for the reader of these memoirs — she does all this in a prose style that is clotted, repetitive, and frequently hectoring. This is a real disappointment for an enthusiastic reader of Laura Riding's poetry. In contrast to the clarity, economy and beauty of lines such as 'Between the word and the world lie / Fading eternities of soon', from Riding's poem 'Echoes', the prosaic quality of these memoirs seems to offer too little and too much at the same time. When one is confronted with the argument 'That literary activity came to have the force of a negation of literature's function of fidelity to the humanly ascertainable meaning of being is explicable in some part by the collapse of the idea of the human being as ideally represented by a male figure of perfectly generalized human identity' (I: 43), one does rather long for the 'fading eternities of soon'.

It is always encouraging to see work by major literary figures that had previously been unpublished, or difficult to access, brought together in an accessible and affordable format for a contemporary readership, and in this context these volumes are very much to be welcomed. It is, however, disappointing that the editors have provided such a modest scholarly apparatus to accompany the memoirs. The editorial introductions to both volumes are very brief, and the notes provided amount simply to pointing out some of the key sources and references in (Riding) Jackson's texts. It would have enhanced the potential usefulness of the memoirs to have had much fuller annotations, outlining the complexities of the literary and philosophical issues and figures to whom (Riding) Jackson refers, as well as introductions to both volumes which present and analyse in much more detail the historical context of the memoirs. The addition of a more substantial scholarly apparatus would have significantly enhanced the importance and utility of these memoirs for a broad range of scholars and readers of modernist literature. As they stand they may, sadly, be seen as of interest only to the reader who is already a committed reader of Laura (Riding) Jackson's work.

Morag Shiach
Queen Mary University of London

Celia Britton, *The Sense of Community in French Caribbean Fiction*. Liverpool: Liverpool University Press, 2008. vii + 190pp. £16.99 pb. ISBN 978-1-84631-500-8.

Any serious attempt to understand the contemporary Caribbean must at some point engage with the question of community. The nature and scope of government in the Caribbean today, the related crises of governance, dominant themes in civil society, jurisprudence and the wider dynamics of social and political culture which define the region all have at their core a conception of community which is pivotal to their relevance and meaning. Of course, the urgency with which present day Caribbean society prioritises (or distances itself from) the idea of community is inseparable from the histories of colonialism, transplantation, slavery and the wholesale ideologies and practices of fracture which were germane to the creation of society in these territories.

Not surprisingly therefore, one of the abiding concerns of Caribbean fiction has been the quest to explore, understand and celebrate community. If decolonisation has been one of the principal goals of Caribbean fiction, the construction of a (mostly Afro-Caribbean) communal identity has been one of the principal conduits through which it has sought to achieve this goal. In both the Anglophone and Hispanophone Caribbean, fiction, whether canonical or emergent, androcentric or woman-centred, continues to be a site which stages a range of anxieties concerning belonging, collective identity and the struggle to assert and protect it.

Celia Britton's book presents a highly cogent analysis of a corpus of seven novels which are all invested in representing community in the French Caribbean. This is not an easy undertaking. The straightforward title of the book masks the complexity of the subject matter and the deftness with which Britton explicates the multiple levels at which the 'sense of community' is encoded in the fiction she discusses. The fictional works investigated in this book were produced over a fifty year period with the first, Jacque Roumain's *Gouverneurs de la rosée*, appearing in 1946 and the last, Maryse Condé's *Desirada*, being published in 1997. The political conception of community in the French Caribbean evolves significantly over those fifty years. Equally, the writers that Britton studies, all of whom seem to subscribe to the idea of literature as a channel for social action, demonstrate a progression from writing community as unified nation to conceiving of community as more flexible groupings with open-ended definitions. The complexity of the subject matter is further amplified by the fact that the book covers Haiti as well as the Département d'Outre-Mer, thus having to take into account radically different political trajectories and their concomitant histories of self-determination.

Britton is acutely aware of the diversity of themes which are encompassed by the concept of community in French Caribbean literary thought. Indeed, she demonstrates that at times the authors convey divergent or irreconcilable imaginings of the communal. Accordingly, the book does not set out to establish any totalising claims or linear approach to understanding the dynamics of community. Taking her cue from the different models of community proposed by the novels themselves, the author explores in intricate detail the narrative worlds of some of the major canonical works of twentieth-century French Caribbean literature. In the process the book offers fresh perspectives on persistent themes in Caribbean literature such as myth, resistance, leadership, social marginalisation, fragmented family structures and the tribulations of kinship.

The re-reading which Britton undertakes of this group of texts is facilitated by her engagement with the work of French philosopher Jean Luc-Nancy. The book provides a considerable analytical summary of Nancy's theorization of community and Britton uses different aspects of his thoughts on community to illuminate the way the subject is encoded in the Caribbean texts which she reads. Britton's use of Nancy is exemplary. She presents highly dense, complicated philosophical ideas with admirable lucidity. More importantly, rather than imposing the theoretical concepts on fiction she puts both into fruitful conversation with each other and thereby produces illuminating readings of a range of concerns that have been central to French Caribbean thinking since the mid twentieth century.

Britton does not provide English translations for the titles of books nor for the quotes used throughout. Neither does she provide much background information on the authors and texts discussed. It is clear, therefore, that her aim is to address specialists in the field of French Caribbean literature. Nonetheless the book has implications for and will be extremely useful to a far wider audience. The productive liaisons which she establishes between French philosophy and Caribbean literature serve as another reminder of the highly regenerative reading possibilities which inhere in cross-disciplinary approaches to postcolonial (and other) cultural products.

Brilliantly erudite, authoritative yet succinct, this book is also a pleasure to read.

Conrad James
University of Birmingham

Notes on Contributors

Elizabeth Allen is a Senior Lecturer in Cultural Studies at Regent's College, London. Her doctoral thesis, *The Dislocated Mind*, is an analysis of the fiction of Raymond Williams. She lives in Hastings and her current research interest is the cultural regeneration of English seaside towns.

Jennifer Birkett is Professor Emeritus in French Studies at the University of Birmingham. Recent publications include *Margaret Storm Jameson: A Life* (OUP, 2009). She is currently completing a biographical and critical study of Samuel Beckett for Irish Academic Press.

Michael Coyle is Professor of English at Colgate University, and is founding President of the Modernist Studies Association and currently serves as Vice President of the T.S. Eliot Society. In the summer of 2003 he guest-edited a special issue of *Key Words* on *Raymond Williams and Modernism*. More recently he co-edited *Broadcasting Modernism*, with Debra Rae Cohen and Jane Lewty (2009) and with Steve Yao co-edited *Ezra Pound and Education* (National Poetry Foundation 2012).

Debra Rae Cohen is Associate Professor of English at the University of South Carolina. She is the author of *Remapping the Home Front* (2002) and co-editor, with Michael Coyle and Jane Lewty, of the collection *Broadcasting Modernism* (2009). Her current project is *Sonic Citizenship: The BBC, Writing, and the Radio Body Politic*.

Hywel Dix is Lecturer in English and Communication at Bournemouth University. Between 2003 and 2006 he was Raymond Williams Research Fellow at the University of Glamorgan, leading to the publication of *After Raymond Williams: Cultural Materialism and the Break-Up of Britain* (University of Wales Press, 2008). He has published extensively on the relationship between literature, culture and political change in contemporary Britain, most notably in the monograph *Postmodern Fiction and the Break-Up of Britain* (Continuum, 2010). His wider research interests include modern and contemporary literature, postmodernism, critical cultural theory and British writing about Republicanism.

Steve Ellis is Professor of English Literature at the University of Birmingham. His most recent books are *Virginia Woolf and the Victorians* (2007) and *T.S. Eliot: A Guide for the Perplexed* (2009). He is at present writing a book on literature and the outbreak of World War II.

Notes on Contributors

Ian Gasse is a freelance editor and arts administrator. He has spent much of his working life in political and socialist theatre, with spells at Red Ladder Theatre, Solent Peoples Theatre and, most recently, with Birmingham-based Banner Theatre. He has also worked in arts journalism and research, local government and teaching. He has a longstanding interest in early Soviet culture.

John Higgins teaches English at the University of Cape Town. His *Raymond Williams: Literature, Marxism and Cultural Materialism* (1999) won both the Altron National Book Award and the UCT Book Prize, and his *Raymond Williams Reader* appeared in 2001. A founding editor of the journal *Pretexts: Literary and Cultural Studies* (1989–2003), he received in 2000 an *Award of Excellence* from the *Cape Tercentenary Foundation* for services to literature and culture, and was elected to the South African Academy of Science in 2009. His study of Karl Marx will shortly be published in the *Routledge Critical Thinkers* series; his *Academic Freedom in the New South Africa* will appear from Wits University Press.

Chris Hopkins is Professor of English Studies and Head of the Humanities Research Centre at Sheffield Hallam University, where he teaches and researches twentieth-century literature. He has published *English Fiction of the 1930s: Language, Genre and History* (Continuum Books, 2006) and has published widely on interwar writers including Eric Ambler, Katherine Burdekin, Cyril Connolly, Ralph Bates, Winifred Holtby, Storm Jameson, Naomi Mitchison and Sylvia Townsend Warner. He is currently working on a book on Walter Greenwood's *Love on the Dole* (1933).

Conrad James lectures in Hispanic Studies at the University of Birmingham. He has published widely on twentieth-century Caribbean Women's Writing, issues of gender and sexuality in the Spanish Caribbean and in the field of Afro-Cuban literature. An edited collection of essays on the culture of Blacks in the Hispanic world, *Writing the Afro-Hispanic*, appeared in 2012. Work in progress includes a project (with David García Vidal) on *Trans-national Negations: Cuba and Galicia,* and a monograph provisionally entitled *Crossing the Line: Caribbean Migration Narratives of the 1990s.*

Jim McGuigan is Professor of Cultural Analysis at Loughborough University, UK. His latest books are *Cool Capitalism* (2009) and *Cultural Analysis* (2010). He is currently working on an edited collection of Raymond Williams's more social-scientific writings and preparing *Towards 2000* for republication.

Don Milligan is the author of *Raymond Williams: Hope and Defeat in the Struggle for Socialism* (Studies in Anti-Capitalism, at www.studiesinanti-capitalism.net,

Notes on Contributors

2007). He blogs on political and social matters at www.donmilligan.net, and is currently writing a monograph on capitalism and its alternatives, *The Ghost of Communism*, which will be available later in the year at www.studiesinanticapitalism.net. He also works on the defence of Israel and the fate of Palestine.

Simon Machin is completing a PhD about masculine codes of behaviour in British juvenile adventure fiction from 1850 to 1925 under the supervision of Professor Nicki Humble in the Department of English and Creative Writing at Roehampton University.

Alan Munton is an Honorary Research Fellow in the Department of English at Exeter University. He is at present engaged in a research project on satire funded by the University of La Rioja, Logroño, Spain. Scholarly websites are a primary interest: he is involved with four at present. He has published recently on 'Modernist Politics: Socialism, Anarchism, Fascism' in *The Oxford Handbook of Modernisms* (2010), and published a critique of Pat Barker's novel *Life Class* in *London, Modernism, and 1914* (CUP, 2010). He writes on art for the *Journal of Wyndham Lewis Studies*, and is a left-Lewisite.

Joseph Pridmore lectures in English at Heilongjiang International University in Harbin, north-east China. He wrote his PhD on working-class writers of the 1930s and has published in *Critical Survey* and *The European English Messenger*. He is co-editor of the book *Textual Variations* and is currently preparing a monograph on the Irish author Jim Phelan.

Morag Shiach is Professor of Cultural History and Vice-Principal (Humanities and Social Sciences) at Queen Mary University of London. Her research interests are in the cultural history of modernism, and her publications include *The Cambridge Companion to the Modernist Novel* (2007) and *Modernism, Labour and Selfhood in British Literature and Culture, 1890–1930* (2004).

Elinor Taylor is a doctoral candidate in English at the University of Salford. Her research concerns left-wing writing in Britain from 1934 to 1939. She has interests in working-class writing, historical novels and genre fiction.

Roberto del Valle is a Lecturer in English Studies at the Universidad de Alcalá (Spain). He has published journal articles and book chapters on radicalism and cultural dissidence in Britain and the United States, and has recently co-edited a volume on gender politics in the Caribbean, *The Cross-Dressed Caribbean: Writing Transvestisms* (University of Virginia Press, forthcoming).

Raymond Williams Foundation (RWF)

The key aim of RWF is 'to commemorate the works of Raymond Williams, in particular in the sphere of adult education for the benefit of the public'. We do this across wide areas, geographically and in terms of themes, by supporting projects. For example, over the past two years our Trustees have approved grants for: the annual RW residential weekend at Barlaston in May 2011 on *The Spirit Level*, with joint-author Richard Wilkinson as the key-note lecturer; an oral history project in West London; a WEA politics course in Stoke-on-Trent; the RWS Day Conference on *People of the Black Mountains* in Abergavenny; Rural Women's Network for Education in Nepal; Community Centres for Women and Youth, Congo, Africa.

Gaining a grant of £5,000 from the Westham House Trust has enabled the development over the last twelve months of 'reading retreats' to assist individuals and groups gain short residential breaks for 'reading, research, writing and discussion'. A major initiative has grown from this, whereby RWF, with partners, has organized 'budget priced' residential seminars at Wortley Hall, near Sheffield (a cooperative, 'The People's Country Mansion'). These have brought together participants from discussion circles (Dcs) and groups such as Philosophy in Pubs (PiPs); Dcs in North Staffs; Sci-bars in Cheshire, and the WEA and U3A nationally.

Following two small-scale but successful Wortley Hall seminars in the autumn of 2011, the annual RW weekend, which ran at the Wedgwood Memorial College, Barlaston for twenty-three years, had to be relocated in May 2012 and ran mid-week at Wortley Hall. The theme was *The Long and the Short of Revolution*, and was based on Anthony Barnett's lecture at the RWS AGM in Oxford last autumn and his introduction to the new edition of *The Long Revolution*. This gained more residential bookings than ever and small-group discussions engaged with a range of '*Long Revolution* big issues'. Full reports on this, including an Opendemocracy posting, can be read on our website. To build on these strengths we have booked The Adelphi Hotel, Liverpool, for the weekend 23–25 November 2012, in partnership with the RW Society, which will hold its AGM and annual lecture on the Saturday, 24 November.

RWF has recently been much involved in trying to save the Wedgwood Memorial College (WMC) – visit www.savewmc.org. The College closed on 1 April 2012 but the campaign will continue to seek to re-open the College as long as the buildings remain empty (and costing tens of thousands of pounds for security cover alone!).

Derek Tatton
www.raymondwilliamsfoundation.org.uk

Style Notes for Contributors

Presentation of Copy
Key Words is an internationally refereed academic journal. In the first instance typescripts for prospective publication should be submitted as an email attachment to the Contributions Editor Dr Catherine Clay, Nottingham Trent University, at catherine.clay@ntu.ac.uk. Articles should normally be no longer than 6,000 words; reviews should typically be between 1,500 and 2,000 words. Articles should be double spaced, with generous margins, and pages should be numbered consecutively. For matters of style not addressed below, please refer to *The Chicago Manual of Style*, 15th ed. or http://www.chicagomanualofstyle.org/contents.html. Contributors who fail to observe these notes may be asked to revise their submission in accordance with them.

Provision of Text in Electronic Format
Key Words is prepared electronically. Consequently, contributors whose work is accepted for publication will be asked to supply a file copy of their work to the Contributions Editor. The preferred word processing format is Microsoft Word (any version).

References and Bibliographic Conventions
Notes should be kept to a minimum, with all discursive material appearing in the text. Citations in *Key Words* appear as endnotes at the conclusion of each contribution. Essays presented for prospective publication should adopt this style. Endnote markers should be given in arabic numerals and positioned after, not before, punctuation marks, e.g. '.¹' rather than '¹.'. With no bibliography, full details must be given in a note at the first mention of any work cited. Subsequent citations can then use the short form or a cross-reference. Headline-style capitalisation is used. In headline style, the first and last words of title and subtitle and all other major words are capitalised. Titles of books and journals should be formatted in italics (not underlined).

Please cite books in the following manner:

On first citation: Raymond Williams and Michael Orrom, *Preface to Film* (London: Film Drama, 1954).

On subsequent citations: Williams and Orrom, *Preface to Film*, 12.

Please cite journal articles in the following manner:

Patrick Parrinder, 'Politics, Letters and the National Curriculum', *Changing English* 2, no. 1 (1994): 29.

Chapters in books should be referenced in the following way:

Andrew McRae, 'The Peripatetic Muse: Internal Travel and the Cultural Production of Space in Pre-Revolutionary England', in *The Country and the City Revisited: England and the Politics of Culture, 1550–1850*, ed. Gerald MacLean, Donna Landry, and Joseph P. Ward (Cambridge: Cambridge University Press, 1999), 41–57.

For internet articles:

Raymond Williams Society Executive, 'About the Raymond Williams Society', Raymond Williams Society, http://www.raymondwilliams.co.uk/ (accessed 26 March 2012).

Please refer to newspaper articles in the following way:

John Mullan, 'Rebel in a Tweed Suit', *The Observer*, 28 May 2005, Features and Reviews section, 37.

A thesis should be referenced in the following manner:

E. Allen, 'The Dislocated Mind: The Fictions of Raymond Williams' (PhD diss., Liverpool John Moores University, 2007), 22–9.

Conference papers should be cited in the following style:

Dai Smith, 'Translating Raymond Williams' (paper presented at the Raymond Williams's Culture and Society@50 conference, Canolfan Dylan Thomas Centre, Swansea, 7 November 2008).

Quotations
For quotations use single quotation marks, and double quotation marks for quotations within quotations. Punctuation is used outside quotations. Ensure that all spellings, punctuation, abbreviations etc. within a quotation are rendered exactly as in the original, including errors, which should be signalled by the authorial interpolation '(*sic*)'.

Style Notes for Contributors

Book Reviews

Book reviews should open with full bibliographic details of the text under review. These details should include (in the following order): in bold type, first name(s) and surname(s) of author(s), or first name(s) and surname(s) of editor(s) followed by a parenthetic '(ed.)' or '(eds)'; in italics, the full title of the volume followed by a period and a hard return; then, in regular type, the place of publication, publisher and date of publication; the page extent of the volume, including front papers numbered in Roman numerals; the price (where available) of the supplied copy and an indication of 'pb.' or 'hb.'; and the ISBN of the supplied copy.

For example:

Dai Smith, *Raymond Williams: A Warriors Tale*. Cardigan: Parthian Books, 2008. xviii + 514 pp. £24.99 hb. ISBN 978 1 905762 56 9.